THE SCOTTISH OFFICE

The Public Inquiry into the Shootings at Dunblane Primary School on 13 March 1996

The Hon Lord Cullen

Presented to Parliament by the Secretary of State for Scotland by Command of Her Majesty
October 1996

Cm 3386

£20.00

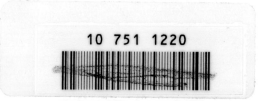

ISBN 0 10 133862 7

Foreword

The Rt Hon Michael Forsyth MP
Secretary of State for Scotland

Dear Secretary of State

On 21 March 1996 it was resolved by both Houses of Parliament that it was "expedient that a Tribunal be established for inquiring into a definite matter of urgent public importance, that is to say, the incident at Dunblane Primary School on Wednesday 13 March 1996, which resulted in the deaths of 18 people."

In terms of the Warrant of Appointment dated 21 March 1996, you appointed me to be a Tribunal for the purposes of this Inquiry in virtue of Section 1 of the Tribunals of Inquiry (Evidence) Act 1921; and you declared that that Act should apply to the Tribunal and that the Tribunal was constituted as a Tribunal within the meaning of Section 1 of that Act.

In a Parliamentary reply to Mr George Robertson MP on 21 March 1996 you set out that the Inquiry's terms of reference should be:–

> "To inquire into the circumstances leading up to and surrounding the events at Dunblane Primary School on Wednesday 13 March 1996, which resulted in the deaths of 18 people; to consider the issues arising therefrom; to make such interim and final recommendations as may seem appropriate; and to report as soon as practicable."

I have carried out the Inquiry and now respectfully submit my Report thereon. A list of the names of the persons who were the victims of the incident, both the dead and the surviving, follows.

W. Douglas Cullen
30 September 1996

List of Victims

Deceased Victims	Surviving Victims
Victoria Elizabeth Clydesdale	Aimie Lauren Adam
Emma Elizabeth Crozier	Coll Austin
Melissa Helen Currie	Matthew Alexander Birnie
Charlotte Louise Dunn	Mary Blake
Kevin Allan Hasell	Scott Elliot Crichton
Ross William Irvine	Eileen Mary Harrild
David Charles Kerr	Steven James Hopper
Mhairi Isabel MacBeath	Robbie Hurst
Gwen Hodson or Mayor	Amy Louise Hutchison
Brett McKinnon	Ryan Thomas Liddell
Abigail Joanne McLennan	Mark James Mullan
Emily Morton	Andrew O'Donnell
Sophie Jane Lockwood North	Victoria Elizabeth Porteous
John Petrie	Robert Raymond Purves
Joanna Caroline Ross	Grace Tweddle
Hannah Louise Scott	Ben Vallance
Megan Turner	Stewart Campbell Weir

Contents

Inside back cover
Aerial view of Dunblane Primary School in March 1996 (provided by Central
Scotland Police, whose assistance is gratefully acknowledged).

Chapter 1   Summary of the Report

1.1   Through the Inquiry I sought the answers to the following questions:

- what were the circumstances leading up to and surrounding the shootings at Dunblane Primary School on 13 March 1996?

- what should I recommend with a view to safeguarding the public against the misuse of firearms and other dangers which the investigation brought to light?

1.2   In **Chapter 2** I give an account of the investigation of the circumstances and the steps which were taken to prepare the way for my consideration of possible recommendations.

1.3   In **Chapter 3** I describe how Thomas Hamilton, having entered the school, shot Mrs Gwen Mayor and 16 members of her Primary 1/13 class and inflicted gunshot wounds on 10 other pupils and three other members of the teaching staff. I then describe the response of the teaching staff, emergency services and police to the incident, with an account of various lessons which have been learned from the experience. I narrate that an examination of the scene showed that, having entered the school with 4 handguns and 743 rounds of ammunition, Thomas Hamilton fired 105 rounds with a 9 mm Browning self-loading pistol over a space of about 3-4 minutes before committing suicide with one shot from a .357 Smith & Wesson revolver.

1.4   In order to provide the full background to this outrage the Inquiry had to investigate events in the life of Thomas Hamilton, and in particular over the last 23 years. The results of that investigation are set out in Chapter 4 with the exception of the last 6 months which are covered by Chapter 5. In **Chapter 4** I describe how the withdrawal of his warrant as a Scout leader in 1974 led to his undying resentment against the Scouts who, he claimed, undermined his work with various boys clubs which he ran from the 1970s onwards. However, the way in which he ran those clubs, and in particular his insistence that the boys should wear brief swimming trunks which he provided and be photographed in them while performing gymnastic exercises caused complaints from parents and led to his coming into contention with a number of local authorities which owned the school premises where his clubs met. His summer camps in 1988 and 1991 and his residential sports training course in 1992 were investigated by the police, but he was never prosecuted. Thomas Hamilton countered these complaints and investigations with complaints of his own against the police and local authority officials. In 1995 Central Regional Council was still endeavouring to find ways of making it more difficult for him to obtain the let of their premises. The chapter also deals with allegations as to his conduct with firearms, and in particular showing them to others and an occasion on which he is said to have threatened Mrs Doreen Hagger with a gun. I do not find it proved that this incident occurred or was reported to the police.

1.5   In **Chapter 5** I deal with a number of possible pointers as to the factors which were at work in the mind of Thomas Hamilton in the period leading up to 13 March 1996. His clubs were then in decline. He was in serious financial difficulties. His mood was low and he was deeply resentful of those who had claimed that he was a pervert and had discouraged boys from attending his clubs. After a gap of about 8 years his interest in firearms was resurgent. There is evidence which points to his making preparations for what he did, including the questions which he put to a boy about the layout and timing of events at the school and his questioning of a retired police officer about the time which the police would take to respond to an incident. In the light of expert evidence from a psychologist and psychiatrist I conclude that Thomas Hamilton was not mentally ill but had a paranoid personality with a desire to control others in which his firearms were the focus of his fantasies. The violence which he used would not have been predictable. His previous conduct showed indications of paedophilia.

1.6   In **Chapter 6** I am concerned with the question—How was it that Thomas Hamilton came to hold the firearms and ammunition which he did on 13 March 1996? I set out the history as from February 1977 of the firearms and ammunition which he was authorised to and did acquire. In the light of the legislation and the official Guidance to the Police I examine the operation of the certification system by Central Scotland Police. I find that the reasons which were given and accepted for his being authorised to hold more than one handgun of the same calibre were unsatisfactory. The authority which he had for the possession of firearms and the acquisition of ammunition was renewed without enquiry as to the use which he was making of the firearms. The underlying reason for this was the unsatisfactory way in which the Guidance was expressed. His fitness to be entrusted with a firearm was challenged by Detective Sergeant Hughes in a memorandum of 11 November 1991 after the police investigation of the summer camp of that year. However, it was decided that no action should be taken against Thomas Hamilton. A similar decision had been taken in 1989 after he had behaved inappropriately in showing firearms to a family in Linlithgow. I reach the conclusion that in the response of senior police officers to the memorandum of Detective Sergeant Hughes an unduly narrow view was taken of "unfitness" as a ground for the revocation of a firearm certificate; and that in view of various considerations Deputy Chief Constable McMurdo should have made further enquiries. On balance there was a case for revocation which should have been acted upon. The same considerations should have led in any event to the refusal of Thomas Hamilton's subsequent applications for renewal of his firearm certificate. However, the eventual outcome would have depended on the outcome of the appeal to the sheriff which I have no doubt that Thomas Hamilton would have taken. The chapter concludes with some observations on what I regard as weaknesses in the system used by Central Scotland Police for the carrying out of enquiries and the making of decisions about firearm applications.

1.7   As I explain in **Chapter 7,** there are essentially two methods of control of firearms and ammunition under the Firearms Acts. The first is the regulation by means of the certification system of the authority to possess, or as the case may be, to purchase or acquire them. The second is the imposition of restrictions on certain categories of firearms and ammunition by reference to their relative dangerousness. At the outset of my discussion of the future of legislative control I consider the submission that all guns should be banned, from which it would follow that there would no longer be a certification system. For the reasons which I give I do not recommend such a wholesale prohibition.

1.8   It is logical that I should next consider what could be achieved by improvements to the certification system. I do this in **Chapter 8**. As regards the work of the police I do not favour the removal from them of any of their functions but I point out that in a number of respects there is a need to strengthen the support which is given to those who carry out enquiries; and to extend the powers available to police officers and civilian licensing and enquiry officers. I also endorse the steps which are being taken to enable police forces to hold and exchange information on computer as to the individuals who hold firearm certificates and those whose firearm applications have been refused or certificates revoked.

1.9   The history of Thomas Hamilton's possession of firearms and ammunition shows that there is a need to ensure that a person does not retain the authority to possess a firearm or ammunition for it when he no longer can show "good reason" for doing so. There requires to be a power to revoke a firearm certificate on this ground, in whole or in part. However, if the police are to have the opportunity to consider revocation it is essential that there should be a means by which the use of firearms and ammunition can be ascertained; and that the police are made aware of circumstances indicating lack of use. This leads me to discuss the need for each holder of a firearm certificate to be a member of at least one club which is approved for the purposes of section 15 of the Firearms (Amendment) Act 1988; and for approved clubs to keep a record of the activities of their members who are holders of firearm certificates and to inform the police of the termination of membership or non-attendance for a substantial period.

1.10   The suitability of a holder of a firearm certificate is linked even more closely with the safety of the public. The fitness of a person to be entrusted with a firearm should become one of the conditions on which the granting and renewal of a firearm certificate depends. I also consider what additional steps should be taken to guard against "prohibited" persons becoming members of an approved club. I discuss the current requirement for a counter-signatory in support of a firearm application, and recommend that it should be replaced by a system for the provision of two references. I turn then to the provision of medical and psychological information. I do not consider that it would be practicable for general practitioners to be required to provide a medical report on each applicant, or for a psychiatric examination or a psychological test to be carried out. In any event in each case there are grounds for considerable reservations as to the effectiveness of such a measure. However, the proposal that general practitioners should provide information as to applicant's medical history for consideration by a forensic medical examiner should be the subject of consultation with the interested bodies. Lastly, I discuss the present system for appeals against the decisions of the chief officer of police, and express the view that it would be more appropriate that the scope for appeal should be restricted to enumerated grounds which did not trench on the exercise of his discretion; and that this be the subject of further study and consultation.

1.11   Despite the fact that there is room for improvement in the certification system I conclude that there are significant limitations in what can be done to exclude those who are unsuitable to have firearms and ammunition. There is no certain means of ruling out the onset of a mental illness of a type which gives rise to danger; or of identifying those whose personalities harbour dangerous propensities. On this ground alone it is insufficient protection for the public merely to tackle the individual rather than the gun. This brings me to the discussion in **Chapter 9** of the availability of section 1 firearms, and in particular handguns held for target shooting, with which the Inquiry was directly concerned. I discuss the uses of such handguns and the dangers which may be posed by their misuse—the part they play in crime and their relative lethality, ease of use and rapidity of fire. I consider the risk which arises from their present legal availability and reach the conclusion that there is a case for restricting the possession by individuals of self-loading pistols and revolvers of whatever calibre which are held for target shooting.

1.12   I then proceed to examine the evidence which was before me as to the practicability and effectiveness of various measures for restricting the availability of handguns in target shooting—(i) limiting the number of handguns or the number of a particular calibre which may be held; (ii) separating the handguns from their ammunition; (iii) restricting the capacity of multi-shot handguns; (iv) temporarily disabling multi-shot handguns; and (v) the banning of the possession by individuals of multi-shot handguns. I then consider the implications of the imposition of a restriction of one kind or another on the availability of handguns.

1.13   In reviewing my conclusions I note that of all the measures which stop short of a ban the one which is open to the least objection on the ground of practicability is the temporary dismantling of self-loading pistols and revolvers by the removal of major components. Any difficulty on this ground could be met by a requirement for the fitting of locked barrel blocks. It does not eliminate all possibility of evasion by a determined would-be killer but such a system would effect a substantial reduction in the opportunity for misuse of lawfully held handguns. I also require to consider what would be proportionate and just, having regard on the one hand to the scale of risk and on the other to the implications of one course of action or another. The banning of multi-shot handguns would have a very damaging effect on the sport of target shooting and would give rise to claims for compensation and adverse effects on the economy. I point out that the ultimate decision raises a number of matters of policy which are peculiarly for the Government and Parliament to decide. For that reason I direct my recommendation to what should be *considered.* My conclusion is that consideration should be given to restricting the availability of self-loading pistols and revolvers of any calibre which are held for use in target shooting preferably by their disablement, while they are not in use, by either (i) the removal of the slide assembly/cylinder, which is to be kept securely on the premises of an approved club of which the owner is a member or by a club official; or (ii) the fitting of a locked barrel block by a club official. If such a system is not adopted, consideration should be given to the banning of the possession of such handguns by individual owners.

1.14   In **Chapter 10** I am concerned with the safety of staff and pupils in schools, and in particular with their protection against violence. Guidance has been published on the subject of violence to staff but little, if any, on tackling the dangers to pupils. However, it is clear that the solution to the problem of protection is to be found through the application of sound principles of safety management. I point out the legal responsibility for safety of employees and pupils which arises from the provisions of the Health and Safety at Work Act 1974. There should be no uncertainty as to the personnel to whom safety roles are allocated. The risks against which staff and pupils at school are to be safeguarded includes the possibility of attack by an intruder, and the existence of that risk calls for the working out of a preventive strategy with an action plan appropriate to the particular features of each school. While the approach to be adopted in such an action plan and the measures which it should include must depend on the particular case I set out an outline of the main points which were put to me in the submissions which I received.

1.15   **Chapter 11** is concerned with the means of protecting children and young people who attend clubs or other groups against abuse by leaders or others who have regular contact with them; and in particular with the steps which can and should be taken to vet such persons and supervise their conduct. Having reviewed existing controls and advice I concentrate on situations in which children and young people under 16 years of age voluntarily attend clubs or groups for their recreation, education or development. It is unsatisfactory that it should be left to individual clubs or groups to carry out their own checks and to adopt whatever practice they please. Parents are not always in a position to make adequate enquiry into the way in which clubs or groups are run or their personnel are checked. There may be difficulties facing smaller organisations in carrying out effective checks. As matters stand there is no system for co-ordinating information between different areas of the country as to persons who are regarded as potentially unsuitable to work with children and young people. As I explain, these and other considerations indicate that, in my view, a system should be instituted to ensure that clubs and groups use adequate checks on the suitability of the leaders and workers who have substantial unsupervised access to them. Having reviewed various possible approaches to such a system I reach the conclusion that what is required is one for the voluntary accreditation of clubs and groups, and that such a system should be operated by means of a national body. Such a body would also be responsible for drawing up or selecting guidelines, collecting information in regard to any matter which might reflect on a person's suitability and monitoring the conduct of clubs and groups which are accredited.

1.16 **Chapter 12** contains a summary of my recommendations.

Chapter 2 The Scope and Conduct of the Inquiry

Preliminary matters

2.1   The preliminary investigation for the Inquiry was carried out under the authority of the Lord Advocate. The bulk of the investigation was carried out by Central Scotland Police under the direction of Mr John Miller, Procurator Fiscal at Stirling. This involved a painstaking and detailed examination of the conduct of Thomas Hamilton over many years; his relationship with a considerable number of bodies and officials; and the actions of the police in investigating his conduct and authorising his holding of firearms and ammunition.   I would like to acknowledge the considerable assistance which the Inquiry derived from being able to draw on the results of that investigation which placed great demands on Central Scotland Police.

2.2   In regard to two subjects, namely (i) the adequacy of the procedures and actions taken by Central Scotland police in regard to Thomas Hamilton's firearm certificate; and (ii) the reports concerning Thomas Hamilton which were made by Strathclyde Police and Central Scotland Police to the Procurators Fiscal at Dumbarton and Stirling, the Lord Advocate very properly decided that it was appropriate to obtain independent evidence for the assistance of the Inquiry. This was provided in the form of reports by Mr J Richardson, Deputy Chief Constable, Strathclyde Police and Mr Alfred D Vannet, Regional Procurator Fiscal of Grampian, Highland and Islands, Aberdeen, respectively.

2.3   In addition to the preliminary investigation, the Lord Advocate, along with counsel appointed by him to act on his behalf, Mr Iain Bonomy QC and Mr Jonathan Lake, Advocate, undertook responsibility in the public interest of presenting evidence to the Inquiry. The general lines to which the evidence should be directed were worked out in consultation with myself. To them I would like to express my profound gratitude for their assistance in achieving the objects of the Inquiry.

2.4   Mrs Glynis McKeand was appointed Clerk to the Inquiry. Her unfailing support and dedication have been invaluable. She has done far more than respond to the call of duty. Mrs Christine McGowan-Smyth assisted me by marshalling information contained in certain parts of the factual evidence. Miss Rachel Gwyon analysed the content of the written submissions relating to matters of school security and the vetting and supervision of adults working with children. Mrs Dorothy Gordon has borne the burden of typing the text of this Report and the preliminary drafts and revisals. To all these members of the Inquiry team I am most grateful.

2.5   From the time when my appointment was announced I received over 1600 letters from a wide variety of correspondents, concerned mainly with the control of firearms and ammunition. While these letters were not intended to be, nor were they, treated as evidence I took account of the concerns which were expressed in them in determining what I would examine. In addition I received petitions supported by 33,739 signatures.

2.6   In order to make myself more familiar with what would be discussed at the Inquiry I took a number of steps. I visited the gymnasium at Dunblane Primary School during the week following the shootings. Arrangements were made for me to see a demonstration of the operation of firearms by Mr Alastair Paton, a firearms expert, who in due course gave evidence at the Inquiry. I also requested that arrangements should be made to enable me to visit Bisley during the holding of the competitions known as Pistol '96 in order to see how they were conducted. I would like to record my thanks to the National Rifle Association for their responding to this request. I also attended as an observer at a meeting of a pistol club near Edinburgh.

2.7   A preliminary hearing was held at the Albert Halls, Stirling on 1 May 1996. At this hearing I disposed of applications by persons who wished to be parties to the Inquiry and dealt with various matters of procedure. Under the Tribunals of Inquiry (Evidence) Act 1921 I had the power to authorise the representation of any person who appeared to me to be "interested", that is to say interested in the circumstances leading up to and surrounding the incident. A list of the parties to the Inquiry and their representatives is contained in Appendix 1. One of the rules of the Inquiry was that if any party formed the intention at any stage to criticise another person, whether or not his or her interests were already protected by representation, that party should promptly inform the Inquiry Office so that whatever steps were appropriate might be taken, including, where necessary, giving the opportunity for representation to be obtained.

2.8   At the preliminary hearing I also invited written submissions in regard to three particular topics and any other topic which was relevant. This invitation was repeated in a press notice on 3 May 1996. The three particular topics were:

     (i) control of the possession and use of firearms and ammunition;

     (ii) school security; and

     (iii) vetting and supervision of adults working with children.

The Inquiry

2.9   The Inquiry was held at the Albert Halls, Stirling. It sat for 26 days, opening on 29 May and closing on 10 July 1996. The whole proceedings were held in public and recorded by shorthand writers, Wm. Hodge & Pollock Ltd, Glasgow. The arrangements for the accommodation of the participants, the public and the press were made by the Scottish Courts Service. I am most grateful to them for their assistance.

2.10   Shortly before the opening of the Inquiry I and the Lord Advocate had a meeting with the relatives of the victims of the shootings in order to discuss any concern or anxiety which they had in regard to the taking of evidence at the Inquiry. With my approval and in accordance with their wishes, details of the injuries suffered by individual victims were not explored in evidence. However, as was stated at the opening of the Inquiry, I was supplied with a set of files relating to the victims for my personal consideration.

2.11   At the opening of the Inquiry the Lord Advocate made a statement that, while it was extremely unlikely that any witness should have any concern about self-incrimination, he considered that it was appropriate in the public interest to give an undertaking that anything which a witness said in evidence at the Inquiry would not be used in evidence against him or her in any criminal proceedings in Scotland, except in relation to any offence of perjury or against the course of justice.

2.12   The witnesses who gave evidence at the Inquiry did so on oath or affirmation. In a few instances the evidence of a witness was submitted in writing and read to the Inquiry. Copies of the statements which had been taken from witnesses before they gave evidence were issued in advance to the parties. In no case did it prove necessary for me to exercise the power to enforce attendance which is contained in section 1 (1) of the 1921 Act. A list of the witnesses is contained in Appendix 2. In all but one instance the witness was led by the Lord Advocate or counsel acting on his behalf.

2.13   Copies of the documents which had been assembled for the Inquiry were made available in advance to the parties. The statements of witnesses and the documents were made available on the basis that they were solely for the use of parties and their representatives in connection with their preparation. The parties were asked to give, and gave, their undertakings for this purpose in the normal way. In no case was it necessary for me to exercise my power to compel the production of a document under section 1(1) of the 1921 Act. I should add that the documents assembled by Central Scotland Police included a copy of the draft (as at February 1996) of the thematic report of Her Majesty's Inspectorate of Constabulary for Scotland on the subject of the Administration of the Firearms Licensing System in 1995. This was referred to during the course of the evidence; and I was also provided with a copy of a later draft of April 1996. I was informed that the decision on whether or not the report should eventually be published would be taken when I had completed my deliberations.

2.14   With my approval and the agreement of parties evidence was taken at the Inquiry in such a way as to avoid the identification of any persons who had come into contact with Thomas Hamilton during their childhood.

2.15   I endeavoured to ensure that the Inquiry had before it the evidence which would enable me to make the findings which are expected of a fatal accident inquiry in Scotland.

2.16   During the course of the Inquiry evidence was led as to information submitted to the Procurators Fiscal of Dumbarton and Stirling by Strathclyde Police and Central Scotland Police during the years from 1988 to 1993; and the reasons stated by the Procurators Fiscal for their decisions in relation to the matters reported to them. As I have already stated the Inquiry was provided with a review by Mr Vannet of the reports and information which were submitted to the Procurators Fiscal by those police forces. On 24 June 1996 Mr Bonomy on behalf of the Lord Advocate made a statement of the Lord Advocate's position in relation to that evidence and the question of enquiring into the decisions taken by those Procurators Fiscal. On the following day I heard submissions from Mr C M Campbell QC and Mr Bonomy in regard to the proper scope for questioning in regard to these matters, after which I gave my decision. The statement made on behalf of the Lord Advocate, a note of the submissions which were addressed to me and the terms of my decision are set out in Appendix 3.

2.17   In the latter part of July it was drawn to my attention that a telephone conversation between two police officers on the morning of 13 March concerning the situation at the school had been accidentally recorded by a telephone answering machine in Motherwell: and that the cassette on which it had been recorded had come into the hands of Central Scotland Police later that day. I was provided with a transcript of the recorded conversation. I was satisfied that it did not contain anything which was of value to the Inquiry.

2.18   As the Inquiry was held not long after the shootings it is not surprising that someone who did not come forward or could not be traced at an earlier stage should claim later that he was able to contribute information about the behaviour of Thomas Hamilton. I deal with a particular instance of this in para 4.15.

Evidence in regard to possible recommendations

2.19   I received a considerable number of contributions in response to the invitation for written submissions which I had issued. In selecting those which were to form part of the written evidence before the Inquiry I had regard to a number of considerations, the most important of which were the qualifications and responsibilities of the contributors and the desirability of obtaining a full range of views. Appendix 4 contains a list of the organisations and persons whose written submissions were selected. Copies were made available for inspection by the press and the public as from 10 June 1996 (Day 10): and thereafter as further written submissions were received and accepted in evidence. I would like to express my appreciation for the high quality of these submissions. They have been of considerable assistance to me in evaluating a wide range of proposals. It is not practicable for me to set out every contention in this Report, let alone all the supporting arguments, but every point has been considered.

2.20   In addition to these written submissions I also had available to me

  (i) evidence submitted on behalf of the Secretary of State for Scotland and the Home Secretary on 30 April 1996, which contained background information about the licensing of firearms and ammunition; together with comments about the advantages and disadvantages of a number of suggestions for changes in the law which had been made since 13 March 1996, which I will refer to in this Report as the "Green Book".

 (ii) the report of the Working Group on School Security for the DfEE, which was published in May 1996, along with a commentary by The Scottish Office Education and Industry Department; and

(iii) a paper by The Scottish Office on the recruitment and supervision of adults working with children which was published in June 1996.

2.21   Since the written submissions raised a number of points which had practical implications I considered that it would be appropriate to obtain certain additional factual evidence. For this purpose the Inquiry heard evidence in regard to the operation and use of firearms and ammunition; the operation of the certification system; the practice of shooting disciplines and the operation of rifle and pistol clubs; and the extent to which medical practitioners could assist in the assessment of applicants for firearm certificates.

2.22   It was clear to me that it would be of assistance to have a contradictor to oral submissions by the parties which had not been anticipated in the written submissions. I invited legal representatives of the British Shooting Sports Council, the Scottish Target Shooting Federation, the Stirling Rifle and Pistol Club and the Callander Rifle and Pistol Club to address the Inquiry at the stage of closing submissions. I am grateful to them for their assistance in helping me to focus the points at issue.

2.23   In connection with possible recommendations I had available to me by way of background a number of publications, which are listed in Appendix 5. In addition I received a number of papers relating to firearms laws in the Republic of Ireland, Northern Ireland, Australia and Japan.

2.24   At an early stage of the Inquiry it was clear that a number of the written submissions were critical of the research material referred to in Annex G to the Green Book which had been provided by the Research and Statistics Directorate of the Home Office. I decided at that stage that I should seek the Directorate's comments on these submissions. A note of their comments was received by the Inquiry Office on 29 July. As their comments had been requested while the Inquiry was in progress I decided that the appropriate course was to treat the note as part of the evidence before me. Copies of the note were supplied to the critics of the research material and arrangements were made for notification of the press. A similar procedure was followed when the results of studies of statistics relating to certain cases involving firearms in England and Wales in 1992-94 and in Scotland in 1993 were submitted to the Inquiry Office in the latter part of August.

The scope of recommendations

2.25   In considering the evidence before me I have endeavoured to identify the lessons of the incident and of the circumstances which led up to it, with a view to avoiding the misuse of firearms and other dangers which the investigation brought to light. Every inquiry of this kind involves an extrapolation from the particular circumstances of the case. However, I have borne in mind, as I said at the Inquiry, that, consistently with my terms of reference, I am concerned with issues which arise from the circumstances leading up to and surrounding the incident. For that reason I have concentrated on matters which have some tenable connection with those circumstances. While this is the approach which I would have adopted in any event it is particularly necessary for me to point this out in view of the range of subjects with which some of the submissions relating to the control of firearms were concerned. How I have followed out that approach will be seen from Chapters 7-11. I did not consider that, in regard to any of the matters with which my recommendations are concerned, it was necessary or appropriate for me to present them as interim recommendations.

2.26   I have worked out my recommendations by reference to the evidence, both oral or written, which was before me. I have applied my own independent judgment to the task. I say that with added emphasis in view of a report in the *Sun* newspaper on 15 August which stated that, following a remark attributed to the Prime Minister, I would abandon a first draft of my report and rewrite my proposals. I would add that at that time no text of my recommendations, draft or otherwise, was in existence.   The shootings also prompted the House of Commons Home Affairs Committee to initiate an inquiry into matters of general public policy relating to the possession of handguns. The Committee received both written evidence and oral evidence at a hearing on 8 May. Their report was published on 13 August. Some of the written evidence which was presented to the Inquiry was also presented to the Committee. I should make it clear that, while there was an overlap with the matters which I considered, I did not feel in any way inhibited in reaching my own conclusions.

Chapter 3   The Events of 13 March 1996

Introduction

3.1   In this chapter I will describe the circumstances of the shootings, and the response of teaching staff, emergency services and police to the incident. I will also set out a number of findings in regard to the firearms, ammunition and other equipment carried by Thomas Hamilton.

The Shootings

3.2   About 8.15 am Thomas Hamilton was seen by a neighbour to be scraping ice off a white van outside his home at 7 Kent Road, Stirling. They had a normal conversation. Some time later he drove off in the van in the direction of Dunblane. At about 9.30 am he parked the van beside a telegraph pole in the lower car park of Dunblane Primary School. (*See inside back cover*). He took out a pair of pliers from a toolwrap and used them to cut the telephone wires at the foot of the telegraph pole. These did not serve the school but a number of adjoining houses. He then crossed the car park, carrying the weapons, ammunition and other equipment which I will describe later, and entered the school by way of a door on its north west side which was next to the toilets beside the gym. Had he used the main entrance to the school it was more likely that he would have been seen as there were many persons in the vicinity of the entrance at that time. The main school building had six entrances and two doors controlled by push bars for emergency exit. In addition to the main school building there were six hutted classrooms in the playground. Most of the huts had two doors, not including fire exits.

3.3   The school day had started at 9 am for all primary classes. Morning assemblies were held in the school's Assembly Hall which was situated between the dining area and the gymnasium. The school had 640 pupils, making it one of the largest primary schools in Scotland. The Assembly Hall was not large enough to accommodate the whole school at one time, with the consequence that assemblies were limited to certain year groups in rotation. On 13 March all primary 1, 2 and 3 classes had attended assembly from 9.10 am to 9.30 am. They consisted of a total of about 250 pupils, together with their teachers and the school chaplain. They included Primary 1/13 which was a class of 28 pupils, along with their teacher Mrs Gwen Mayor. This class had already changed for their gym lesson before attending assembly. 25 members of the class were 5 years of age: and 3 were 6 years of age. Mrs Mayor was 47 years of age.

3.4   At the conclusion of assembly all those present had dispersed to their respective classrooms, with the exception of Primary 1/13 who with Mrs Mayor had made their way to the gymnasium, passing the entrance which Thomas Hamilton used to gain access to the school, and entering the gymnasium by the doorway at its north end. A physical education teacher, Mrs Eileen Harrild, had already arrived there along with Mrs Mary Blake, a supervisory assistant, who was to relieve Mrs Mayor in order to enable her to attend a meeting. The children had been instructed to go to the centre and away from the equipment which was at the south end. Mrs Harrild had been talking to Mrs Mayor for a few minutes. As she was about to attend to the waiting class she heard a noise behind her that caused her to turn round. This was probably the sound of Thomas Hamilton firing two shots into the stage of the Assembly Hall and the girls toilet outside the gym. He then entered the gym. He was wearing a dark jacket, black corduroy trousers and a woolly hat with ear defenders. He had a pistol in his hand. He advanced a couple of steps into the gym and fired indiscriminately and in rapid succession. Mrs Harrild was hit in both forearms, the right hand and left breast. She stumbled into the open-plan store area which adjoined the gym, followed by a number of the children. Mrs Mayor was also shot several times and died instantly. Mrs Blake was then shot but also managed to reach the store, ushering some children in ahead of her.

3.5   From his position near the entrance doorway of the gym Hamilton fired a total of 29 shots in rapid succession. From that position he killed one child and injured others. During this shooting four injured children made their way to the store. In the store Mrs Blake and Mrs Harrild tried to console and calm the terrified children who had taken refuge there. The children cowered on the floor, lying helplessly in pools of blood hearing the screams and moans of their classmates in the gym, and waiting for the end or for help. Thomas Hamilton walked up the east side of the gym firing six shots. At a point midway along it he discharged 8 shots in the direction of the opposite side of the gym. He then advanced to the middle of the gym and walked in a semi-circle systematically firing 16 shots at a group of children who had either been disabled by the firing or who had been thrown to the floor. He stood over them and fired at point-blank range.

3.6   Meanwhile a child from Primary 7 class who had been sent on an errand by his teacher, and was walking along the west side of the gym heard loud banging and screaming. He looked in and saw Thomas Hamilton shooting. Thomas Hamilton shot at him. The child was struck by flying glass and ran off. It appears that Thomas Hamilton then advanced to the south end of the gym. From that position he fired 24 rounds in various directions. He shot through the window adjacent to the fire escape door at the south-east end of the gym. This may have been at an adult who was walking across the playground. Thomas Hamilton then opened the fire escape door and discharged a further 4 shots in the same direction from within the gym.

3.7   He then went outside the doorway and fired 4 more shots towards the library cloakroom, striking Mrs Grace Tweddle, a member of the staff, a glancing blow on the head. A teacher, Mrs Catherine Gordon, and her Primary 7 class who were using hut number 7 which was the classroom closest to the fire escape door saw and heard Thomas Hamilton firing from that direction. She immediately instructed her class to get down on the floor, just in time before he discharged 9 shots into her classroom. Most became embedded in books and equipment. One passed through a chair which seconds before had been used by a child.

3.8   Thomas Hamilton then re-entered the gym where he shot again. He then released the pistol and drew a revolver. He placed the muzzle of the revolver in his mouth, pointing upwards and pulled the trigger. His death followed quickly.

3.9   Mrs Mayor and 15 children lay dead in the gym and one further child was close to death. They had sustained a total of 58 gun shot wounds. 26 of these wounds were of such a nature that individually they would have proved fatal.

3.10 In the result the deaths of the victims listed in the left hand column of the Annex to the Foreword to this Report were caused by gunshot wounds caused by Thomas Hamilton's unlawful actions in shooting them. All of these victims died within the gym, with the exception of the sixteenth child, Mhairi Isabel MacBeath, who was found to be dead on arrival at Stirling Royal Infirmary at 10.30 am. While it is not possible to be precise as to the times at which the shootings took place, it is likely that they occurred within a period of 3-4 minutes, starting between 9.35 am and 9.40 am.

3.11 The survivors of the incident were taken to Stirling Royal Infirmary. They are listed in the right hand column of the Annex. They consisted of the remaining 12 members of the class; two pupils aged 11 who were elsewhere than in the gym when they were injured; and Mrs Harrild, Mrs Blake and Mrs Tweddle. 13 of them had sustained gunshot wounds, 4 being serious, 6 very serious and 3 minor. Of the remaining 4, 2 had sustained minor injuries and 2 were uninjured.

The response to the incident

The school staff 3.12 Mrs Agnes Awlson, the Assistant Headmistress, was making her way across the playground from her classroom when she heard several sharp metallic noises and screaming coming from the gym. She ran along a corridor and saw what she thought were cartridges lying outside its doorway. Realising that something dreadful was happening she ran back to the office of the Headmaster, Mr Ronald Taylor, who was making a telephone call. The call began at 9.38 am. He was conscious of hearing noises like indistinct bangs. This puzzled him and his reaction was to think that there were builders on the premises about whom he had not been informed. Mrs Awlson entered his office in a crouched position saying that there was a man in the school with a gun. Mr Taylor cut short his call and made an emergency call to the police, which was received at 9.41 am. He then ran along the corridor to the gym. On the way he heard no further noises. A student teacher told him that he had seen the gunman shooting himself. Mr Taylor's estimate was that some 3 minutes had lapsed between his first hearing the noises and being told this by the student teacher.

3.13 Mr Taylor burst into the gym. He was met by what he described in evidence as "a scene of unimaginable carnage, one's worst nightmare". He saw a group of children on the right hand side of the gym who were crying and obviously less injured than the others. He asked the student teacher to take them out of the gym and give them comfort. He then ran back to his office and instructed the Deputy Headmistress, Mrs Fiona Eadington, to telephone for ambulances. That call was made at 9.43 am. He then ran back to the gym calling for adults, and in particular the kitchen staff, to come and help. He moved through the gym along with the janitor Mr John Currie. He noticed Thomas Hamilton lying at the south end of the gym. He seemed to be moving. He noticed a gun on the floor beside him and told Mr Currie to kick it away, which he did. He also removed the revolver from Thomas Hamilton's hand and threw that aside. By this time the Assistant Headmaster, Mr Stuart McCombie, and members of the kitchen staff were in the gym endeavouring to help the injured children until the arrival of the police. When Mr Taylor went to the store area he discovered the injured who were there. Other members of staff arrived and endeavoured to attend to the injured, who were taken to the Assembly Hall.

3.14 By this time the police and medical teams had arrived. Attention was turned to the difficult problem of identifying the children. Since Mrs Mayor was dead, help was sought from members of staff, including nursery staff, who had looked after the children during the previous year. However, not all of the children had been through the nursery. This was an extremely harrowing experience for all the members of staff who were involved. They had to be taken into and out of the gym on several occasions. The record cards were consulted in order to aid identification. Unfortunately the class register had not been marked for Mrs Mayor's class as the class had proceeded directly to the gym after assembly. A further difficulty was encountered when it was discovered that one child was wearing clothing with the name tag of another child. The record card for another child was not in its expected place but this did not delay identification. Mr Taylor and his staff did everything that they possibly could to assist, far beyond what might reasonably have been expected of them.

Emergency Services 3.15   The first ambulance arrived at the school at 9.57 am in response to the call at 9.43 am. It left at 10.15 am with the first patient for Stirling Royal Infirmary, and returned later for more patient transfers.

3.16   A team of doctors and a nurse from the Health Centre at Dunblane arrived on the scene at about 10.04 am, followed shortly thereafter by a community nursing sister from the Health Centre. They were involved in immediate resuscitation of injured teachers and children. They were joined by doctors from the Doune Health Centre and from Callander.

3.17   At 9.48 am the accident and emergency department at Stirling Royal Infirmary was notified of the incident and within a few minutes it was known that multiple casualties or fatalities were possible. A major incident was declared and the planned response to such an event was put into operation. At 10.15 am the first of a number of teams from Stirling Royal Infirmary arrived at the school and took up the process of triage which had been initiated by the doctors from Dunblane. This involved working out the priorities according to an assessment of each victim's needs. A decision was then taken as to fitness for evacuation and the order in which evacuation should take place. At the Infirmary operating theatres had been cleared of planned surgical cases. On their arrival at hospital the victims were handed over to the care of teams of surgeons and anaesthetists. Four of the children had sustained potentially fatal wounds. A team from Falkirk and District Royal Infirmary also arrived about 10.35 am. All of the injured victims had arrived at Stirling Royal Infirmary by about 11.10 am. After initial examination some were sent to the Falkirk and District Royal Infirmary and others required to be transferred to the Royal Hospital for Sick Children, Yorkhill, Glasgow, for specialist treatment.

The Police 3.18   The first police officers arrived from Dunblane Police Office at about 9.50 am in response to the telephone call from Mr Taylor. They immediately summoned further police assistance and these officers assisted in the gym and took steps to clear the way for the arrival of ambulances. By about 10.10 am senior police officers were on the scene, including the Chief Constable who had put into force the strategy for major incidents. In accordance with this a casualty bureau was set up at police headquarters in Stirling. The Chief Constable also delegated various tasks to his commanders. DCS John Ogg was appointed to be senior investigating officer. The police were faced with a very considerable task in dealing with the incident and its consequences. On 13 March over 100 police officers out of a total force of 658 were involved.

3.19   The first action of the police was to put a cordon around the school buildings with an outer cordon around the road access to the school, in order to restrict admittance to those who could be of assistance. By 10.30 am a considerable number of people had approached the school, not merely anxious relatives of school children but also representatives of the media. The emergency services had to make their way through some 200-300 people in proceeding to and from the school.

3.20   The police then gave priority to ensuring that the injured were taken to hospital. A deliberate decision was taken to refrain from noting their names before they left in order to ensure that they were given medical attention as soon as possible and in order to avoid insensitive intrusion. The next objective of the police was to endeavour to identify the deceased, then institute enquiries, followed by the appointment of production officers and the setting up of an administrative system.

3.21   As I have already indicated the task of identifying the victims was complicated by a number of factors. In addition it was found that two members of Mrs Mayor's class were absent that day. At one point it appeared that a particular child had been apparently identified as being at Stirling Royal Infirmary as well as lying dead in the gym.

3.22   In order to determine the identity of the dead it was necessary for the police to obtain identification of the survivors who had been removed to hospital. However, they had extreme difficulty in communicating with the hospital or the casualty bureau in the manner intended. Apart from a line in the library which was used for the internet facility there was only one telephone line into the school. This was engaged for virtually the whole time by calls from anxious parents or from the media. When the police used mobile telephones they soon found that they also became completely blocked. They decided not to resort to their radio system as the information in which they were interested was extremely sensitive and could have been picked up by scanners. The police did not receive information from the hospital until after mid-day when they obtained two or three names at a time with the use of mobile telephones. They requested British Telecom for additional telephone lines into the school but it was not until 3 pm that the first of these was installed.

3.23   In the meantime arrangements had to be made by the police for the relatives of children who attended the school. They were taken to a private house. From there the parents of children in Primary 1/13 were escorted to a second house before being transferred to a staff room at the school. The process of reuniting parents with children in other classes took up some 2-3 hours. As regards the parents of children in Primary 1/13, the police began to inform the parents of children who were injured and arranged for them to be driven to hospital. By about 1.15-1.30 pm all the injured children had been identified and the necessary information conveyed to their parents.

3.24   In order to communicate information to the parents of children who had died a family liaison team consisting of two police officers and a social worker was organised for each family. These teams required to be assembled and briefed before they spoke to the families and they were also instructed to provide them with continuing counsel and support. The police decided that they should be entirely certain as to the identity of the deceased children before informing their families lest any parents be misinformed. Their concern in this respect was increased by the fact that, as I have already narrated a child had been apparently identified as being both in the gym and at hospital. This necessitated a second round of physical identification of the children in the gym by members of staff. This served only to make their task the more harrowing. As this doubt had arisen the police took the deliberate decision to withhold information about any of the deceased until all of them had been identified.

3.25 Although these procedures were protracted for the reasons that I have explained the parents were not told of the problem and were given no explanation of the reason for the delay. The process of breaking the news to the parents of deceased children did not begin until 1.45 pm. It was not completed until about 3.30 pm. In the meantime doctors from the Health Centre at Dunblane had remained with the families in order to give them whatever comfort they could. The families of each child were called out of the staff room and then escorted by members of their liaison team to one of seventeen rooms which had been made available for the purpose of enabling news to be broken in privacy. The last family remained in the staff room with the members of their team. After the families had received the news they were escorted home by the members of their team who stayed with them as long as was required. It may be noted that at one stage before individual families had been informed there were broadcasts by the media as to the number of children who were thought to have been killed. This had a serious effect on the credibility of the work of the police.

3.26 Mrs Mayor's daughter, Esther, went to Stirling Royal Infirmary where she heard people enquiring about her mother's class at around 12.30 pm. She then left immediately for the school where she was put into the staff room with the parents. Mrs Mayor's husband arrived at the school about 1 pm and was taken to the school library. He was extremely upset and suspected from various media reports that his wife was among the dead. The police officer who escorted him knew that one teacher had been killed but did not know that teacher's identity. Mr Mayor threatened to obtain information from the media if the police would not provide him with it. The officer then left him alone in the library while he sought confirmation of the teacher's identity. After receiving confirmation of Mrs Mayor's death he returned to the library and broke the news to Mr Mayor. This was at least half an hour after he had arrived at the school. The officer then left Mr Mayor in the library in order to go to the briefing room where he was allocated as a member of one of the liaison teams. It appears that neither Mr Mayor nor his daughter was informed of the other's presence in the same building and that it was not until 2.45 pm that they were brought together and informed of what had happened.

3.27 A delay occurred later at Stirling Royal Infirmary where families and their supporters had to wait for some time before they were able to see their child in the mortuary.

Lessons from the Incident

3.28 Although the police had received training for emergencies and had participated in disaster planning they could never have envisaged an incident of such magnitude and involving such distressing circumstances as the massacre which Thomas Hamilton perpetrated. During the course of their evidence police officers who were concerned with the maintenance of access and communication to the school and with the provision of information to the parents of victims accepted that there were a number of lessons to be learned from what happened. In addition, during closing submissions, Mr James Taylor for Central Scotland Police presented me with a written submission by the Chief Constable dated 26

June. I have not thought it necessary to make any recommendations of my own in this respect but it may be of assistance if I draw attention to a number of matters which are to receive attention.

3.29   As regards the use of a cordon it appears to have been accepted that it would have been possible to move it further back from the school so as to enable police officers to speak to the families without their being under the gaze of the press and other members of the media. That was clearly desirable.

3.30   It is clearly better that the names of injured should be noted before they leave the scene of an incident involving multiple victims unless this creates a clear risk of prejudice to their treatment. This point has been noted in the Chief Constable's submission at 4.5.

3.31   A number of important points in regard to communications require future attention. In part 5 of his submission the Chief Constable refers to the importance of emergency services having the ability to limit the number of incoming calls in order that operators can continue to make outgoing calls; the use of a facility for re-configuring domestic telephones in order to give priority to outgoing callers; the dedication of several lines for use by emergency services at localised junction boxes; the value to emergency services of message pagers; the use by the police of encrypted radios; the use by family liaison teams of mobile telephones; the need for a communications vehicle for command purposes; and the need for a statement of best practice for adoption by the Association of Chief Police Officers of Scotland.

3.32   As regards the operation of the casualty bureau the Chief Constable has noted (at 9.3 and 9.4) that it is important for the future to ensure the recording of the times when casualties are positively identified and the times when relatives are notified; and that it would be of greater value to the police service if the processes of the casualty bureau were computerised.

3.33   A major incident puts a heavy premium on close co-ordination between the police and emergency services. I note from his submission at 4.8 that the Chief Constable considers that a closer liaison between his own press team and that of other emergency services would be beneficial.

3.34   However, the point which was of most concern to the families in the present case was the delay in their being informed of the fate of their children, and in particular the time which it took before the families of those who had been killed were informed of that fact. These delays were entirely unacceptable, especially when they were combined with the distressing effect of lack of any information, even an explanation that there was a problem and something was being done about it. It should be accepted that the provision of information even of a limited nature should be one of the aims in setting up adequate systems in the immediate aftermath of a major incident. I can appreciate that in the present case the police wanted to ensure that they were in a position to provide accurate information to the parents but the need, as they saw it, to wait until their information was considered accurate in every case, along with the time taken up by the formation of the liaison teams meant that a considerable time elapsed while the parents were left in what was described as a cramped and overcrowded room, experiencing intense frustration, concern and even anger. It is important not merely that as much information should be provided to relatives but also that the means by which that information is provided should be as sensitive and reassuring as possible. I note with approval that the Chief Constable intends (11.7 and 11.8) to consider allocation of officers with particular expertise for this purpose.

3.35   At the same time it is important to keep in view the general quality of the work which was done by Central Scotland Police. At the end of the Inquiry my attention was drawn to the letters in which the school board and Mr Taylor, the Head Teacher, had expressed their gratitude for the help, support and professionalism of the force. Further, as was made plain at the Inquiry the sensitivity and support which were provided to relatives by members of the liaison teams were warmly appreciated.

The firearms, ammunition and other equipment carried by Thomas Hamilton

3.36   It is now necessary for me to return to the scene of the shootings. Some time after 11.30 am Mr Malcolm Chisholm, scenes of crime officer and firearms examiner with the Tayside Police Force began a detailed examination of the area in conjunction with DC Donald Scobie, another member of the identification branch of that police force. The examination of the scene was interrupted for some time while the gym was checked for booby traps. The examination of the scene provided the Inquiry with a very detailed account of what was found. For the purposes of this report it is not necessary for me to go into every detail but to mention a number of findings which are of importance.

3.37   It was clear that Thomas Hamilton had with him two 9 mm Browning self-loading (or semi-automatic) pistols and two .357 Smith & Wesson revolvers. These firearms were found beside his body. They were in good condition and full working order. Thomas Hamilton was wearing four holsters of the right-hand draw variety strapped to his waist and a pouch over each of his shoulders. He had also brought with him a large camera bag.

3.38   As regards the pistols, Thomas Hamilton had used one of them in order to fire all of his shots at his victims. This pistol (pistol A) was a competition model with an extended barrel and barrel weight, and an adjustable rear sight. The spur of the hammer had been removed. The reason for its removal is not clear. It could have been done as a consequence of the pistol being damaged or to reduce the time for which the pistol had to be held on aim. In any event the absence of a spur did not impair its use in target shooting to any significant extent. Pistol A had a light trigger pull but not unusually so for a well-tuned competition model. The other pistol (pistol B) was a standard model which was fitted with a device which prevented it from being fired when the magazine was not fitted. As between the two revolvers there were only minor differences, including the fact that in one of them the standard wooden handgrips had been replaced with rubber handgrips.

3.39   The examination of the scene showed that Thomas Hamilton had fired 105 rounds of 9 mm ammunition by means of pistol A. He had with him 25 extended box-type magazines, each of which was capable of holding 20 rounds of 9 mm ammunition and suitable for use with either pistol. (The standard magazine for such pistols was capable of holding 13 cartridges.) Stickers had been attached to each magazine, a yellow sticker to the front and an orange to the back, presumably in order to ensure that it was inserted into the butt of the pistol the correct way round. The magazines were found to contain a total of 393 cartridges, 18 of the magazines being fully loaded with cartridges and 3 being partially loaded. The remaining 4 were empty. Mr Chisholm and DC Scobie reached the conclusion that Thomas Hamilton had arrived at the school with a total of 501 rounds of 9 mm ammunition which, with the exception of one round in the chamber of pistol B, were contained in the 25 magazines. They noted that in the majority of the magazines which still contained ammunition the cartridges had been loaded in uniform sequence—with metal jacket soft-nosed hollow point type at the bottom of the magazine; full metal jacket semi-wadcutter types in the middle; and full metal jacket round-nosed types at the top. In evidence Mr Chisholm and Mr Alastair Paton, another firearms expert, stated that they had never come across such an arrangement in the course of their experience. However Mr Paton accepted that putting round-nosed types at the top of the magazine could have been done with a view to avoiding the risk of a cartridge sticking between the magazine and the chamber.

3.40   Mr Chisholm and DC Scobie later carried out tests on the pistols at the firing range at the headquarters of Tayside Police. These included an exercise in which pistol A, in the cocked and ready to fire position, was used to fire off a full magazine of 20 shots as quickly as possible. The time taken to accomplish this was 5.46 seconds. Also, using pistol A and the 7 magazines which had been used by Thomas Hamilton and the appropriate number of cartridges, they carried out an exercise of firing off 105 rounds and ejecting 6 magazines in the course of doing so, all as quickly as possible. The time taken to accomplish this was 50.4 seconds. Too much should not be read into the evidence about 5.46 seconds. While he had not carried out a similar exercise Mr Paton gave evidence that in general terms it was consistent with his experience for a magazine of 20 rounds to be fired off in 5 or 6 seconds with some degree of accuracy. However, this depended on the expertise and physical make-up of the person firing. It would be unusual for 20 shots to be fired off at any one time. I accept Mr Paton's evidence as a broad indication. However, I note that Mr D J Penn, who is a highly experienced shooter, expressed the opinion that an averagely competent shot could not achieve 20 rounds of aimed fire in 5.46 seconds with an unmodified 9 mm Browning pistol: and that 10 to 12 shots in that time would be a more realistic figure. (This was expressed in a list of points submitted to the Inquiry after he gave his evidence.)

3.41   As regards the revolvers, an examination of the scene showed the presence of 230 live rounds of .357 magnum cartridges suitable for use in either of them. In addition each of the revolvers was fully loaded with six of such cartridges, apart from the single round which Thomas Hamilton had fired in order to kill himself.

3.42   It follows from the above that when Thomas Hamilton arrived at the school he had with him a total of 743 rounds of ammunition, consisting of 501 rounds of 9 mm and 242 rounds of .357 ammunition. He fired 105 rounds of the former and 1 round of the latter. At para 5.38 I will refer to evidence which was given in an interpretation of his intentions.

Chapter 4   Events in the life of Thomas Hamilton

Introduction

4.1   The events of 13 March 1996 should be seen against the background of certain events in Thomas Hamilton's life and in particular the last 23 years. In this chapter, which of necessity is somewhat protracted, I will endeavour to set out the main events which appear to have a bearing on the outcome, leaving the events of the last 6 months of his life to Chapter 5. After dealing with his family, education and livelihood I will go on to his relationship with the Scouts, his long-standing operation of boys clubs and the circumstances in which he came into contention with local authorities and the police. Finally I will examine his alleged conduct in regard to firearms.

Family, education and livelihood

4.2   Thomas Hamilton was born in Glasgow on 10 May 1952. He was the son of Thomas Watt and Agnes Graham Hamilton or Watt. He was named Thomas Watt. Shortly after his birth his parents separated and in 1955 they were divorced. He and his mother moved to the home of his maternal grandparents in Cranhill, Glasgow. On 26 March 1956 he was adopted by them and his name was changed to Thomas Watt Hamilton. In 1963 he accompanied his adoptive parents when they moved to 11 Upper Bridge Street, Stirling. He grew up in the belief that his natural mother was his sister. In 1985 she moved to live in a house of her own. In 1987 Thomas Hamilton and his adoptive parents moved to 7 Kent Road, where he continued to live until 13 March 1996. In August 1987 his adoptive mother died; and 5 years later his adoptive father moved into sheltered housing, so leaving Thomas Hamilton in sole occupation. He remained in contact with his natural mother, visiting her about twice a week.

4.3   After a primary education in Cranhill and Stirling Thomas Hamilton attended Riverside Secondary School, Stirling and Falkirk Technical College, obtaining a number of O Grades in 1968. In that year he became an apprentice draughtsman in the County Architect's Office in Stirling. In 1972 he opened a shop at 49 Cowane Street, Stirling known as "Woodcraft", which specialised in the sale of DIY goods and supplies, ironmongery, and latterly the sale of fitted kitchens. After about 13 years he gave up the shop and registered as unemployed. He received state benefits until November 1993. However, at the same time he carried on the activity of buying and selling cameras and camera equipment and carrying out some free-lance photography.

Thomas Hamilton's involvement with the Scouts

4.4   In July 1973 Thomas Hamilton, who was then a Venture Scout, was appointed as Assistant Scout Leader of the 4th/6th Stirling Troop. This followed the normal checks into an appointee's suitability. He seemed very keen and willing and did not present any problems. On one occasion he volunteered to take some boys on his boat on Loch Lomond for their proficiency badge work but this was not permitted as the boat had insufficient lifejackets and no distress flares or oars, and he had inadequate knowledge of the waters. In the autumn of 1973 he was seconded to be leader of the 24th Stirlingshire troop which was to be revived at Bannockburn.

4.5   A number of complaints were made about his leadership, the most serious of which were concerned with two occasions when the boys who were in his charge were forced to sleep overnight in his company in a van during very cold weather at Aviemore. His excuse on the first occasion was that the intended accommodation had been double-booked and he was warned of the need to double-check such arrangements. On the latter occasion it was found that no booking had been made by him on either of these occasions. The County Commissioner, Mr Brian D Fairgrieve had a discussion with the District Commissioner, Mr R C H Deuchars, in which they agreed that Thomas Hamilton should be asked to resign. Thereafter Mr Fairgrieve had a meeting with him. He did not think that Thomas Hamilton was a particularly stable person. He said in evidence "I formed the impression that he had a persecution complex, that he had delusions of grandeur and I felt his actions were almost paranoia". He was doubtful about his moral intention towards boys. Thomas Hamilton was informed that in view of his lack of qualities in leadership his warrant was being withdrawn. On 13 May 1974 Mr Deuchars wrote to him requiring that he return his warrant book. Despite repeated requests he did not do so for some months.

4.6   Mr Fairgrieve wrote to the Scottish Scout Headquarters in order to give them his views about Thomas Hamilton as he considered that he should not be a member of the Scout movement. In this letter dated 29 June 1974 he wrote:

> "While unable to give concrete evidence against this man I feel that too many 'incidents' relate to him such that I am far from happy about his having any association with Scouts. He has displayed irresponsible acts on outdoor activities by taking young 'favourite' Scouts for weekends during the winter and sleeping in his van, the excuse for these outings being hill-walking expeditions. The lack of precautions for such outdoor activities displays either irresponsibility or an ulterior motive for sleeping with the boys...... His personality displays evidence of a persecution complex coupled with rather grandiose delusions of his own abilities. As a doctor, and with my clinical acumen only, I am suspicious of his moral intentions towards boys".

Mr Deuchars also submitted a form to Scout Headquarters to the effect that Thomas Hamilton was not considered to be a suitable applicant due to his immaturity and irresponsibility. This resulted in his name being entered on the "blacklist" which is intended to ensure that unsuitable applicants are denied an appointment in the Scout Association. Such a record is also consulted on occasions when an outside enquiry is made as to whether a former Scout leader has provided satisfactory service. In the case of Thomas Hamilton it was effective in preventing him in his attempt to become a Scout leader in Clackmannanshire.

4.7   During the Inquiry reference was made to a copy of what purported to be a letter written by Thomas Hamilton, dated 28 April 1974 and addressed to Mr Deuchars. In that letter he tendered his resignation as Scout leader of the 24th Stirlingshire troop, criticised the conduct of Mr Deuchars and stated his intention to transfer to another district. Mr Deuchars had no recollection of receiving the letter and there is no record of it on the Scout files. The copy was retrieved from the records of Central Regional Council. I am satisfied that Thomas Hamilton did not write or send the letter on the date which it bears and that it was written by him in order to create a false impression that through his own resignation he had anticipated the withdrawal of his warrant.

4.8   In February 1977 after making a number of attempts to return to Scouting Thomas Hamilton requested the Scout Association to hold a Committee of Inquiry into his complaint that he had been victimised. This request was denied. After some correspondence he stated in April 1977 that he was discontinuing the thought of holding a warrant "as I do not want my good name to be part of this so-called organisation in this district". However, his letters of complaint continued. The response of the Scout Association was that the warrant had been withdrawn on the basis of lack of preparation and planning for his adventure activities at Aviemore. In 1978 he approached Mr David Vass, the District Commissioner for the Trossachs, offering his services as a Scout Leader. After consulting with Mr Fairgrieve Mr Vass responded that they were unable to make use of his services. Thomas Hamilton persistently maintained that the Scouts had not only ruined his reputation by terminating his appointment but that they were linked with the actions taken by other organisations, and in particular the police. In para 4.23 I narrate his later approaches to Scout officials.

Thomas Hamilton's boys clubs

4.9   After the withdrawal of his warrant Thomas Hamilton became increasingly involved in the setting up and running of boys clubs. It is not clear when he began this activity but it appears that in the late 1970s he was running the "Dunblane Rovers" in the Duckburn Centre in Dunblane. He also ran a Rovers Group in Bannockburn. There was some evidence that at this time he was permitted to use school premises. In any event it is clear that during the period from November 1981 until his death he organised and operated 15 boys clubs for various periods and that these clubs used school premises in Central, Lothian, Fife and Strathclyde Regions. The clubs, the periods within which they were active and their locations are set out in the accompanying table.

CLUBS OPERATED BY THOMAS HAMILTON BETWEEN NOVEMBER 1981 AND MARCH 1996

Club	Period Active	Location
Dunblane Rovers Group*	Nov.1981-Oct 1983	Dunblane H.S.
Dunblane Boys Club*	Oct 1985-March 1996	Dunblane H.S.
Bannockburn Boys Club*	May 1983-March 1996 (No information Oct 1983-1992)	Bannockburn H.S.
Lynburn Gymnastics Club/Lynburn Boys Club*	Feb.1985-Feb.1986	Woodmill Centre and Dunfermline Centre
Dunfermline Boys Sports Club*	May 1987-Aug 1992	Woodmill Centre & Queen Anne H.S.

Falkirk Boys Club*	May 1987-March 1966 (Intemittent)	Graeme H.S. & Falkirk H.S.
Linlithgow Boys Club	April 1988-May 1989	Linlithgow Academy
Menstrie, Alva & Tillicoultry Boys Club	March 1989-March 1995	Alva Academy
Stirling Boys Club	May 1989-June 1993	Wallace H.S. & Stirling H.S.
Alloa Boys Club*	Nov.1992-June 1994	Alloa Academy
Lornshill Boys Club	Oct. 1992-June 1994	Lornshill Academy
Denny Boys Club	Oct. 1992-Jan 1994	Denny H.S.
Balfron Boys Club	April 1993-June 1993	Balfron H.S.
Callander Boys Club	March 1995-April 1995	McLaren H.S.
Bishopbriggs Boys Club*	Sept.1995-March 1996	Thomas Muir H.S.

The symbol * indicates clubs in respect of which there is evidence of others assisting him to some extent.

4.10   The typical way in which Thomas Hamilton sought to obtain support for such clubs was to send leaflets to houses and primary schools in the area which the club was intended to serve. In general head teachers, who had a discretion as to whether leaflets from voluntary organisations should be allowed to be distributed through their schools, endeavoured to prevent their schools being used in this way. The clubs were aimed mainly at boys between the ages of 7 and 11. The club activities consisted of games, such as football, along with an element of gymnastics. Thomas Hamilton held a Grade 5 certificate from the British Amateur Gymnastics Association which qualified him to provide coaching in gymnastics, subject to being supervised by someone who held a higher qualification. He was occasionally assisted by persons with sporting qualifications who had responded to an advertisement; or by volunteer helpers, including parents, but this was not regularly the case. In general Thomas Hamilton ran each of the clubs entirely on his own. In a few instances he represented that there was a club committee. In these cases it appears that a few individuals gave him temporary assistance but there was no satisfactory evidence that the members of the committee controlled or managed anything. From about 1989 he used the title "Boys' Clubs Sports Group Committee", so creating the impression that others were participating in the running of the clubs. In reality this was a title for his own activities. From the running of the clubs he obtained a modest income which in the early days enabled him to finance his trading in cameras. Boys were initially charged 20p or 30p per night but these charges rose to £1 or £1.50. Most of the clubs were initially extremely popular, attracting as many as 70 boys. However, over the lifetime of a club the numbers dropped, typically to less than a dozen. In the early days Thomas Hamilton put this down to lack of patience or determination on the part of the boys. However, it is more likely that this was due to the accumulated effect of reactions to his behaviour and the rumours which it generated.

4.11   Thomas Hamilton's explanation of his objectives was that he wanted to give the boys something to do and keep them off the streets, and that the discipline was a useful preparation for life. He said that he put his boys through fitness schemes; that he hated fat children and blamed parents for allowing them to eat junk food. However, his style of running the clubs attracted the comment from parents and helpers that it was over-regimented and even militaristic. Witnesses described him as tending to be domineering. There was too much use of shouting. It suggested to some that he was getting something out of dominating the boys. His approach was in any event not in line with modern methods. The evidence also indicated that the exercises which the boys were asked to perform were over-strenuous for their age. Parents were also concerned that he was running the clubs without any apparent adult help. He said that he was authorised to be in sole charge of up to 30 boys but this was known to be untrue.

4.12   At the same time Thomas Hamilton appeared to show an unusual interest in individual boys after only one appearance at the club and to put pressure on them to obtain parental permission to attend one of his summer camps. He appeared to helpers to have favourites. He was also very eager to collect boys from their homes and was keen to find out more about their family background than was acceptable to their parents after a short acquaintance. Parents were particularly concerned about Thomas Hamilton's insistence that for gymnastics the boys wore black (and ill fitting) swimming trunks which he provided and that they changed into them in the gym rather than in the changing rooms. He argued that they often arrived in unsuitable clothing and hence this "uniform" was needed. The colour eliminated the problem of matching different colours. He also argued that since the Regional Council had changed the colour of its vehicles he was justified in deciding on a uniform colour.

4.13   Another matter which was of concern to parents was his practice of taking photographs of the boys posing in their black trunks while taking deep breaths, without the knowledge or permission of their parents. For this purpose he used not only a still camera but also a video camera which he acquired about 1989 and possessed for about 5 years. He argued that it was quite normal for photographs to be taken for training and advertising purposes and said that parents could obtain copies from him. On a number of occasions he offered parents a videotape so that they could see what kind of activities he ran. These only served to increase their concern. Their overriding impression was that there was something unnatural. The boys did not seem to be enjoying themselves but appeared silent and even frightened. There was also an over-concentration on parts of the boys' bodies, especially the naked upper parts along with long lingering shots of the area between the waist and the knees. When confronted with complaints about this Thomas Hamilton argued that it was necessary to identify what muscles were being used so that wrong movements could be corrected. When challenged about videotapes being made and photographs taken without parental knowledge or consent he responded that parental consent was not necessary but that parents could have access to any photographs which he had taken. Individual parents through contact with each other discovered that their anxieties were shared. At home Thomas Hamilton kept a large collection of photographs of boys, many of them wearing black swimming trunks. These were in albums or attached to the walls of his rooms. On one occasion he attempted without success to interest a neighbour in a videotape showing "his boys" performing gymnastics in small black bathing trunks. In the same way as with the parents it made her feel uneasy. Evidence was also given that he attempted without success to take photographs of a neighbour's children, including his 5 year old son. The neighbour explained in evidence: "I just didn't like the look of the guy".

4.14   Some parents, rather than having specific complaints, simply felt that they did not like the way in which he ran the club. Some boys complained of feeling uncomfortable in his presence and said that he was "weird". When he was asked about the way in which he ran his clubs Thomas Hamilton would often speak with pride of what he was doing for the benefit of the boys. On closer questioning he would quickly become defensive and even aggressive and angry, leaving parents with the impression that he was hiding something. When a child was withdrawn from one of his clubs he would tend to react by writing to the parents long and repeated letters in which he stated that rumour and innuendoes were rife about him and it was up to them to stamp out this type of falsity. Some of the letters were hand-delivered at night and were seen by parents as intimidating. On occasion Thomas Hamilton would make use of the names of people in official positions as "contacts" in his promotional leaflets, but without their permission. Thus, for example, in 1993 he used the name of a police inspector, the Chief Executive of Central Regional Council and Mr Michael Forsyth, MP in this way. Naturally this was objected to.

4.15   The only evidence which the Inquiry heard as to any act of indecency on the part of Thomas Hamilton comprised two incidents. Firstly, one witness gave evidence at the Inquiry that about 1979-80 when he was 12 years of age he attended the Dunblane Rovers at the Duckburn Centre on one occasion. At one point Thomas Hamilton sat down close beside him and rubbed him on the inside of his leg, asking him why he wanted to be one of his boys and join the club. The boy pulled away from him and said that he was just interested in firing weapons, which they had done earlier. The boy told his father that he did not like the way Thomas Hamilton had touched and spoken to him but he went back to the club the next week. However, Thomas Hamilton said that he was not mature enough and would not let him in. Secondly, another person, whose statement was read to the Inquiry, stated that when he was about 12 years of age (in 1985) he attended Thomas Hamilton's club at Bannockburn. In the summer he was one of a party of eight boys who went to Loch Lomond with him and stayed in his cabin cruiser. He described an occasion when Thomas Hamilton in his cabin touched him between his legs and on his private parts; told him to lie face down on a bed where he started to push his fingers into his rectum and stroked his back. Thomas Hamilton's shorts were off and his penis was erect. He then told him to face the side of the cabin and ran his hand up and down his back while breathing heavily. Up to that point Thomas Hamilton was striking him from time to time with a telescopic pointer. He then told him that he could go. The witness did not report this incident to anyone else. I do not have difficulty in accepting the evidence in regard to the first of these incidents. The second is in a rather different position. The witness was unwilling to be identified and accordingly his evidence was available only in written form. Thus he could not be cross-examined and I had no opportunity of observing his demeanour for myself. Further Mr Bonomy advised me that there were certain further matters in the statement of the witness which, if they were true, would be expected to be corroborated by independent evidence. However, efforts to obtain such corroboration had met with no success. In addition the witness had in the past been convicted of a serious crime of dishonesty. I also noted that the witness stated that the boat blew up about a week after the trip. However, other evidence showed that Thomas Hamilton received his insurance payment for his loss of the boat in December 1983 While there may well be an element of truth in this account I do not consider that it would be wise for me to treat it as entirely reliable. Accordingly I do not find this allegation to have been proved. I would also mention that in the BBC *Panorama* programme broadcast on 16 September a young man alleged that at a summer camp at Loch Lomond in the early 1980s he had been touched indecently by Thomas Hamilton. I understand that a subsequent investigation which was carried out by the Crown showed that the police had been unable to trace him in connection with the Inquiry: that his allegation was not supported by other evidence and was not consistent with a newspaper article dated 17 March which was based on information supplied by him: that he had received payment for both the article and the broadcast: and that he had a considerable list of convictions for crimes of dishonesty, the latest of which had led to his imprisonment on 20 August 1996. I consider that evidence of his allegation would not have assisted the Inquiry.

Clubs in Central Regional Council premises in the 1980s

4.16   It appears that Thomas Hamilton first obtained a let of Central Regional Council premises in or about 1980 at Borestone Primary School. In October 1981, describing himself as principal leader of the Dunblane Rovers Troop, he applied for a let of the gymnasium at Dunblane High School. Such lets were dealt with by the clerk to the School Council. The Region's policy was designed to encourage the use of council premises by the community. No checks were carried out on the applicants. The application was granted. In the same month Mr I Collie, Director of Education, received a memorandum in regard to an enquiry about Thomas Hamilton's activities at Dunblane High School in which it was stated that Thomas Hamilton was not affiliated in any way to the Scout movement. It continued: "Mr Hamilton appears to be the subject of a confidential report at national level which shows him to be totally undesirable in relation to working for the Scout movement. The report is based on his homosexual tendencies, and he was for obvious reasons discreetly removed from the Scout movement". This information was said to have been provided by Mr T Mack who was then a District Commissioner. However, in evidence Mr Mack denied being the source of this information. He was aware that it had been rumoured that Thomas Hamilton was taking young people on camping expeditions which were not properly supervised, but he was not aware that he was suspected of any sexual impropriety. After making certain enquiries of Thomas Hamilton Mr Collie took the view that there was nothing which could be queried by the education authority. It may be noted that the name "Rovers" created the impression that there was some connection between the club and the Scout movement; and the fact that the club was being operated on school premises gave the impression that it was respectable and approved by the local authority.

4.17   In the summer of 1983 complaints from parents and head teachers led to the club's activities being considered at a meeting of the Further Education and General Purposes Sub-Committee on 15 August. At that meeting the junior deputy Director of Education referred to complaints about confusion with the Scout movement and lack of supervision. He also stated that he had learned that Thomas Hamilton had been removed from the Scouts for homosexual tendencies although they were not prepared to say so formally. The Committee decided that the lets in favour of Thomas Hamilton at Dunblane and Bannockburn High Schools should be cancelled. Thomas Hamilton was informed of this decision but not of the reasons for it.

4.18   Thomas Hamilton reacted by lodging a complaint on 10 October 1983 with the Commissioner for Local Administration in Scotland, to whom I will refer as the "Ombudsman", on the ground that the Council had acted on "malicious gossip and unfounded allegations without investigation". His councillor Mr Robert Ball was concerned that the decision was a breach of natural justice in that no formal complaints had been made against him. Thomas Hamilton also appealed against the decision to terminate the let of Dunblane High School and obtained the support of 30 letters from parents together with a petition dated 2 November 1983 bearing 70 signatures in his favour. The latter ended with the words: "We are all proud to have Mr Hamilton in charge of our boys; he has a most activated, excellent quality of leadership and integrity and absolutely devoted to his lads; above all he cares". These were considered by the sub-committee on 7 November 1983 when by a majority it was decided that the *status quo* should be maintained.

4.19   Local opinion was divided over Thomas Hamilton. Some parents had a "gut feeling" that something was amiss about his activities. They included Mr George Robertson MP who took up the matter informally with Mr Michael Forsyth MP, the local Member of Parliament since April 1983. Earlier in that year Thomas Hamilton had demanded an explanation from Mr Robertson's son why he was absent from the club and sought an interview with the boy. This aroused Mr Robertson's suspicions. As a result he and another parent had visited the club and had been dismayed to see "a large number of small boys in shorts stripped to the waist being bossed around by two or three middle-aged men, swaggering around in a very military-type way". Mr Robertson also described it as "looking like the Hitler youth". They had decided on the spot that their sons were not going to return to the club. Their unease had been shared by other parents, although it was difficult to identify exactly what was wrong. Mr Forsyth, who had already been approached by Thomas Hamilton for his support, was aware that rumours were circulating in Dunblane about him but was also aware that he was supported by a number of parents and that there was no hard evidence of wrongdoing on his part. Thomas Hamilton made a fresh application for a let of Dunblane High School, this time in the name of the Dunblane Boys Club but on 12 March 1984 the sub-committee decided to defer consideration of this application pending the decision of the Ombudsman.

4.20   On 15 November 1984 the Ombudsman found that there had been maladministration on the part of the Regional Council and that injustice had been caused as a result. The grounds for this decision appear to have been that there was not adequate evidence to substantiate the complaints against Thomas Hamilton; and that he had not been given an opportunity to put his side of the case before the decision was taken. The reasoning which the Ombudsman provided for his decision is not wholly satisfactory. Firstly, his jurisdiction to enter into a consideration of the merits of a decision depended upon whether he had found in the first place that there had been maladministration and this in turn depended on whether the local authority had acted in accordance with good administrative practice. However, it is clear from his conclusions that the Ombudsman became involved in a consideration of the weight to be attached to the complaints before determining whether the Regional Council had acted unfairly. Secondly it is not clear why the Ombudsman adopted the view of the complaints which he did, and in particular why they should have been, in his words, "heavily discounted". If he was well-founded in becoming involved in the merits of the decision it is difficult to understand why no consideration was given to the potential risk to the children whose parents had complained. It was open to him to take into account questions of child protection and parental complaints. In the result he stated that on the evidence available he saw no reason why the Council should not now grant a let and that in any case he would be unable to record that their future action was a satisfactory response until he was convinced that they had made a decision "on the basis of a proper examination of the relevant factors and only those". The Ombudsman's report also referred to the fact that in October 1981 a Scout official had expressed displeasure to a local councillor about the fact that Thomas Hamilton's "Boys Group" was using the name "Rovers", which had previously been used by the Scouts. Enquiries made by the councillor had confirmed that there was no affiliation to the Scouts and that Thomas Hamilton had been required some years before to give up his activities with them. The report also stated that Thomas Hamilton had sent to the Regional Council in October 1983 a copy of a letter by which he had resigned his Scout leadership in April 1974 (cf para 4.7); and that the Scout Association had informed the Ombudsman that it had not been received by them.

4.21   The Regional Council were dismayed at the outcome but took the view that if they were obliged to grant a let to Thomas Hamilton they should insist upon the safeguard of a constitution for what was now to be named as the Dunblane Boys Club; a committee formed by named adults; and a meeting with the committee. Thomas Hamilton considered that the outcome was a complete vindication of his position; and, fortified by Mr Forsyth's congratulations, made a practice in future of forwarding him copies of correspondence about further investigations of his activities.

4.22   A meeting between the committee of the Dunblane Boys Club and the Sub-Committee of the Education Committee did not take place until 23 September 1985, principally due to a delay on the part of Thomas Hamilton. However, the sub-committee was provided with information on a number of matters together with evidence of appropriate insurance cover and gymnastics qualification. The sub-committee agreed that there was no reason for refusing the let of Dunblane High School and it was reinstated as from 24 October 1985.

4.23   It should be added that after the publication of the Ombudsman's report Thomas Hamilton visited Mr David Vass once more. In the course of a conversation between them which was quite vigorous Thomas Hamilton gave him the impression that he believed that the Ombudsman had condemned Mr Vass, and the latter became aware that Thomas Hamilton was recording their conversation on a portable machine. In August 1986 Thomas Hamilton sought a meeting with Mr Fairgrieve at which he maintained that his life had been ruined by malicious rumours about his behaviour and his views which had been spread by the Scout Commissioner in the area of Dunblane. He refused to substantiate his complaint, claiming that the matter was in the hands of his solicitor. Mr Fairgrieve formed the view that he was even more obsessional and even had the appearance of being on psychiatric drugs. This was followed by various telephone calls in which he sought without success to rejoin the Scout movement and to see the confidential report which related to him. He also contacted various senior officials in the Scout movement with complaints about what he referred to as a grapevine of innuendo and unattributable comments about him.

Summer camp on Inchmoan Island, Loch Lomond in July 1988

4.24   On a number of occasions Thomas Hamilton organised summer camps which were aimed at catering for boys. Some of them took place on Loch

Lomond where he had a small speedboat and later, as I mentioned before, a cabin cruiser, until it caught fire and sank in the early 1980s. He organised a camp on Inchmoan Island for several weeks as from 3 July 1988. He claimed later that this was his 55th summer camp for boys but there is no way in which this can be confirmed. Depending on the arrangements made with the individual parents, boys of about 9 years of age came for one or two weeks at a time. It appears that for much of the time Thomas Hamilton was running the camp with no additional adult help. After one boy arrived home unhappy about the camp the complaints of several families came to the attention of Strathclyde Police, in whose area the island was situated. At the request of Chief Inspector Hay of Dumbarton CID, PC George Gunn and PC Donna Duncan visited the Island on 20 July.

4.25   They found the site was generally messy, the tables strewn with dirty dishes. The sleeping bags in the tents were damp to the touch. The food was not very wholesome. There was no sign of fresh food and the only source of nutrition was tinned and powdered food. The boys were 13 in number and appeared to be cold and inadequately dressed for the weather conditions. Some were playing unsupervised in and around the water about 30 yards from the camp dressed in swimming trunks, some with tee-shirts. They had scratches on their legs. These were explained as being due to their going through bracken on the island. Thomas Hamilton would not allow them to wear trousers, saying that legs dried more easily than trousers. When questioned, 3 boys said unreservedly that they were enjoying themselves; the others were generally somewhat homesick, complaining of the food and the fact that they were not allowed to send postcards home or to contact their parents by telephone when they made a trip to Luss on the shore of the loch. The means of reaching the shore was a rowing boat with an inadequate number of lifejackets. However, none of the boys was sufficiently upset to accept PC Gunn's offer to take them home. Thomas Hamilton was pleasant in his manner but PC Gunn was uneasy about him in a vague and indefinable way. He did not consider that the children were in any particular danger but regarded the camp as very basic and badly run. Thomas Hamilton was alleged to have slapped one or two boys. He did not deny doing so but maintained that they had been disruptive, bullying and cheeky.

4.26   PC Gunn submitted a report to Dumbarton Police Office. Thomas Hamilton was not charged with any offence. The parents were contacted by the police. In due course six of them came to Dumbarton Police Office where the boys and Thomas Hamilton had been taken after they had been found on a trip to Alexandria. Some of the boys felt homesick and were taken home, but none of the boys or the parents on that occasion made any complaint against Thomas Hamilton. Some indeed praised him.

4.27   DS Ian McBain submitted a report on the investigation dated 30 August 1988 to the Procurator Fiscal at Dumbarton, Mr James Cardle. Mr Cardle decided that some of the witnesses from whom statements had been obtained should be precognosced before he reached a decision. His purpose in doing so was to obtain full information about the alleged assaults and to see if some of the discrepancies between the accounts given by the boys could be reconciled. Virtually all the boys spoke to being struck by Thomas Hamilton and/or seeing other boys being struck. In a number of statements some of the boys were unable to name the boys they had seen being struck. Some boys described events happening to other boys which these boys did not refer to themselves. After precognition Mr Cardle, according to his recollection, found that the discrepancies between some of the boys' accounts were even greater than they had been. Assaults were either not corroborated or there were discrepancies between accounts. Thus boy A would speak to boy B being slapped in his presence but boy B would not recall this—and vice versa. Not all the boys spoke up to the police statements and some of the accounts at precognition were vague. He also recollected that while after precognition there may have been one or two incidents for which there was corroborated evidence there were many others where accounts were vague or inconsistent. He did not consider it appropriate to select from the whole picture one or two incidents where there was on paper an apparent sufficiency of evidence. In any event his recollection was that the one or two incidents for which there was corroborative and consistent evidence were very minor indeed and did not merit criminal prosecution. Having considered the papers he reached the decision that he would not institute criminal proceedings against Thomas Hamilton. As he remained concerned at the situation which had been revealed in the papers he indicated to the police that they should take these matters up with the social work department, the Reporter to the Children's Panel and also the education authorities involved in the letting of the school premises for the clubs. His recollection was that he was informed that these other agencies were already aware of these matters. In this context the role of the Reporter is, of course, not concerned with initiating proceedings against an adult.

4.28 Miss Laura Dunlop submitted at the close of the Inquiry that the Procurator Fiscal could have taken steps to prosecute Thomas Hamilton in regard to assaulting two of the boys and for a breach of section 12 of the Children and Young Persons (Scotland) Act 1937. In response Mr Bonomy pointed out that the Inquiry did not have available to it the precognitions which had been obtained by Mr Cardle. Furthermore there was no evidence that the children had sustained any injury. Any striking of them was exclusively in connection with Thomas Hamilton's attempts to maintain discipline. There was no question of the children being in physical or moral danger. The attitude of the parents towards Thomas Hamilton was far from uniform. For the reasons which I set out in Appendix 3 to this report I am not concerned with reviewing decisions taken by a Procurator Fiscal. If Mr Cardle's decision had hinged on whether or not there was enough evidence as a matter of law on which to frame a charge or charges there might be some point in my considering the question whether there was enough evidence on which charges could have been based. However, it is clear from the account of Mr Cardle's actions that his decision was based upon an assessment of the quality and significance of the evidence. In these circumstances I see no point on which I can properly express any view on the decision taken by him.

4.29 Meanwhile Thomas Hamilton made an informal complaint against PC Gunn, claiming that he was incompetent and untruthful in making his report. He sent a series of letters to his superior officer, Inspector Michael Mill, and other officers of Central Scotland Police. These were widely circulated through Dunblane and reached his local MP. In August Thomas Hamilton called at Balfron Police Office intending to discuss PC Gunn's report with him. PC Gunn refused to do so and had great difficulty in getting Thomas Hamilton to leave, even having to resort to the threat of having him arrested. It was clear that the incident had become an obsession as far as he was concerned. His initial complaint was that police officers were not qualified to make a proper judgment. He sent letters to Inspector Mill indicating the type of activity which took place at the camp and enclosing receipts to show the kind of food that he had bought. His complaint was thoroughly investigated and rejected in a letter written on behalf of the Chief Constable dated 19 October 1988. Initially Thomas Hamilton appeared to accept what had been said. However, almost immediately he changed his mind and wrote to the Chief Constable objecting to the fact that PC Gunn had been appointed to investigate his camp "in view of a long resentment shown to our group by many adult members of the Dunblane Scouts". He claimed, incorrectly, that PC Gunn was a Scout leader. This was a demonstration of a fixation on the part of Thomas Hamilton that there was a "brotherhood" conspiracy between the police and the Scouts in Dunblane. This fixation was pursued in a stream of letters to the police, his MP, The Scottish Office, his local newspaper and circulars to parents of boys and to the public.

4.30   On 30 November 1988 Thomas Hamilton made his complaint official. It was then formally investigated on behalf of the Deputy Chief Constable of Central Scotland Police, Douglas McMurdo, who appointed Inspector (now Supt) James Keenan to investigate. The charges made by Thomas Hamilton were that PC Gunn had made a false and misleading statement to Strathclyde Police, and that he had made an unlawful and unnecessary exercise of his authority in the investigation of the Inchmoan camp. A barrage of letters from Thomas Hamilton continued, becoming personalised and critical of the competence and professionalism of the police officers. Inspector Keenan carried out a thorough investigation of Thomas Hamilton's complaint, having taken a formal statement of it from him. Thomas Hamilton took some 3 hours to deliver it. Inspector Keenan's investigations included the taking of additional statements from witnesses in regard to allegations of a similar type to those investigated by PC Gunn. He also interviewed a number of persons who had camped in the same area as Thomas Hamilton and spoke highly of his organisation and capabilities as a leader, and the food and equipment provided by him. On 22 May 1989 Inspector Keenan submitted his report in which he exonerated PC Gunn and PC Duncan. Thomas Hamilton subsequently complained that this investigation was a whitewash and that he had not got to the truth. PC Gunn expressed the view in his evidence that Thomas Hamilton was untrustworthy, vindictive, wholly unreasonable, malicious and obsessive. He had considered suing him for defamation but decided that there would be little point in doing so.

4.31   In his report Inspector Keenan suggested to DCC McMurdo that numerous points which had been elicited might be worthy of consideration by Strathclyde Police. The Deputy Chief Constable submitted the report to the Deputy Chief Constable of Strathclyde Police, and on his behalf it was passed on 16 June 1989 to the Chief Superintendent responsible for disciplinary matters asking that a senior officer take the report to the Procurator Fiscal at Dumbarton and have any further enquiry necessary carried out. However, when the report reached Mr Cardle he realised at once that it concerned a complaint against police officers which was a matter which could not be dealt with by him but only by the Regional Procurator Fiscal at Paisley. Accordingly he forwarded the report to him. It should be understood that as a matter of long standing practice which has had the approval of the High Court of Justiciary (*MacLeod v Tiffney* 1994 SCCR 169) information which is elicited in the course of the investigation of a complaint against a police officer remains confidential to the Regional Procurator Fiscal and is not disclosed to the Procurator Fiscal or his staff who may be considering a report against the person making the complaint. This applies, of course, to matters arising out of the same incident. Accordingly I see no ground whatever for imputing any criticism to the Procurator Fiscal at Dumbarton. The Regional Procurator Fiscal having considered the report of Inspector Keenan reached the view that it disclosed nothing of a criminal nature so far as the conduct of the police was concerned and marked the papers "no proceedings".

He confirmed his decision in a letter to the discipline branch dated 10 October 1989.

Linlithgow Boys' Club

4.32   In April 1988 Thomas Hamilton registered the Linlithgow Boys Club with Lothian Regional Council. Registration depended on whether the applicant organisation was to be run for the benefit of young people and details of the members of the organisation required to be provided. Registration qualified the organisation for reduced rates. An application was normally investigated. However, due to an oversight no check was made in this case. Accordingly a follow-up check was made by Mr D G Jeffrey, a senior youth educational worker, who had responsibility for youth and children's work development. On his visit to the club, which met at Linlithgow Academy, he saw nothing to give him cause for concern. He found about 30 boys aged between 8 and 11 in PE kit in the school gym doing football training. He was also concerned with a complaint from a parent who had withdrawn her son from the summer camp and had complained of being intimidated by Thomas Hamilton who was seeking payment of money due for the booking. The Inquiry also heard evidence that a parent had been against her son going to his camp as she had heard that Thomas Hamilton stood at the entrance to the showers at Linlithgow Academy on the pretext that this was to stop any trouble there.

4.33   Mr Jeffrey took the opportunity to discuss the summer camps, the programme and nature of the activities and contact points with parents. The information which Thomas Hamilton gave him caused him some concern. He felt uneasy about such young boys being on an island in Loch Lomond with the only access to parents being a telephone link. He felt ill at ease during this meeting. Thomas Hamilton was immediately on the defensive when he was asked about the club and wanted to know who had made complaints against him. When he was questioned about whether there was a club committee and/or parental involvement in the club, he said he intended to form a parents' committee after a trial period (in fact he never did so). Later in the same week Mr Jeffrey made enquiries about Thomas Hamilton with the Scout Association, the Scottish Association of Boys Clubs and Mr G Baxter, Head of the Woodmill Centre, Dunfermline. From all these sources came the same impression, a feeling of uneasiness and concern which was difficult to define. He was concerned as to why Thomas Hamilton refused to have his clubs affiliated to a larger organisation such as the Scottish Association of Boys Clubs. There was no tangible evidence that something was amiss but the general recommendation was that it was better to have nothing to do with him. He was also concerned at learning that it was unlikely that Thomas Hamilton would receive any help in running the club at Linlithgow or at Dunfermline. Shortly after his visit he received a very detailed letter from Thomas Hamilton which sought to justify his activities, along with copies of letters to public figures including his appeal to the Ombudsman to which I have referred already. Mr Jeffrey felt that Thomas Hamilton was attempting to deter him from further investigation. However, he was aware of "innuendo and unhappiness" rather than objective details.

4.34   Thereafter a recommendation was made to the Head of the Community Education Service in Lothian Region Council that the club should be de-registered on the grounds that the ratio of leader to members was unsatisfactory; that there was no parental committee; that other regional councils could not recommend Thomas Hamilton's clubs; that he was not affiliated to the Scottish Association of Boys Clubs; and that there was no insurance. However despite this Thomas Hamilton was granted a further let for the year starting in the autumn of 1988.

4.35   In May 1989 a further complaint was made about Thomas Hamilton and was later presented on behalf of Mrs Doreen Hagger by her councillor. The complaint was that there had been inappropriate activities at the camp on Inchmoan Island to which I have already referred. Mrs Hagger was one of the parents of boys who had attended that camp and, following her son making a complaint, she had gone to the island and eventually agreed to assist Thomas Hamilton with the camp. At a later stage when Inspector Keenan interviewed her son it emerged that Thomas Hamilton had allegedly rubbed suntan oil on the boys at the camp and had asked them to do so all over his body, on some occasions when he was not wearing pants. She did not witness this herself. She became extremely opposed to his activities and decided to do her utmost to persuade others of his unsuitability to supervise boys clubs.

4.36   On 16 May 1989 Mrs Hagger, along with Mrs Janet Reilly who had also assisted at the camp on Inchmoan Island, assaulted Thomas Hamilton by pouring various substances including suntan oil over him as he was leaving Linlithgow Academy at the end of one of the meetings of the club. In her evidence Mrs Hagger said that she wanted to stop Thomas Hamilton organising another camp. She wanted to be taken to court for assaulting him so that there would be a proper investigation. She arranged for a press reporter to be present with a photographer so that she could obtain the maximum publicity from the incident. She also wanted Lothian Regional Council to revoke the let at Linlithgow Academy. To her great disappointment Thomas Hamilton refused to make any complaint against her and remained calm and polite.

4.37   It is reasonably plain that Mrs Hagger's actions led to the Regional Council becoming aware that the 1988 camp had been the subject of police investigations. Through the confusion between the original report to the Procurator Fiscal at Dumbarton (who had already decided to take no proceedings) and the report by Inspector Keenan the education department of the Regional Council was given to understand that a decision on proceedings against Thomas Hamilton was still pending. On this basis the Regional Council considered that it had a duty to protect the children which justified them in suspending the let while investigations were proceeding. In these circumstances they suspended the let in May 1989.

4.38   Thomas Hamilton responded by making a complaint to the Ombudsman, but the latter decided not to carry out an investigation. He stated that he did not consider that any criticism could be levelled at the Regional Council having regard to the high duty of care where children were involved. It may be noted that in this case the existence of parental complaints, in combination with the fact that there had been a police investigation, were sufficient to tip the balance against the complaint. In due course the Regional Council was informed that no action was to be taken against Thomas Hamilton. He was told that if he submitted an application it would be considered. Despite this the Regional Council had developed a policy whereby any space which he sought would be allocated for community use so as to be unavailable for him. The assistant Director of Education, Mr J Perry, said in evidence that they had a feeling that his organisation was not suitable but they could not prove it.

Summer camp at Mullarochy Bay, Loch Lomond in July 1991

4.39   On 23 July 1991 DS (now Chief Inspector) Paul Hughes, who was in charge of the Child Protection Unit at Bannockburn was informed of a complaint by a parent about Thomas Hamilton's camp at Mullarochy Bay which was within the area of Central Scotland Police. This camp was held for a period of 2 weeks with some 20 boys in the age range of 6-11 years attending for part or all of the time. It had been understood that the camp would be supervised by 4-6 adults. In fact the only assistance which Thomas Hamilton had was one other adult who arrived after the first week. There were complaints about assault and the videotaping of boys. DS Hughes assigned DC Grant Kirk and a social work colleague. They went to the camp on 23 July and interviewed Thomas Hamilton under caution. He effectively admitted the assault but sought to justify it. Once more there was concern about boys being required to wear black swimming trunks.

4.40   DS Hughes had not encountered Thomas Hamilton before but learned that he would be likely to be quick to complain. He therefore decided to become involved in the investigation and visited the camp on 25 July in the company of DC Kirk. The main purpose of this visit was to return camera equipment which Thomas Hamilton had surrendered 2 days before, but it also provided DS Hughes with an opportunity to look at the camp himself. As regards the assault Thomas Hamilton admitted under caution to slapping a child across the face. His justification was that the boy had been disruptive, a bully, had assaulted another child, had thrown a stone which hit another child in the eye and needed chastisement. He also admitted to slapping the same boy across the leg and grabbing him. Concerns had also been raised about the nature of the photographs which he had taken and about a trip to an island where the children had been forced to take part in the making of a videofilm on the lines of "The Lord of the Flies". In particular one child was forced to lie in cold water against his will. The children were cold and wet and were dressed only in swimming trunks during a rain shower as Thomas Hamilton prevented them from putting their clothes on. When he was asked to provide photographs he had taken Thomas Hamilton denied that he had taken any still photographs.

4.41   During his visit DS Hughes became concerned about the lack of supervision at the camp. Half a dozen boys were running around the camp area but the others were out of sight. They were about 400-500 yards away at a jetty and out of clear view of the camp. It took DS Hughes some 3 or 4 minutes to walk down to the jetty where he found the boys, the youngest being only 6 years old, jumping from the jetty into a boat and back out again. The water there was deep and not one of the boys was wearing a life jacket. Thomas Hamilton did not know the boys were there. When he was questioned about the potential for accidents he said that they were capable of looking after themselves and that he could provide any assistance in the event of an accident. Some of the parents had removed their children after DC Kirk's first visit to the camp.

4.42   One of the boys who was interviewed later said that he had been singled out by Thomas Hamilton, taken alone to an individual tent and photographed in red-coloured swimming trunks. DS Hughes feared that this boy was being singled out for special treatment and perhaps for future abuse. Thomas Hamilton denied any such intention and denied taking such photographs. On 30 July and in response to a request from the police he handed over 6 boxes of slides and about 150 still photographs. There was reason to believe that he deceived the police.

DS Hughes discovered at the shop in Stirling where Thomas Hamilton had handed in what was to be developed that he had in fact received eight boxes of slides: and that a ninth had recently arrived for him. DS Hughes did not take possession of that box at that time, but at a later date when it was handed over by Thomas Hamilton. In the result there were two boxes of slides which were never recovered by the police. Among the photographs which were recovered there were a large number of the particular boy who was plainly a favourite and had been given special jobs on the camp. However, there were no photographs of him wearing red swimming trunks. A processor in Livingston had also contacted the shop in Stirling in order to express her concern about the content of some of the photographs. It is impossible to know whether the boxes which were not recovered by the police contained photographs which would have given rise to even greater concern. As regards the photographs which were recovered by the police, although there were various different poses by boys wearing black swimming trunks there was no explicit indecency. DS Hughes considered that Thomas Hamilton had been untruthful about the photographs. The nature of them made him concerned about the "stability" of his personality and his unhealthy interest in children.

4.43 At this stage DS Hughes himself became the target of complaints by Thomas Hamilton who wrote to the Chief Constable, the Deputy Chief Constable, his MP and other persons about him. DS Hughes continued his investigations and when he had gathered all the information which he considered relevant he decided to try to interview Thomas Hamilton under caution and give him an opportunity to respond to the allegations. As he himself was the subject of a complaint he sought advice from colleagues and the Procurator Fiscal at Stirling as to how he should proceed. The Procurator Fiscal, Mr K Valentine, advised him to invite Thomas Hamilton to the police office on a voluntary basis for an interview under caution. Thomas Hamilton refused to be interviewed. DS Hughes then delivered his very substantial report to the Procurator Fiscal on 6 September 1991. This report included 10 charges drafted against Thomas Hamilton. They had a brief discussion. Mr Valentine doubted whether the report revealed sufficient evidence of criminality to merit court proceedings. However he decided to have further enquiries made and to have the boys precognosced before reaching a final decision. He was troubled by the contents of the report and the situation that was revealed. He was concerned to have it confirmed that the situation had been drawn to the attention of other agencies that might have an interest. One of the Procurator Fiscal Deputes prepared a note indicating that, in his view, there was not a great deal to substantiate many of the charges proposed by the police, with the possible exception of the charges of assault and a charge of breach of the peace based on Thomas Hamilton shouting and swearing at the boys. When the precognitions were obtained it was noted that none of the parents had anything to add to their statements and some of them had shown concern at the thought that Thomas Hamilton was being suspected of anything untoward. They had not stopped their children going to his clubs. On 18 November 1991 having considered all the material Mr W Gallagher, Procurator Fiscal Depute, decided that no criminal proceedings should be taken, marking the papers "no pro:no crime libelled: not in the public interest". On the same date he wrote to Thomas Hamilton advising him of his decision and informing him that the police had been instructed to return his photographs to him. Mr Gallagher's view was that in relation to some of the allegations the evidence did not indicate criminality and, where criminality was indicated, the circumstances, taken at their highest were not such as to require prosecution in the public interest. Mr Valentine and Mr Gallagher had discussed DS Hughes' report on several occasions. Both took the view that while the contents of the report had troubled them they were of the view that the conduct had approached but not crossed the border of criminality.

4.44   Miss Laura Dunlop in her closing submission also maintained that proceedings could have been taken against Thomas Hamilton in respect of charges 2-7 of those framed by DS Hughes. Mr Bonomy pointed out that the evidence plainly indicated that the child who had been struck by Thomas Hamilton had obviously been behaving in a violent and bullying manner. Once again the question of whether proceedings could have been taken against Thomas Hamilton does not turn on any matter which is properly within my province to review. There is no question of the decision not to prosecute turning on any view of the law which can be seen to be mistaken. Thus there is no basis for my entertaining criticism of the decision taken by the Procurator Fiscal.

4.45   During the course of these investigations DS Hughes discovered that Thomas Hamilton had a firearm certificate. While the papers were before the Procurators Fiscal and anticipating that no proceedings would be taken against Thomas Hamilton, he submitted a memorandum dated 11 November 1991 to the Detective Superintendent, CID Headquarters, in which he requested that serious consideration should be given to withdrawing the firearm certificate as a precautionary measure. I will discuss the implications of this memorandum later in this Report (paras 6.41-6.42 and 6.48 *et seq*).

4.46   Thomas Hamilton made a formal complaint about DS Hughes which was investigated by Chief Inspector Ferguson. His report completely exonerated DS Hughes. In his report Chief Inspector Ferguson stated: "I have completed 30 years police service, a long number of these as a CID Officer. Throughout these years I interviewed many hard criminals, many aggressive people, many reluctant witnesses, many complainers against the police but I can honestly say the interviews with Mr Hamilton were the most exasperating of my career". Not satisfied with this result Thomas Hamilton complained about the way in which Chief Inspector Ferguson had carried out his investigation but nothing came of this. The Chief Constable sought advice from the department of Administration and Legal Services of Central Regional Council about the raising of proceedings for defamation against Thomas Hamilton in respect of his statements about officers of Central Scotland Police, but it was considered that such proceedings would not deter him and would give him the opportunity to air his views about a conspiracy between the Scouts, the police and the Regional Council.

4.47   Thomas Hamilton also complained to the Ombudsman about the conduct of Central Scotland Police and to the Social Work Department claiming that his activities had been harassed and disrupted and his character had been defamed. The Ombudsman dealt with this complaint by pointing out that the police lay outside his jurisdiction, and that defamation was a matter for a court of law.

Residential sports training course, Dunblane in June 1992

4.48   Following the problems which Thomas Hamilton had experienced with his summer camps he ran the series of what came to be known as residential sports training courses during the summer holidays at Dunblane High School. Central Regional Council considered that these courses represented an improvement as compared with his summer camps as they had better facilities and could be supervised. On the evening of 29 June P C Gunn came across three young boys walking down Old Doune Road, Dunblane dressed in their pyjamas. They told him that they had been at a boys' camp at Dunblane High School and that they were wanting to go home. They were home-sick and did not like the discipline which Thomas Hamilton was imposing on them. They did not complain of any violence or criminal behaviour. P C Gunn took them to the police office, but having heard the name of Thomas Hamilton he felt that it was best that he should not become personally involved. Contact was made with the parents who took the boys home.

4.49 On the following day Thomas Hamilton explained to police officers who visited the school that the boys slept in sleeping bags on the dining hall floor. After settling down for the night they were not allowed to go anywhere without his permission, except to the toilets. Three boys had gone there and had probably left the building by the fire exit. At that stage the police were satisfied by his explanation and no further action was taken.

4.50 On 2 July the police received a complaint from a parent about regimentation and lack of supervision. Arrangements were then made to take statements from the three boys. One of the parents expressed herself as concerned about the lack of supervision, the circumstances in which her son left the school and Thomas Hamilton's discouragement of any telephone contact with home and any parental access. A report was made to the Child Protection Unit, which contacted the corresponding unit in Fife from whence the boys had come. Copies were also sent to the Reporters to the Children's Panels for Central Region and Fife Region. The latter Reporter, Mr A Kelly, was concerned about the risk to which the three boys might have been exposed, the conditions at the school and the general lack of supervision. He communicated his concerns to Mr D Somerville, the Senior Assistant Director of Education of Fife Regional Council. In a memorandum to him he wrote: "I feel that the events of 29 June 1992 in Dunblane in a sense serve as a warning. If the kind of circumstances as described are allowed to continue without some kind of intervention, I consider that other children may be placed at risk. In like situations arising unchecked, I fear that a tragedy to a child or children is almost waiting to happen."

4.51 A copy of the police report was submitted to the Procurator Fiscal at Stirling, Mr Valentine, for information only. He was satisfied that it required no action to be taken and marked the copy "no pro: not a crime". There plainly was no evidence of any criminal act.

Lynburn Gymnastics Club/Dunfermline Boys Club

4.52 In the case of Fife Regional Council applications for lets at school premises required to be made to the area office of the Regional Council but might be referred to the headmaster for consideration. Thomas Hamilton obtained a let for the Lynburn Gymnastics Club at the Woodmill Centre in Dunfermline. The club included swimming under the supervision of qualified attendants employed by the Regional Council. At first Thomas Hamilton had an assistant, but when attendances started to diminish he could not afford to keep him on. Thereafter a number of parents assisted him but from about 1990 he was there on his own.

4.53 While the club was at the Woodmill Centre it was monitored by the full-time staff employed at the Centre who would watch activities once a fortnight for about ten minutes. The staff described activities as being "a gymnastics class from about 1945 or the 1950s". Mr G Baxter, the Head of the Woodmill Centre, said in evidence that: "It just wasn't the type of gymnastics they were being taught in the 1990s but there was nothing else wrong with it". The boys wore only gym shoes and shorts, but this was not considered to be unusual. Thomas Hamilton took photographs of the boys and some of these were passed to Mr Baxter for display in the Centre. They did not contain anything unusual.

4.54   A number of complaints came to the attention of Mr Baxter. A number of these related to camps run by Thomas Hamilton. In 1985 it was reported that he had left some boys unsupervised at night on an island in Loch Lomond while he stayed on a barge with other boys. They were left with a rowing boat and the youngest was hardly able to swim. They were given little to eat and were not able to wear warm clothing. One boy was assaulted by three others and Thomas Hamilton apparently watched without intervening. A further complaint was made in regard to a camp in 1990. This was that a boy had sustained a serious chest infection there. However, in this instance the parent did not pursue the complaint. In each instance the Regional Council considered withdrawing the lets, but took the view that they could not do so as nothing untoward was occurring in the Centre.

4.55   As regards the club there was a complaint in 1990, by which time it was referred to as the Dunfermline Boys Sports Club. The complaint was that a boy was excluded from the Club for being too big. Following correspondence Thomas Hamilton agreed not to prevent boys from joining on the basis of their build. As far as Mr Baxter was aware this was the only complaint received by Fife Region in regard to activities within the Woodmill Centre.

4.56   Following the memorandum from the Reporter to the Children's Panel to which I have referred in para 4.50, Mr Somerville prepared a detailed report considering the issues raised by the 1992 training course. His report incorporated the findings of Mr E Liddell, a PE Instructor, who had viewed a videotape of the gymnastics run by Thomas Hamilton. Mr Liddell's view was that the activities were inappropriate and in some cases dangerous. As a result of this report it was decided that the Regional Council would not provide further lets to Thomas Hamilton. The concern was that children might suffer harm through carelessness on his part. The Council were not aware of any rumours regarding possible abuse of boys. The lets were terminated as from 28 August 1992.

4.57   Thomas Hamilton complained about this to the Ombudsman, but on 7 September 1992 he declined to proceed with the complaint as the Regional Council had offered to meet Thomas Hamilton. However, Thomas Hamilton did not receive any further let from the Regional Council.

Further complaints about Thomas Hamilton during 1993—1995

4.58   In January 1993 a complaint was made to Central Regional Council that Thomas Hamilton was solely in charge of the club at Denny High School. This led to the Regional Council investigating his qualifications and methods and the *bona fides* of the Boys Sports Club Group Committee. In May and June 1993 the Family Unit (formerly the Child Protection Unit) received two further complaints about Thomas Hamilton's conduct at Denny High School and Dunblane High

School. The complaints were that he had required boys to change into black swimming trunks and had photographed them. In one case the boy was photographed on his own in a locked gym. In the other the boy was photographed while carrying out exercises with another boy. Another complaint was made that a boy had attended at Stirling High School with a view to playing five-a-side football but instead had been required to change into ill-fitting trunks and perform gymnastic exercises. The nature of the exercises caused concern to the police. In each case an investigation was carried out by the Family Unit, but as the boys were then withdrawn from the clubs no further action was taken under the child protection procedures. However, the investigation was continued as a police matter and a report was submitted to the Procurator Fiscal on 9 June 1993 with a request for a warrant to search Thomas Hamilton's house for photographs, photographic equipment, documentation and other items which might be relevant to police enquiries. The police were concerned about Thomas Hamilton's access to boys, especially those who were vulnerable. They thought that photographs of them performing certain exercises were open to being interpreted as lewd. While Thomas Hamilton provided parents with photographs of their children fully clothed, he did not include photographs of them wearing only swimming trunks. The police also were concerned about Thomas Hamilton overworking the boys. DC (now DS) Gordon Taylor who brought the report to the Procurator Fiscal's office had the opportunity of discussing it with Mr W Gallagher. Mr Gallagher, having considered the information provided, reached the view that there was insufficient material to file the application. He was of the view that while the conduct was of concern it did not yet cross the border into criminality. However, he expressed the view that the police should continue their enquiries and report further to him if any more evidence came to light. In these circumstances he marked the report so as to indicate that the matter should be reviewed in three months' time. So far as he was concerned he was concentrating on whether some form of indecency was going on. None of the photographs appeared to be indecent. He advised the police that they need not report further instances of the same conduct unless there was a change in the character of the circumstances indicating criminality. In his evidence DS Taylor stated that he had suggested to Mr Gallagher that, while the children were not alarmed by Thomas Hamilton's conduct, the parents' alarm would possibly have amounted to a breach of the peace but that Mr Gallagher did not think that it did. In his evidence Mr Gallagher said that he would have been surprised if he had said that a breach of the peace could not be constituted where alarm had been caused to a third party. I accept that he would not have said that. On 10 September 1993 Mr Gallagher reviewed the papers adding to them a marking which indicated that no proceedings were to be taken. In the meantime no further information had come to light. It is likely that he would have been in contact with the police before making this decision. In her closing submissions Miss Dunlop argued that a case of breach of the peace could have been based on the parents' reactions to Thomas Hamilton's conduct. While I accept that a case of breach of the peace may arise where alarm is caused to a third party the question in each case, which is one of fact, is whether the action complained of was of such a nature to be likely to give rise to such reactions on the part of those witnessing it. This was a matter which was left to the discretion of the Procurator Fiscal to assess. It is in any event clear that in this case the concentration was upon whether there was evidence indicative of indecency.

4.59 In the meantime the Regional Council was investigating the activities of Thomas Hamilton. In February 1993 Mr Flett, Assistant Director of Administration and Legal Services, had obtained a report by Mrs T Chillas,

Sports Development Officer, on three videotapes which had come into the hands of the Regional Council and showed boys club activities. In her report she criticised the gymnastic exercises and trampolining shown in the videotapes and made critical observations about the manner in which the club was conducted by Thomas Hamilton. That report was made available to DS Moffat who had been endeavouring to gather more information about his activities. His qualifications were checked and found to meet the requirements of the Regional Council. In June 1993 Mr Flett asked Thomas Hamilton for a copy of the minutes of the most recent AGM of the Boys Sports Club Group Committee. These were never furnished, but by letter dated 31 July 1993 Thomas Hamilton sent to Mr Flett what purported to be minutes of an A G M held on 8 August 1993. Mr Flett wrote again to Thomas Hamilton pointing out that the minutes which had been supplied were of a meeting subsequent to that requested. In order to see whether the parents' complaints could be backed up by 'hard' evidence DC Taylor obtained the consent of the Scout Association to examine their file on Thomas Hamilton on 20 October 1993. From this file he was able to read that he had been suspected of improper behaviour towards boys. A letter in the file also attributed to Mr B D Fairgrieve the view that Thomas Hamilton was "mentally unbalanced", but Mr Fairgrieve said to him that he could not substantiate that particular comment about him, which was purely a personal opinion.

4.60 Arising from the summer camp organised by Thomas Hamilton in 1993 at Dunblane High School, a further complaint was received by the police. It was similar in nature to previous complaints: children who were scantily clad in black swimming trunks were the subject of photographs which the parents considered to be inappropriate. On the instruction of the Deputy Chief Constable, DS (now Superintendent) Holden and DS Moffat interviewed Thomas Hamilton at his home in October 1993 in regard to the organisation and composition of his committee and the complaint which had been made about his methods and use of photography. Thomas Hamilton refused to supply details of people who were on his committee, despite reminders. During the interview, which lasted two hours or more, DS Holden gained the impression that the clubs filled most of Thomas Hamilton's life. He was quite obsessive about his methods and manner of organising the exercises. He would tolerate no criticism of his conduct of the clubs or of the boys' dress. A short question on the methods of training he used would elicit a lengthy reply and a very persuasive argument in favour of his methods. He gave the impression that he had rehearsed these arguments many times. He was quite calm and articulate, very polite but extremely evasive on the subject of the members of the club committee. DS Holden considered that he was lying on that point. He reported back to the Deputy Chief Constable who by that stage was well aware of complaints about children being required to dress in swimming trunks with bare tops and inappropriate photographs being taken of them.

4.61 It may be noted that throughout the years Thomas Hamilton's stream of letters of complaint and self-justification continued unabated. He expressed a complete lack of faith in any of the complaints procedures and tried on various occasions to enlist the help of his MP. He frequently wrote to parents defending himself and attacking the police. He tried to involve The Scottish Office, complaining about the way that the police were handling his complaints, with the result that the police had to keep The Scottish Office regularly up to date on what was happening. DCC McMurdo became obviously exasperated at what he described as his irrational outpourings in vindictive correspondence. The police were obliged to follow up persistent complaints which were quite absurd. He considered Thomas Hamilton to be bitter and petty-minded, perverting the healthy relationship between police officers and the Scout movement into something sleazy and dishonourable. He found it difficult to try to reason with a person whom he described as a zealot (cf para 6.43).

4.62   In October 1993 a yet further complaint was received from parents, in this instance in regard to a boy who had attended Balfron Boys Club. The parents asked for reassurance about the running of the club and posed a number of specific questions. They too expressed concern that Thomas Hamilton had insisted that the children were topless, that he had required the children to change into black swimming trunks, and that he had taken photographs of them. This letter was followed up DS Moffat, but he had to explain to them that there was nothing in their letter which was not already known to him and to the Procurator Fiscal.

4.63   Further similar complaints about clubs on the premises of Central Regional Council were expressed in December 1994. These were referred to the police, but were not reported to the Procurator Fiscal because of his previous decision to take no proceedings against Thomas Hamilton in similar circumstances. The Regional Council wrote to Thomas Hamilton asking why swimming trunks were essential and whether he had made it clear to parents that photographs would be taken. His reply contained a lengthy justification of his methods but did not provide straight answers to the questions. Thomas Hamilton continued to enjoy the general support of Councillor Ball. In 1995 the Regional Council had frequent discussions as to how they could make it more difficult for Thomas Hamilton to obtain a let of school premises. Some of their discussions involved DS Moffat. In May 1995 the Regional Council required Thomas Hamilton to give parents advance information that their children might be photographed: and in June they declined to accede to his request that teachers at Bannockburn Primary School should be instructed not to make comments about him and that a letter of apology about such comments should be sent to all parents. The fact that the Regional Council did not terminate his lets resulted from the belief that, in the absence of more substantial evidence, termination would not be sustainable. The Regional Council were also wary of encountering the repetition of an adverse report by the Ombudsman.

Alleged incidents involving firearms

4.64   In this part of the Chapter I will consider evidence relating to allegations that Thomas Hamilton used firearms in what was, or may have been, an improper manner prior to 13 March 1996.

4.65   In Chapter 6 I will set out a history of the firearms which Thomas Hamilton was authorised to, and did, acquire and use. For present purposes it suffices to say by way of background that he had a long-standing interest in firearms. There was evidence that he had possessed an air rifle with which he practised at the rear of his shop in Cowane Street, Stirling. On 14 February 1977 he was granted a firearm certificate. At the outset he acquired small-bore firearms. In December 1979 he moved on to full-bore.

4.66   While he was running the Dunblane Rovers Group he took a number of boys on Friday evenings to the range of the Dunblane Rifle and Pistol Club for tuition in the use of air rifles and air pistols. There is no reason to doubt the reliability of the evidence that he saw that strict discipline was observed. At that stage he was a member of that club. After it was disbanded he became a member of the Stirling Rifle and Pistol Club in 1986 or 1987. It also appears likely that he was for a few years a member of the Callander Rifle and Pistol Club (which was mentioned in his original application for a firearm certificate) and of the Clyde Valley Pistol Club.

4.67 He was not a very frequent attender at the meetings of the Stirling Rifle and Pistol Club. There was evidence that he was a "loner" who would stand to one side rather than join in the conversation between members. One observer said: "Nobody in the club knew very much about him". He was described as being "not competition-orientated". It was found that when he was taking part in the discipline known as police pistol, he did not follow the course of fire. When the command at twenty metres distance was to fire six rounds in a given time, he would "blast off" twelve. He was not endangering the others, but was disturbing them by his rate of fire. It was not in the spirit of a competition, and he was not prepared to listen to advice. Since he observed safety procedures, there was no occasion for him to be reported to the police.

4.68 There was evidence that on a number of occasions he brought firearms to homes of other people in order to show them off. This happened in the case of a parent of a boy who was attending the Dunblane Boys Club in the middle 1980s. Thomas Hamilton brought a .357 revolver and a semi-automatic pistol to his home on one occasion after he had asked the son if he would be interested in seeing them. However, the parent was impressed with Thomas Hamilton's approach to safety.

4.69 One of these occasions was reported to the police. Towards the end of 1988 Thomas Hamilton took two handguns and a semi-automatic machine gun to the home of a family in Linlithgow. The boys in the family attended Linlithgow Boys Club and one of them had attended his camp on Inchmoan Island that year. Thomas Hamilton had been in the habit of visiting the house and had mentioned his interest in guns. When the boys showed an interest in them he offered to bring them to the house. On this occasion he told the family how the firearms were held and used. He did not have any ammunition with him. The father took photographs of his wife and the boys holding the firearms. This incident was reported to the police at Stirling on 20 May 1989. Sergeant McGrane of the Lothian and Borders Police stationed at Bathgate was instructed to take statements as to what had happened. He attended their home on the evening of that day for that purpose. He ascertained from them that they had not been distressed by what had happened and had not complained to the police about it. However, he had the impression that they had not been at ease with someone bringing guns into their house. He did not pass on this impression with the statements. In evidence he said that he did not consider that Thomas Hamilton's behaviour was normal. He did not think that a firearm certificate holder should act in that way. He sent the statements and photographs which he had obtained to Inspector Nimmo of the Stirling Police who had instructed him. She felt that it was not very wise for Thomas Hamilton to take the firearms and show them to the children. She passed the papers on to Chief Supt Gunn on 30 June 1989. He in turn wrote a memorandum to the DCC McMurdo, stating:- "It may be quite a harmless display of weapons, but nevertheless an action which leaves a lot to be desired". This is a matter which was taken up in due course with Mr McMurdo when he was giving evidence (para.6.40).

4.70   One curious feature of this episode is that the report to the police which set off their enquiries was an incident log which showed that the report had been made by Mrs Doreen Hagger and contained a correct note of her then address and telephone number, as well as the address of the family to whom the firearms had been shown. However, in her evidence, Mrs Hagger said that she did not report the matter to the police. She could not do so because she did not have the family's address, but merely their telephone number. The mother had phoned her and told her that Thomas Hamilton had come to her house in Linlithgow with two or three guns. She did not know what kind of guns they were. The last she heard of this matter was when the mother had spoken to her on the telephone. She had no recollection of saying to a police officer that, as stated in the incident log, Thomas Hamilton could become violent and use weapons against her as she was involved in reporting him for complaints involving children. I do not understand how particulars relating to Mrs Hagger as the informant could realistically have been entered on the log unless she did make a report to the police. Whatever may be the explanation for the evidence which she gave, I do not accept her denial as reliable.

4.71   Another episode concerning Thomas Hamilton was spoken to by Inspector Ralph. He gave evidence that some 7-10 years before his death, Thomas Hamilton made an informal complaint to him about the behaviour of two police officers who had come across him with an air weapon in Stirling and told him that he could be charged with recklessly discharging it. He was particularly indignant because the police officers had taken hold of the weapon and waved it about. Since Thomas Hamilton had made no formal complaint the Inspector took no further action. Enquiries made after 13 March 1996 revealed no record by the police of any such incident as was alleged by Thomas Hamilton.

4.72   In the course of her evidence Mrs Doreen Hagger gave an account of an occasion on which Thomas Hamilton pointed a gun at her. This account was the subject of considerable publicity after she was interviewed by members of the press on 14 March 1996. The incident she alleged, had occurred at Bridgend, Linlithgow some time after she had been interviewed by Inspector Keenan in January 1989 in connection with his report on Thomas Hamilton's complaint. She said that she and Mrs Janet Reilly, had been coming back from the shops and had picked up her daughter Vicky after she had been dropped off the school bus in the main street. They were just getting to her gate when a light coloured transit van driven by Thomas Hamilton "slammed up at the pavement". She then said:-

> "He rolled the window down and he said 'I hear you have been making statements about me to Keenan'. I said 'That's right'. I said 'I just told him about the state of the camp, how you treated the kids, and my own personal opinion of you'. And at that he leaned forward, his face was all puffy. When he used to get in a rage his face would go puffy, would blow up and really bulge.... He leant forward and I thought he was going to start the engine up, after the mouthful I gave him, and the next thing I heard a click of metal hitting glass, and I looked down and there was a bit of metal there. It didn't register with me right away, and I just looked at him and he said 'My friends don't like it'..... I looked again and that is when I realised that it was a barrel, and I said 'Dinnae point that f'ng thing at me. I will ram it down your throat'. He just got really bulging and never said a word, off he went."

Mrs Hagger said that she used to pick up Vicky from the bus at about 2.45—2.50 pm. She was quite clear that the date of this encounter was before the incident at Linlithgow Academy on 16 May when she and Mrs Reilly assaulted Thomas Hamilton. Vicky was then seven years of age. Later in her evidence she described the barrel of the gun as having "a bit sticking up at the end of it". After Thomas Hamilton had driven off, she went into the house with Mrs Reilly. After they had talked together they agreed that the police station should be telephoned about what had happened. Later a couple of officers in uniform came round and she told them what had happened. They returned in one or two days and told her that Thomas Hamilton had been going to a gun club and had not meant to scare them. As far as she was concerned Thomas Hamilton had not threatened to shoot her, but she was meant to be a bit worried about him. She said: "I thought the man was a complete idiot. He didn't bother me".

4.73   There are a number of considerable problems about this account which were explored both in evidence and in parties' closing submissions. The Dean of Faculty on behalf of Lothian and Borders Police invited me to treat her evidence as lacking both reliability and credibility. In the first place the account given by Mrs Hagger was not supported by that given by Mrs Reilly where one would have expected it to be if Mrs Hagger's account was correct. According to Mrs Hagger, Mrs Reilly was beside her at the gate when Thomas Hamilton drew up outside her house. The gun was protruding and both Mrs Reilly and Vicky would have been in a position to see the window if they had been looking. However, Mrs Reilly's evidence was that Thomas Hamilton was just ready to drive away by the time that she reached Mrs Hagger's gate. She did not see anything protruding out of the van. Thomas Hamilton had something covered up on the passenger seat. I should add that Vicky Hagger did not give evidence at the inquiry. On Day 13 Mr Bonomy drew my attention to a report in the press that she was missing from home. He said that having considered the position very carefully he had formed the view that the inquiry would be put at no disadvantage by not hearing her evidence. He stated that from what he could tell of the police investigation, it appeared to him that all the evidence that the inquiry needed was covered by other evidence already before it. In these circumstances he proposed that her attendance should not be required. None of the parties made any representation against that proposal. I was entirely satisfied with Mr Bonomy's assessment. I had the opportunity of reading Vicky Hagger's statement to the police which had been taken from her in connection with the Inquiry. I also noted that when Mrs Hagger was being interviewed by members of the press on 14 March 1996 Vicky Hagger was present in the same house as her mother but did not give any information about seeing a gun. In these circumstances, intimation was made to Mrs Hagger that the attendance of Vicky Hagger was not required. In making his closing submissions Mr Bonomy confirmed that he knew of no further evidence which could assist me in arriving at a conclusion about whether the incident occurred and whether it was reported to the police. Secondly, leaving aside for the moment Mrs Hagger's evidence that she reported the incident to the police, I find it quite extraordinary that she made no reference to it, either when she was interviewed further by Inspector Keenan, or when she was enlisting the attendance of a reporter to witness the incident on 16 May 1989 at Linlithgow Academy. If she was intent on making his misbehaviour a matter of public knowledge it is remarkable that she made no mention of it to the reporter. On her own evidence she made no reference to it until she was being interviewed by members of the press on 14 March. Even then, according to her, it would not have been brought up if it had not been for Vicky saying: "Do you remember, he pointed a gun at you?" Thirdly, considerable efforts were made in order to ascertain whether there is any record of the reporting of this alleged incident. The Inquiry heard of the examination of log-books and notebooks and the questioning of all the police officers who might have been involved in dealing with such a report, with negative results. Evidence was also given by the sergeants who might have been expected to have been aware of such a complaint, having regard to its seriousness, but none of them had any recollection of it. I am quite unable to accept the suggestion that police officers would have regarded the pointing of a gun as not meriting recording, even if Mrs Hagger's attitude to Thomas Hamilton's behaviour was at that time the same as it was when she was giving evidence. Fourthly, there are more general reasons for questioning the reliability of Mrs Hagger's evidence. According to her when she was at the camp on Inchmoan Island she did not get on well with Thomas Hamilton. She left the island when "he threatened me once too often". His threat was "I hope your tent doesn't catch fire tonight". However, when she was interviewed by DS McBain in August 1988 in regard to the report of what happened on the island, she made no mention of Thomas Hamilton threatening to burn her tent, but stated that another adult who had been assisting with the camp at that stage had threatened Mrs Reilly. According to Mrs Reilly Mrs Hagger left the island because Thomas Hamilton had threatened Mrs Hagger with a gun, but the basis for this was that she had seen that Mrs Hagger was frightened. She told her that Thomas Hamilton had had a gun in his hand. The adult referred to by Mrs Hagger had threatened to kill Mrs Hagger with an axe and set fire to the tent. She appeared to accept that when she was interviewed by the police in April 1996 she made no mention of a gun. In his closing submission, Mr C M Campbell submitted that for Thomas Hamilton to have referred to his guns as his "friends" had a ring of truth about it. It may well be true that on some occasion Thomas Hamilton told Mrs Hagger that his guns were his "friends": and indeed Mrs Hagger gave evidence that he said this at the camp. However, this does not appear to me to lend any significant support to what she said happened at Bridgend.

4.74   For all these reasons I have come to the conclusion that the account given by Mrs Hagger is lacking in both reliability and credibility. I do not accept her evidence that Thomas Hamilton pointed a gun at her or that she reported such an incident to the police. It follows that there is no question of such an incident coming to the knowledge of the police.

Chapter 5   The Last Six Months

Introduction

5.1   In this chapter I will endeavour to put together the picture of Thomas Hamilton's character and attitudes which emerged from the evidence, before turning to an account of events during the last six months of his life. While this cannot provide a full explanation as to what led him to perpetrate the outrage on 13 March 1996, it may provide some pointers as to the factors which were at work in his mind. The chapter concludes with an assessment of Thomas Hamilton which has been derived from expert evidence given by a psychologist and a psychiatrist .

Thomas Hamilton's character and attitudes

5.2   Thomas Hamilton claimed in a number of letters that the rumours about him in 1983 caused the collapse of his shop business. However, it is more likely that this was due to the effect of competition from modern DIY stores and to his preoccupation with boys clubs and camps. He saw the clubs as a means of making a success of the camps. Mr D G McGregor, a former employee of Central Regional Council, whom he consulted about 1980 in regard to the qualifications required by someone running a gymnastics club, recalled that "he was interested in running camps during the summer months, but in order to ...get recruits, you might say, along to the camps he felt it necessary that he would have to run clubs during the winter".

5.3   The evidence showed that Thomas Hamilton was constantly engaged in recruiting boys and that he could be abusive to parents who withdrew their sons.

5.4   He was not averse to using deceitful or at any rate questionable methods of attracting support. His description as to the intended activities, his own qualifications, the number of helpers and the charges which would be made for membership not infrequently bore little relation to what happened. In order to gain an appearance of respectability he represented that a committee was responsible for the running of clubs and he made use of the names of officials as "contacts". He took photographs of boys without their parents' knowledge or consent. He issued misleading information as to the circumstances in which he had left the Scouts.

5.5   At the same time he was extremely intolerant of those who questioned the way in which he ran the clubs and camps. It is also clear that he had an inflated view of his own importance and that of his activities. Mr B D Fairgrieve said of a meeting with Thomas Hamilton in 1974, where he had been subjected to a long and rambling discourse: "I formed the impression that he had a persecution complex, that he had delusions of grandeur and I felt his actions were almost paranoia." When DCC McMurdo wrote to The Scottish Office on 14 January

1992 he made a number of remarks which showed that he was plainly exasperated with Thomas Hamilton's statements. His remarks included: "For Mr Hamilton to see his tiny local organisation as a serious rival to the Scouting movement indicates a certain lack of perspective". When Thomas Hamilton was criticised he would reply with elaborate self-justification and often adopted attack as a means of defence.

5.6   Thomas Hamilton harboured a long-standing grievance against the Scouts and the police. In the large volume of correspondence which he generated a recurring theme is his assertion that the police were biased in favour of the "brotherhood of masons" and that there was a "brotherhood" link between the Scouts and the police. In passing it may be noted that this together with evidence given by Mr Deuchars indicated that Thomas Hamilton had never been a freemason. I am satisfied that he was not a member of the masons. Evidence was given by a number of his acquaintances of his bitter complaints of having been victimised by the police and having suffered hard treatment at the hands of local authorities. When Mr W B McFarlane met him from time to time during the last 7 or 8 years of his life he found that Thomas Hamilton's conversation was "all one way..... he was anti-police, he was anti-establishment, he was anti- the education authority, he seemed to be anti-anybody who opposed his views on how the clubs should be run or whether they should be run". Thomas Hamilton knew that he was being referred to as a pervert and thought that teachers and parents had been discouraging boys from attending his clubs. He told an acquaintance that, if he stopped running the clubs, people would have considered that rumours about him were true.

5.7   I will refer later to expert evidence which was given as to the nature of Thomas Hamilton's sexuality, but for the present it may be of some significance to note some of the observations as to the way in which he treated the boys. There are a number of indications that he sought to domineer and that he was insensitive to their comfort and safety. I have already referred to the general methods which he adopted in the clubs (para 4.11 *et seq*). At the camps there was a general lack of adequate supervision; the boys were found to have insufficient clothing for the prevailing weather; he insisted on making a videofilm when the boys were cold and wet; and he insisted that the boys should be denied contact with their parents. It was not surprising that they became homesick and upset.

5.8   Thomas Hamilton did not form any close relationship with an adult of either sex. His natural mother, Mrs Agnes Watt, stated that he had had a girlfriend a long time ago. However, after she got too serious "he didn't want to know". Mr F B Cullen, who assisted him in his shop, said that he was nervous among adults and very uncomfortable amongst females in particular. The events on 13 March 1996 may have made some people reluctant to admit that they were friends of Thomas Hamilton, but I am satisfied that he had few friends but more than a few acquaintances. The impression which he made on people varied. He was "a generous man to work with and a kind man", according to Mr Cullen. Mr E J E Anderson, who was associated with him in the running of the Dunblane Rovers Group and the Dunblane Boys' Club, referred to him as "a very shy, lonely person.... a very quiet, kind individual"; and Mr D MacDonald who had been a member of one of his clubs and who was regularly in touch with him said that he was "quite an intelligent man .... interesting enough to talk to". On the other hand some found that he made them feel uncomfortable and did not like talking to him. They were uneasy about the way in which he walked and spoke. A neighbour described him as follows: "He sort of crept. He was very head-down". He spoke slowly, softly and precisely but without expression in his voice. Mr G S Crawford, Secretary of the Stirling Rifle and Pistol Club said: "Hamilton was a loner, he wouldn't engage in social conversation with anybody; it is known also that women members didn't particularly like being around him. He was a bit of a creep in their eyes". Mr J S B Wilson said: "He was unusual....effeminate. He had a tendency to sort of wring his hands. There was a bit of a feeling of discomfort". Mr G Baxter, Head of the Woodmill Centre, Dunfermline, found that Thomas Hamilton was unusual in that "he didn't laugh at anything. He didn't joke at anything. He was far too polite". Some neighbours referred to him as sly and devious. A number of witnesses remarked that the only thing that he was interested in was boys clubs, so that it was difficult to carry on a conversation with him. A number of witnesses described him as being peculiarly calm in the face of adversity. Thus Mr George Robertson MP so described him in the face of hostile questioning from parents. His reaction to the incident on 16 May 1989 when he was assaulted by Mrs Hagger and Mrs Reilly is particularly striking. Finally while there were some boys who regarded him as a nice man, others found him "weird".

Events during the last 6 months of Thomas Hamilton's life

Thomas Hamilton's Boys' Clubs

5.9   By September 1995 there had been a substantial decline in his clubs. The Menstrie, Alva and Tillicoultry Club had ended in March; and a proposed club at Callander had come to grief when only one boy had attended. On 18 August he had issued a large number of circular letters to parents in Dunblane in order to deal, he said, with the false and misleading gossip about him which had been circulated by Scout officials. The letter stated that it was rumoured that he had been put out of the Scouts or asked to leave in sinister circumstances, whereas it was he who had left the Scouts. The letter went on to say that despite the severe and obvious difficulties the Dunblane Group had operated for 15 years. He added that "many young athletes had been lost needlessly over the years and others deterred from attending". However 25 boys had attended the sports training course at Dunblane High School in the summer of 1995.

5.10   It is clear that Thomas Hamilton intended to make up for the difficulties nearer home by going further afield. In the autumn of 1995 he obtained a let in Thomas Muir High School, Bishopbriggs for a newly formed Bishopbriggs Boys Club. In order to obtain the let at an advantageous rate he obtained recognition as an approved youth organisation. For this purpose he had to comply with a number of conditions, the most important of which was to provide two references in support of his application, each referee stating that "the leaders are known to me and are worthy of support". One of the references was signed by Councillor Ball, who by then had become the convenor of the Education Committee of Central Regional Council. In evidence Councillor Ball said that he had had misgivings about signing but felt that it was difficult to refuse. He accepted that he had not given the matter as much attention as he should have done. In his application Thomas Hamilton said that there was to be a committee of 12 adults, mostly parents. His natural mother was shown as the treasurer and a young assistant, Ian Boal, as secretary. The application was granted after an official of Central Regional Council had advised Strathclyde Regional Council that Thomas Hamilton's activities should be monitored.

5.11   In the meantime Thomas Hamilton decided that he would withdraw from personal involvement in the Falkirk Boys Club. He persuaded a parent, Mr D P

Jones, to take over the leadership of the club from the second week in November. This arrangement ended in early March when Mr Jones was unable to continue on account of his work commitments. Thomas Hamilton looked in from time to time at the meetings of the Club, the last time being in January or February 1996.

5.12 Meanwhile Mr Boal, who was an undergraduate student in sport in the community, began running the Bishopbriggs Boys Club. He said in evidence that he never met the members of its committee. He had expected to be running the club himself but Thomas Hamilton appeared every week. To his annoyance Mr Boal found that Thomas Hamilton had distributed leaflets which not only named him as club coach but also gave his telephone number. In January he wrote to Mr Boal criticising his coaching methods. In response Mr Boal said that he would go on only until Easter. In evidence he said: "I wasn't going to put up with the hassle he was giving me through writing a letter like that to me". At this stage boys were being bussed to Dunblane from not only Bishopbriggs but also Callander and Bannockburn. It is known from a letter which Thomas Hamilton wrote to Mr Michael Forsyth MP on 11 February 1996, to which I will refer later, that only 5 boys from Dunblane still attended the Dunblane Boys Club, and that only one of them had attended the sports training course in July 1995. Mr Boal last saw Thomas Hamilton on 11 March when his parting words to him were "Thanks very much, Ian, see you next Monday". Mr Boal had not noticed any change in him. He said: "His personality was very dry. He wasn't the most interesting person to have a conversation with".

5.13 Thomas Hamilton applied for the use of Dunblane High School for a summer training course in 1996. Mr R Mercer who was then caretaker at the Menstrie Community Centre, gave evidence that on 12 March in a telephone conversation Thomas Hamilton requested the use of the Centre's minibus on 14 March. However, I was informed later in the Inquiry that the witness had since giving evidence indicated to the Crown that, to the best of his recollection, the accurate date for this conversation was 7 March. Little turns on this but it indicates that to outward appearances Thomas Hamilton was still actively planning for his club activities.

Thomas Hamilton's activities with firearms

5.14 While Thomas Hamilton's activities with boys were going into decline his interest in firearms was resurgent. As I will explain in Chapter 6 he appears to have been relatively inactive for a number of years until 1995. His firearm certificate did not contain any record of a purchase of ammunition between 22 October 1987 and 22 September 1995. The evidence strongly indicates that Thomas Hamilton did not reload his ammunition (an operation which would not require to be recorded on the firearm certificate) but that he purchased commercially-made ammunition. Purchases of ammunition from clubs did not require to be entered in the firearm certificate unless the ammunition was not used on the occasion when it was purchased and was taken away. Accordingly it seems unlikely that Thomas Hamilton was actively shooting to any significant extent during this period. On various occasions between 22 September 1995 and 27 February 1996 he purchased a total of 1700 rounds of 9 mm and 500 rounds of .357 ammunition. On 11 September 1995 and 23 January 1996 he purchased a 9 mm Browning pistol and a .357 Smith & Wesson revolver. He had had the authority to acquire such firearms since February 1992. These were two of the handguns which he took with him to the school on 13 March; and the 9 mm Browning pistol was the competition model (pistol A) with which he shot his victims. In January 1996 Thomas Hamilton bought two holsters, apparently for the two revolvers which he now owned.

5.15   Thomas Hamilton now became much more active as a shooter. In January 1996 he shot at the Whitestone range used by the Stirling Rifle and Pistol Club. When he attended a meeting there in February Mr G F Smith, the president of the club, noted that his shooting was reasonably good. It surprised him that he fired very rapidly all the time but he knew that this was what he always seemed to do. He said to Thomas Hamilton that with a bit of practice he ought to be going in for competitions. While he was giving him a lift home Thomas Hamilton told him that he was a coach. This surprised Mr Smith as it didn't seem to him that he was the sort of person who could get children interested. He didn't find him very interesting himself. He found him slightly effeminate and didn't particularly like him.

5.16   On 2 March Thomas Hamilton was given a lift to Largs, where the club members were to shoot. At that meeting he again fired very rapidly. He used red or orange stickers on paper targets, apparently as guides for him to aim at. Mr G S Crawford told him that that was not what they were there for and took them down. Thomas Hamilton had used similar stickers at the Whitestone Range. When Thomas Hamilton was taking part in the service pistol discipline, which includes the firing of three rounds at each of two targets at 10 metres in 6 seconds Thomas Hamilton expended 12 rounds on one target with one pistol, at which Mr Crawford said to him "that is out of order". At that meeting he was using principally the 9 mm Browning pistol which was the competition model. Mr W P Campbell, a member of the club who drove Thomas Hamilton back to Stirling, recalled that when he got out of the car in Stirling, his cousin Alexis Fawcett, who was a probationary member, and had been in the back of the car with Thomas Hamilton, referred to him saying: "That is a right weirdo, that one" and she said that he had referred to stroking his gun. She added: "He talks about guns as though they were babies".

5.17   On 24 February 1996 Thomas Hamilton approached an official of Callander Rifle and Pistol Club with a view to regularly shooting with them. Two days later after passing a marksmanship test he was allowed to shoot on their range. He put up his own target sheets with similar stickers on them and took them home afterwards. On 28 February he took part in a police pistol 1. It was observed that at 25 metres distance, where 12 shots were required within two minutes, he let forth "a fusillade of shots". At 10 metres distance, where 2 shots required to be fired within two seconds, he let off 4 shots before he could be stopped. He handed in a form applying for probationary membership but it lacked a supporting signature.

5.18   On 6 March he informed a club official that there had been "a bit of a hold up" about obtaining the signature. He told the official, Mr J A C Moffat, that he had been away from shooting for quite a while and wanted to get back into it, now that he had more time on his hands. On that day Thomas Hamilton also used stickers and put the sheets in a book after he had used them. Mr N K Bell, a probationary member, noticed that Thomas Hamilton fired off a lot more rounds than he had ever seen anyone else doing. He felt very uncomfortable about him. Thomas Hamilton had insisted Mr Bell should try his Browning (not the murder weapon) although the latter was quite happy with his .22 pistol. He appeared to be angry when Mr Bell queried whether his club was using the gymnasium at Dunblane High School on Thursdays. Mr Bell mentioned to his wife that he was concerned about Thomas Hamilton—more in relation to his being involved with children than in regard to firearms. His wife told him that there was no point in doing anything about it because the Regional Council would never have allowed him to run a club unless it was appropriate.

5.19 Mr Mercer, to whom I have referred in para 5.13, gave evidence that Thomas Hamilton hired the minibus from Menstrie Community Centre about 6 or 7 times at the end of 1995 and beginning of 1996. On one occasion he noticed that Thomas Hamilton had left a tin of gun oil on the minibus. When he spoke to him about it Thomas Hamilton said he needed it to oil some hinges on the bus. Thomas Hamilton also asked him if he had ever had guns or fired guns. He brought gun magazines for him to look at. On one occasion he brought an unloaded handgun with him when he came to pick up the minibus. He said that he had thousands of rounds of ammunition in his house. Mr Mercer did not tell anybody about being shown the gun. He didn't think anything of it. Thomas Hamilton assured him at the time that he had a firearm certificate.

5.20 Mr Boal noticed that while he was working for Thomas Hamilton the camera equipment disappeared, and guns took over the conversation. At Christmas 1995 Thomas Hamilton said that he was heavily involved in them. Three or four weeks before he last saw him he kept talking about bullets and what certain bullets could do. Looking back on the conversation Mr Boal thought it quite strange that he talked about the "spray" of a bullet which disintegrated rather than passed through its target. He was also testing to see which bullets were best to prevent jamming of his handgun. He had experimented with shooting at books when he would see the "spray" of the bullets going through the thickness. He said that he liked the videos of *Alien* and *Terminator* because of the guns. On one occasion Mr Boal discovered from speaking to the boys that Thomas Hamilton had told them that he had shot a moose and had showed them an ammunition catalogue. When Mr Boal said to him that he should not be talking to children about guns Thomas Hamilton replied to this effect: "It's O.K., kids play soldiers all the time".

5.21 Mr J O Gillespie was a reasonably frequent visitor to the house of Thomas Hamilton until about 4-5 weeks before 13 March. On that last occasion Thomas Hamilton had a 9 mm pistol in his hand. He asked Mr Gillespie whether, if he had any kids, he would allow them to attend his club. When Mr Gillespie replied in the negative, Thomas Hamilton pointed the pistol at him and pulled the trigger. Nothing was in the chamber. Mr Gillespie got a fright, called him a "stupid bastard", threw coffee at him and walked out smartly. He would not have allowed his children to attend as Thomas Hamilton was·"too military". Mr Gillespie did not report this incident to the police as he knew that Thomas Hamilton would have denied it. It gave him the idea that he was dangerous. He had too many guns in the house for anyone to have.

5.22 On 1 March Isobel Martin, the Head Teacher at a primary school, who had become aware of Thomas Hamilton's setting up of the Bishopbriggs Boys Club, received a complaint from the parent of one of her pupils about Thomas Hamilton's behaviour. According to this complaint he appeared to be taking an exceptional interest in her son and one of his friends. He had offered to pick up the boy to take him to a different club in Stirling. The parent had been informed that Thomas Hamilton had shown the boys photographs of wild animals, and had shown them a gun which he kept in the minibus which he used to transport the boys. He had been increasing the amount of time between picking up the boy and collecting the other children. He also asked her son if he liked the film *Alien* and offered to give him a videotape of it to take home to watch. He also said to her son that he went shooting and offered to take him with him. Her son was 11 years of age. The Head Teacher noted this complaint. After obtaining some advice from the local education officer she addressed a letter to the Social Work

Department in Bishopbriggs. Having received no response to that letter she made a telephone call to that department on 12 March to check that her letter had been received. Later that day the department contacted her and said that they would send a social worker to visit the parent who had been wondering why no one from the department had been in touch with her. The events of 13 March intervened before any further steps could be taken.

Thomas Hamilton's finances

5.23   It is clear that during the last 6 months of his life Thomas Hamilton was in serious financial difficulties. In previous years he had consumed any free capital which became available to him. In 1983 he had received a payment from the insurers of his boat which was destroyed; and in 1985 he received a substantial payment from the sale of his shop business. In each case the payments were used to meet existing overdrafts and his current expenditure. It appears that he regularly made a loss in the running of his boys clubs and camps. At one stage he had a substantial number of cameras in his house but his trading in them led to him losing his right to claim unemployment benefit in November 1993. By the end of 1995 there had been a considerable reduction in his camera business. He also suffered a setback when the *Amateur Photographer* refused to carry his advertisements.

5.24   An examination of his finances as at the date of his death was carried out by Chief Inspector Hughes. This showed that he had made heavy use of accounts with Debenhams and Barclaycard in order to provide finance for his everyday living. At his death he owed £737.74 to Debenhams and on 8 March he had reached the limit of £1,500 on his Barclaycard account. He had no capital in a bank or building society. He had a total overdraft of £3,511. He was in receipt of housing benefit for 7 Kent Road. He owed £2,350 in respect of a loan which had been made to him in 1994 to provide finance for his camera business. His application for a further loan in 1996 had been refused. He did not have much income from cameras. He was in arrears with payment of the council tax.

Thomas Hamilton's mood

5.25   To a number of those who gave evidence he appeared to be his normal self. His natural mother met him on 11 March; and on 12 March he came round for four hours in the afternoon, had a bath and something to eat and "blethered" with her. However, other witnesses were aware of a change in his mood. Mr R P C Allston, a photographer, who only knew Thomas Hamilton from telephone conversations with him, described him as being very subdued and depressed at the end of February. Thomas Hamilton told him that he was shooting more and more as this took his mind off his problems. On 6 March he hardly spoke. The last thing he said was "I am going back to my guns", and then he rang off. Mr D Macdonald spoke to him on the evening of 12 March. He said that he was lonely and it was not good to be alone. Mr Macdonald said that the telephone conversation "went flat". Over the past 6 months Thomas Hamilton had been less enthusiastic about his camera business. Mr A J Togneri said that on 11 March Thomas Hamilton sounded very unhappy and subdued. He said that the numbers at his clubs were down. Mr G E Macdonald said that Thomas Hamilton did not answer at his door when he called on 10 March but he knew that he definitely was in. Some 5 or 6 weeks earlier Thomas Hamilton had telephoned him and seemed "awful down". He said that he had hassle in Dunblane and the club there was not doing very well. When he ran him home on 6 March he had a lot of letters with him. He had a "slight grudge" against the people who were slandering him.

5.26 On 26 January 1996 Thomas Hamilton wrote a letter to Councillor Ball. Although it was headed "Private and Confidential" he sent copies to a number of Head Teachers of primary schools in the area, in particular St Francis Primary School, Falkirk, Bannockburn Primary School and Dunblane Primary School; and to the Scout Association and Mr David Vass. He complained in the letter that teachers at Bannockburn Primary School were informing pupils and parents that he was a pervert. As a result all of the 26 pupils who were members of his Bannockburn Boys Club had left immediately and local gossip followed. He complained that the Education Department had done nothing to correct the situation which was widespread. He added: "At Dunblane Primary School where teachers have contaminated all of the older boys with this poison even former cleaners and dinner ladies have been told by the teachers at school that I am a pervert. There have been reports at many schools of our boys being rounded up by the staff and even warnings given to entire schools by Head Teachers during assembly". He said that this had been extremely damaging not only to his clubs but to his own public standing and had resulted in a complete loss of his ability to earn a living. He said: "I have no criminal record nor have I ever been accused of sexual child abuse by any child and I am not a pervert". He had called at Bannockburn Primary School and Dunblane Primary School and expressed a similar complaint to the Head Teachers about members of staff discouraging boys from attending his clubs and suggesting that he was a pervert. Thomas Hamilton went on to say in his letter that the matter had originated in 1983 when an official of the Education Department had warned Head Teachers that he was a pervert, was currently interfering with boys and had been put out of the Scouts for this and had a long criminal record for this type of offence. He said that this official and his reported source in the Scouts were fully discredited and the clubs' use of schools was returned. However, the information which the official had passed to Head Teachers had never been corrected "and has over the years reached epidemic proportions". He blamed the malicious work of the Scout official in his attempt to undermine "what he considers to be a rival group". He claimed that all this serious damage had resulted from the maladministration of Central Regional Council and its failure to correct the false information. In evidence Councillor Ball commented that Thomas Hamilton never seemed to be able to put the past behind him. Judged by his letter "his mental state" was slightly deteriorating. He had last met Thomas Hamilton in the summer of 1995 when he "sounded fine". But this letter was a bit worrying. Mr Vass telephoned Councillor Ball in order to make it clear that at no time had he suggested that anything improper had taken place between Thomas Hamilton and Scouts.

5.27 On 11 February 1996 Thomas Hamilton wrote to Mr Michael Forsyth MP complaining of many serious problems which he had experienced over the years of which the root cause was "malicious gossip" circulated by certain Scout officials. He referred to the problem in 1983 with the Central Regional Council which, he said, resulted from Scout officials approaching a councillor. He referred once more to the disruption to his camps in 1988 and 1991. Although he understood that senior officers of Central Scotland Police were satisfied that everything was all right, he had been unable to recover from the very serious damage caused by the police which had compounded the very difficult situation which already existed. The long term effect "has been a death blow to my already difficult work in providing sports and leisure activities to local children as well as my public standing in the community".

5.28 On 6 March Thomas Hamilton made a telephone call to the headquarters of the Scout Association in Scotland and asked who was its patron. He also enquired about the names of other high ranking officials but was told that these were not to hand. In the conversation Thomas Hamilton went on to say he wanted the Queen, who was the patron, or other high ranking officials to know about the maladministration of the Scouts. It was being put about that he was a pervert. A certain official was going around the schools telling everybody that he was a pervert when he was only an enthusiastic and friendly leader. He had tried to start up boys clubs on numerous occasions but because the official had gone into the schools it was very difficult for him. As a result of the rumours he could no longer walk down the street, his reputation had been ruined and he was close to bankruptcy. This telephone conversation was followed by a letter from Thomas Hamilton to the Queen dated 7 March in which he rehearsed the complaints which he had repeatedly made in correspondence. His letter closed with the words: "I turn to you as a last resort and am appealing for some kind of intervention in the hope that I may be able to regain my self-esteem in society". Copies of this letter were sent by him to Councillor Ball, Mr Forsyth, the Scout Association and certain senior Scout officials and the Head Teachers of Bannockburn and Dunblane Primary Schools.

Preparation   5.29   The Inquiry heard the written statement of a boy of 9 years of age who attended Dunblane Primary School and was a member of the Dunblane Boys Club. He stated that on 7 March when he had been playing football at the club Thomas Hamilton took him out and sat him on a bench in order to speak to him. He then continued: "He asked me the way to the gym and the way to the hall. He asked what time certain classes went to the gym and the main way into the school. He asked directions about once he was in the main hall, how to get to the gym and where the stage was. He asked how to get to the Assembly Hall, and I told him to turn right after the main entrance. He said what day do all people go on the stage to do the play. I didn't know and he said to ask the P7s to find out. He asked if the younger children, like the primary 1s to 4s go to the assembly at a different time to the primary 5s to 7s. I told him that the assembly was on a Wednesday morning and that the younger ones went after us. He asked me what time did assembly start and gym, I said 9.30 for assembly. I didn't tell him the time for gym....... The other question was something to do with the gym fire exit. I think it was how many fire exits there were to get out of the gym. Mr Hamilton asked me these questions every single week. He had been asking me these questions for a long time, about 2 years. He didn't ask me any more questions and said I could go back to playing football". According to his father the boy's first reaction to hearing that Thomas Hamilton had been involved in the shooting was: "It can't be Mr Hamilton, he was a nice guy". Later he told his father about Thomas Hamilton asking him about the school. His father queried whether Thomas Hamilton had asked him for directions every week. The boy replied "Well, for quite a while".

5.30   Mr J S B Wilson, who is a retired police officer, met Thomas Hamilton on 7 or 8 March in Stirling. In the course of conversation Thomas Hamilton said that he could do with some instruction in shooting at a distance of 10 yards. He went on to say that the authorities were against him and he seemed to be anti-police. He then said that as far as he was concerned the police were scared to go in when Michael Ryan started shooting at Hungerford. He went on to talk about a firearms incident at Cowie, just outside Stirling, where a police vehicle had been blasted by a shot gun after the police had responded to a call about someone running about with it. He said that the police firearms team should have taken care of it. He then asked whether firearms were kept at all police offices. Mr Wilson responded that this certainly was not the case while he was a police officer. It applied only to places which were manned 24 hours a day. Thomas

Hamilton then said that there should be a permanent firearms response unit available so that they could get to the scene very quickly. It was obvious to Mr Wilson that he had read quite a bit about the subject but he did not get the impression at the time that Thomas Hamilton was looking for information.

5.31   On 2 or 3 March Mr R M Ure saw Thomas Hamilton coming out of the grounds of Braehead Primary School in Stirling. Thomas Hamilton said that he had been away organising another boys club and "seemed agitated as if he had been caught out". On 10 March when he met him in Stirling he was carrying a briefcase of the type which is fitted out for carrying guns. On 4 March he came to the office of Mr D G McGregor and in the course of conversation said that he had bought two shirts in Debenhams. He passed the remark: "the beauty of it is I will never have to pay for them ever".

5.32   In January Thomas Hamilton had purchased the pliers with which he cut the telephone wires near Dunblane Primary School on 13 March.

5.33   On 12 March he travelled to Dunblane from Stirling in the middle of the day. About 3 o'clock in the afternoon of the same day he was in Stirling again and hired the van which he drove to the school on the following day. The hire was for a single day as from about 3 pm. He wanted to pay the entire charge in advance but he was told that it should be paid on return. He left a deposit of £50. The receptionist at the hire company said that "he unnerved me quite a bit .... the way he spoke mainly. He spoke very slowly, very clearly, precisely, but with no emotion or expression ..... there was just nothing, nothing in there. You couldn't have held a conversation with him".

5.34   It may be noted that in the course of his evidence Mr W B MacFarlane said that Thomas Hamilton "was very methodical, he was nobody's fool .... I think his life and everything he did was well thought out in advance before he actually did it".

5.35   As was pointed out by Dr J A Baird, consultant forensic psychiatrist in one of his reports, it appears that Thomas Hamilton planned carefully in order to ensure that nothing would go wrong at the school on 13 March. As I mentioned at para 3.39, each of the magazines was marked in such a way as to ensure that it was inserted the correct way round. The manner in which cartridges were loaded into the magazines may suggest that this was intended to avoid any risk of the pistol jamming. Over each shoulder he had a canvas bag which contained ammunition. The bags had been tied open so that they could not close accidentally. They also had cardboard inserts so that they would not collapse. Further the route which he took when approaching the school buildings appears to show pre-planning and local knowledge. In view of the evidence to which I referred in para 5.29 it may be that his original intention had been to enter the Assembly Hall while assembly was in progress. See also para 5.38.

What was found at 7 Kent Road

5.36   After the shootings the police found at 7 Kent Road 715 rounds of 9 mm and 280 rounds of .357 ammunition, along with 11 rounds of .38 special. If the 501 rounds of 9 mm and 242 rounds of .357 ammunition taken to Dunblane Primary School are added, it follows that before he departed for the school he had a total of 1216 rounds of 9 mm and 522 rounds of .357 ammunition. The police also found a telephone directory open at the page containing the telephone number of Dunblane Primary School; and on the walls of the rear bedroom a number of targets with stickers of the type which Thomas Hamilton had used at the club meetings as I have already described. There were no photographs hanging on the walls of any of the rooms but a total of 445 slides, 542 photographs and 4,260 negatives were found during a search of the house. The majority of these showed boys with their tops bare. There were also 37 videotapes of the type which I have described earlier. There was also a collection of swimming trunks, most of which were black.

Psychological and psychiatric evidence

5.37   The Inquiry was provided with a report on Thomas Hamilton by Professor David J Cooke, Head of Forensic Clinical Psychology for the Greater Glasgow Health Board, Community and Mental Health Trust and Professor of Forensic Psychology at Glasgow Caledonian University; along with a further report by him on the subject of prediction of violent behaviour from the psychological perspective. In addition the Inquiry had the benefit of three reports prepared by Dr J A Baird, Consultant Forensic Psychiatrist and former Consultant Forensic Psychiatrist and Physician Superintendent at the State Hospital, Carstairs containing a psychiatric assessment of Thomas Hamilton. These witnesses were given sight of various productions and were supplied with other information which provided an insight into the life of Thomas Hamilton. They also had the opportunity to read transcripts of evidence given at the Inquiry.

5.38   Before coming to their views as to Thomas Hamilton's state of mind it is convenient for me to set out what they inferred as to his intentions. Professor Cooke said that there were major difficulties in Thomas Hamilton's life which threatened his self-esteem. He was in debt. He was refused a loan. He was being refused access to premises to hold his boys clubs and fewer boys were attending the clubs. It may have been the case that, like many mass killers, he obtained feelings of power and mastery by fantasising his revenge on those whom he perceived as persecuting him. It is likely that his fantasies became more complex and compelling after "behavioural tryouts" when firing at his gun club. He believed that school staff were telling families not to send children to his clubs and that parents were spreading rumours that he was a pervert. Professor Cooke commented on Thomas Hamilton's actions: "Perhaps the most powerful way of getting back at people like that is to kill their children. That is a very traumatic thing to happen. Perhaps he thought he would make maximum impact by doing that. Again, that is speculation". There had been meticulous planning and preparation, so he did not think that Thomas Hamilton had "flipped". Dr Baird accepted that after the event it was possible to formulate explanations for the commission of the murders but he was still at a loss to express any reason which would satisfy himself as to why they were committed. In his first report he observed that a number of pieces of evidence showed that Thomas Hamilton had planned the events very carefully in order that nothing would go wrong. He appeared to have taken pride and almost to have enjoyed the preparation for his crimes. His single specific intention was to kill himself but once he embarked on his murderous spree his victims appeared to have been entirely random. It was possible that he had selected a school because of his association with schools or because, unlike with adults, he would have been much less likely to experience opposition and his victims were the most vulnerable and the most defenceless he could have selected. He went on to state: "It was not my impression that he particularly relished in the killing spree or wanted to prolong it as there was no reason for him to have killed himself at the moment when he did other than to avoid running the risk that emergency services might arrive on the scene and prevent him from killing himself".

5.39   Both Professor Cooke and Dr Baird ruled out any form of mental illness. In particular Dr Baird said that there was no evidence of changes which would have been expected with the onset of mental illness. Furthermore, mental conditions could be quite disabling. It is clear from the evidence that Thomas Hamilton had no history of mental illness or anything suggestive of such an illness. In passing I note that he did not attend a doctor between January 1974 and the date of his death, apart from attendance at hospital for a sprained ankle in March 1993. He did not smoke or drink. A post mortem examination disclosed no form of physical abnormality which could account for his behaviour. Tests on samples from his body showed no evidence of intoxication with alcohol or of drugs abuse; and no evidence of chronic lead poisoning or chronic misuse of androgenic steroids.

5.40   Each of these experts detected what they regarded as signs or traits of abnormal personality in Thomas Hamilton, although they did not fully agree as to how that personality disorder should be categorised. Dr Baird pointed out every adult displayed features of personality which were particular to himself or herself. They tended to be enduring features and often, although not always, appeared to have originated from upbringing and early formative experiences. When undesirable features were prominent this could cause problems and it was in this context that the concept of personality disorder had arisen.

5.41   Professor Cooke pointed out at the outset that in drawing any conclusion about Thomas Hamilton it was necessary to adopt a cautious approach. Unlike the ordinary case it was impossible for him to have access to the person concerned with the result that he could not check hypotheses or obtain information about fantasies and unusual thoughts and ideas. After such a heinous crime the recall of informants and witnesses might not be totally reliable. There was a natural human tendency to explain events—"effort after meaning"—which might result in significant distortion of the recall of events. Further it was difficult to assess the relative credibility of evidence given by witnesses. It was not possible for him to provide a full explanation of the factors which had influenced Thomas Hamilton's behaviour.

5.42   While it was not possible for him to make an absolute diagnosis his conclusion was primarily that Thomas Hamilton was suffering from some form of personality disorder characterised by lack of empathy, and perhaps by a sadistic personality disorder in which he had a desire to have control over others. It was possible that he dealt with distress by fantasising about control over others. As other pressures in his life built up his fantasies about control and revenge over society grew, fostered by planning and practice shots at his gun club. In his report Professor Cooke referred to a definition of sadistic personality as involving a disorder in which the subject used violence or cruelty as a way of establishing dominance. Persons with such a personality humiliated and demeaned others, used harsh discipline, took pleasure in the suffering of others, used terror to get others to do as they wish, and were fascinated by violence, weapons, martial arts, injury or torture. In the case of Thomas Hamilton he referred to his behaviour at the boys clubs, as shown on the videotapes, which suggested that he was very strict in his approach and that he liked to dominate those who were in his charge. The boys appeared to be cowed and in some distress while carrying out the exercises. A physical education expert had noted that they were pushed far beyond their abilities. Other witnesses suggested that he was over-strict and militaristic in his approach. There was also some evidence that he might have been amused by or gained pleasure from the psychological suffering of others. He referred to evidence which had been given that some years before he telephoned his natural mother saying she would have to go to Inverness by ambulance for medical treatment. This had caused her great distress. Professor Cooke said that his neighbour Grace Ogilvie implied that he deliberately frightened her by creeping up behind her when she was hanging out her washing. Mr Gillespie indicated that he had fired an empty gun at him. Mr Deuchars reported that he kept his adoptive father outside their house at night for up to 20 minutes. There also had been an incident at a camp in which it was alleged that he made a boy stay in the cold water of Loch Lomond for too long. There was also some limited evidence that he restricted the freedom of people who were close to him. He controlled the access which his adoptive father had to his own house; and within the house he prevented him from watching a new television set. There was also strong evidence of a fascination with weapons and perhaps with violence. He referred to evidence that Thomas Hamilton had talked about his guns "as if they were babies" and that he took great care in selecting and preparing the weapons, bullets and cartridges which he was eventually to use in the shootings. He displayed used shooting targets in a bedroom of his house. He was allegedly interested in violent films including *Alien* and *Terminator* because of the guns involved. Professor Cooke went on to suggest that Thomas Hamilton displayed many of the characteristics of sexual sadism as it had been described by R P Brittain in 1970 (*The sadistic murderer*, Medicine, Science and the Law Vol.10 pages 198-207). He referred in this context to the fact that Thomas Hamilton had few friends and was described as "overly well mannered". He was perceived by several witnesses as being odd or a misfit in society. As already noted he appeared to lack empathy. He had no apparent interest in girlfriends or adult sexual contact.

5.43   I am bound to say that I have some reservation about the importance which Professor Cooke attached to some of the factors which he took into account in reaching the conclusion that the evidence indicated that he may have had features of a sadistic personality disorder. In particular it seems to me that he attached undue significance to the way in which Thomas Hamilton behaved towards his natural mother, his adoptive father and the neighbour, Grace Ogilvie. The telephone call about the ambulance seemed to me to be no more than an unkind prank. On the other hand his reference to Thomas Hamilton's attitude to weapons seemed to me to be of some significance. The following extract from the work by Brittain to which I have already referred seemed particularly striking: "They (weapons) have an attraction for him far beyond what they have for an ordinary collector and he may "love" them, handling, and in the case of firearms, dismantling them and cleaning them for long periods of time. He has strong feelings about them, may have special favourites and he can even have "pet" names for these" (page 201).

5.44   Dr Baird considered that Thomas Hamilton showed signs of a paranoid personality and a psychopathic personality. In the latter respect he differed from the opinion of Professor Cooke. In his first report he stated that "persons of a paranoid personality are over-sensitive to set-backs and difficulties in their lives, tend to bear grudges and are habitually suspicious and mistrustful. They can have a tenacious sense of their own personal rights which is out of keeping with the actual situation, can be rather self-important and show a tendency to consider that events around them are specifically directed towards themselves and can believe that others around them are conspiring against them...... a person with a psychopathic personality disorder can show callous unconcern for the feeling of others, an incapacity to maintain enduring relationships despite having no difficulty in establishing them, and a low tolerance to frustration and a low threshold for aggression or violence. They are not liable to experience feelings of guilt or to learn from experience and they tend to blame others rather than themselves for anything which may happen". In support of this view Dr Baird referred to Thomas Hamilton's persistent beliefs that others were thinking ill of him and not giving him the status and the trust that he deserved; his persistent complaints about the ways that people were talking about him; the absence of any particularly close relationships; and the fact that he seemed to "use" people with whom he was involved.

5.45   Again while I fully appreciate the basis for a finding that Thomas Hamilton showed signs of a paranoid personality, I am more doubtful about a psychopathic one, in the absence of any history of his tending to resort to violence.

5.46   Mr James Taylor, Solicitor Advocate, who appeared for Central Scotland Police, submitted that the evidence did not provide sufficient factual support for the opinions expressed by either Professor Cooke or Dr Baird. In any event they were not in agreement. In these circumstances it was unsafe to conclude that Thomas Hamilton suffered from any personality disorder. I am not persuaded of that. While I have reservations about aspects of the evidence given by each of the witnesses I am entirely satisfied that Thomas Hamilton did suffer from a personality disorder, as distinct from a mental illness. It may be unrealistic and undesirable to require that every case should fit into a precise category. All that the two experts were endeavouring to do, without going so far as to provide an exact diagnosis, was to identify those features which suggested the type of disorder from which he suffered. I am satisfied that Dr Baird was well founded in describing his personality as paranoid; and to that I would add that his personality was characterised by a desire to control others in which his guns were the focus of his fantasies. It seems to me that he lacked any real insight into the fact that his conduct had led to the decline in his fortunes and in his reputation. In that situation he turned his fantasy into reality in order to achieve control in a one final and terrible manner.

5.47   Both Professor Cooke and Dr Baird expressed the view that it was unlikely that any psychological or psychiatric examination of Thomas Hamilton would have alerted the examiner to his dangerousness. Professor Cooke emphasised that extreme violence was very rare and was virtually impossible to predict. A person assessing Thomas Hamilton would probably not have regarded him as a high risk. Dr Baird pointed out that the various actions and statements of Thomas Hamilton when taken together gave strong suggestions as to what was being planned by him "but it is only after the event that it has been possible for these all to be linked. Each on its own and at the time was trivial and unremarkable".

5.48   Both Professor Cooke and Dr Baird expressed the view that Thomas Hamilton demonstrated paedophilia, which is a sexual interest by an adult in children—an opinion which was clearly confirmed by the evidence of the sexual abuse of a boy (see para 4.15), if this was true. Professor Cooke said that one indication was the evidence provided by the videotapes. Such material was often used by paedophiles. They featured, in tedious detail, boys of a particular age and body-type posing semi-naked in stereotype poses. They contained long, lingering shots of boys' torsos, and many of the boys were in the same posture with hands held above their heads or suspended from wall bars or rings. The videotapes and the provision of the swimming costumes were suggestive of a fetishistic interest in boys. Paedophilia was consistent with an absence of direct physical contact since it included those who fell in love with children and yearned for their company but avoided the physical manifestations of sexual attraction. Dr Baird stated that he had no doubt that Thomas Hamilton was a paedophile. "The nature of his sexual fantasies can still only be a matter of speculation but his boys club activities were not innocent, had sinister undercurrents and were unhealthy". He went on to state that there was no indication whatsoever that at any time he had been subjected to anyone who confronted his paedophilia or challenged him about it. Indeed from what was written of him this would not have been by any means an easy task and he would have tirelessly argued his own position. Since paedophiles could be very persistent, plausible, persuasive and manipulative it was necessary to begin with confronting them with the belief that they had a paedophile tendency and to keep confronting them with what was known until they came to accept that they had a problem.

5.49 Neither Professor Cooke nor Dr Baird considered that there was a necessary link between paedophile interests and violence. In the view of Dr Baird it was a coincidence that someone who was interested in boys was also interested in guns.

Chapter 6 Thomas Hamilton's Possession of Firearms and Ammunition

Introduction

6.1 In this chapter I will be concerned with this question—How was it that Thomas Hamilton came to hold the firearms and ammunition which he did on 13 March 1996? After setting out the history of what he was authorised to, and did acquire, from 1977 until his death, I will examine the system of certification as operated by Central Scotland Police; and against that background the circumstances in which it has been maintained that his firearms certificate should have been revoked, or at any rate not renewed, before 13 March 1996. I will conclude with some observations on the system.

History of authorisation and acquisition

6.2 I set out below the history of the granting, variation and renewal of his firearm certificate (in italics); his purchases and sales of firearms; and the general level of his purchases of ammunition, as shown on his firearm certificate. The evidence indicates that he did not reload ammunition. With the possible exception of some purchases at clubs, which did not require to be recorded, his purchases of ammunition can be taken to be those shown on the certificate.

6.3 *On 14 February 1977 Thomas Hamilton was granted a firearm certificate authorising him to purchase or acquire a .22 target pistol; and to hold 1,000 rounds of .22 ammunition, and to purchase or acquire 500 rounds at any one time.*

In his application "good reason" was given as target shooting at Callander Shooting Club or other suitable clubs and ranges.

On 20 February 1977 he purchased a .22 Vostok semi-automatic pistol. On 17 March 1977 he sold it and purchased a .22 Smith & Wesson revolver.

On 30 August 1977 the certificate was varied retrospectively to cover the purchase of the revolver; and to authorise him to purchase or acquire a .22 rifle and a .22 semi-automatic pistol.

On 13 September 1977 and 1 August 1978 he purchased a .22 Anschutz rifle and a .22 Browning pistol respectively.

On 3 December 1979 the certificate was varied to enable him to purchase or acquire a .357 revolver and a .270 rifle; and to hold 100 rounds each of .357 and .270 ammunition, and to purchase or acquire 50 rounds each at any one time.

In his application "good reason" was given as full-bore target shooting at ranges at Dunblane and under Hamilton Police Office. He also stated that he was a member of the Dunblane Rifle Club, and that he was awaiting membership of the Clyde Valley Pistol Club.

On 4 and 5 December 1979 he purchased a .357 Smith and Wesson revolver and a .270 Sako rifle. He owned the revolver until his death when he used it to commit suicide.

In 1977, 1978 and 1979 he purchased 6,500, 2,000 and 3,800 rounds of .22 ammunition respectively; and in 1979 190 rounds of .357 and 220 of .270.

6.4 *On 14 February 1980 the certificate was renewed on the existing basis.*

In his application "good reason" was given as target shooting per condition 5 on the certificate (ie on ranges covered by a safety certificate or by permission from the Ministry of Defence), with Dunblane Rifle Club and Clyde Valley Pistol Club, and other clubs on invitation.

In 1980, 1981 and 1982 he purchased 2,000, 1,000 and 4,000 rounds of .22 ammunition respectively.

6.5 *On 17 January 1983 the certificate was varied to enable him to purchase or acquire a .22 LR rifle. On 14 February 1983 the certificate was renewed on the existing basis.*

On 15 January 1983 he purchased a .22 Browning LR rifle.

On 26 October 1984 he sold the .270 Sako rifle and the .22 Browning LR rifle; and on 27 October 1984 he sold the .22 Browning pistol and the .22 Smith & Wesson revolver which he had purchased on 17 March 1977.

On 6 November 1984 the certificate was varied to enable him to purchase or acquire a 9 mm pistol and a .223 rifle; and to hold 200 rounds each of 9 mm, .223 and .38 special ammunition, and to purchase or acquire 100 rounds of each at any one time.

In his application "good reason" was stated as per condition 5. Thereafter no further specification was provided.

On 7 November and 7 December 1984 he purchased a 9 mm Browning pistol and a .223 Browning rifle respectively.

In 1983 and 1984 he purchased 1,500 and 3,000 rounds of .22 ammunition respectively; and in 1984 350 rounds of 9 mm, 200 of .223 and 200 of .38 special. On 17 December 1984 he was issued with a replacement certificate as the ammunition table on his existing certificate was full.

On 3 June 1985 he sold the .22 Anschutz rifle.

6.6 *On 30 January 1986 the certificate was varied to enable him to purchase or acquire a 7.62 rifle and another 9 mm pistol; and to hold 200 rounds of 7.62 ammunition, and to purchase or acquire 100 rounds at any one time. On 14 February 1986 the certificate was renewed on the existing basis.*

On 18 February 1986 he purchased a 9 mm Beretta pistol.

In 1985 and 1986 respectively he purchased 850 and 500 rounds of 9 mm ammunition; 100 and 50 of .357; 900 and 350 of .38 special; and 320 and 440 of .223. In 1986 he also purchased 100 rounds of 7.62 ammunition.

On 31 March 1987 the certificate was varied to enable him to purchase or acquire a .22 rifle. The authority to hold ammunition (9 mm, .223, .38 special, .357 and 7.62) was increased to 1,500 rounds of each; and to purchase or acquire to 1000 rounds of each at any one time.

In 1987 he purchased 900 rounds of 9 mm ammunition, 250 of .357 and 620 of .223. Between 22 October 1987 and 22 September 1995 he purchased no ammunition.

6.7   *The certificate was renewed on 14 February 1989, with continuing authority to purchase or acquire a .22 rifle and a 7.62 rifle.*

On 18 March 1989 he surrendered the .223 Browning rifle, as a consequence of the Firearms (Amendment) Act 1988; and on 27 November 1990 he sold the 9 mm Beretta pistol.

6.8   *The certificate was renewed as from 17 February 1992 and he was given authority to purchase or acquire a .357 revolver and a 9 mm pistol; with authority to hold 1,500 rounds each of 9 mm, .357, .38 special, 7.62 and .22 ammunition; and to purchase or acquire 1,000 rounds of each at any one time.*

6.9   *On 28 February 1995 the certificate was renewed on the existing basis.*

On 11 September 1995 and 23 January 1996 he purchased a 9 mm Browning pistol and a .357 Smith & Wesson revolver.

Between 22 September 1995 and 27 February 1996 he purchased a total of 1,700 rounds of 9 mm and 500 rounds of .357 ammunition. He made no purchase after the latter date.

6.10   From the above it may be noted that

    (i)   of the 4 handguns which Thomas Hamilton had with him at the school on 13 March 1996, he acquired the two 9 mm Browning pistols on 7 November 1984 and 11 September 1995; and the two Smith & Wesson revolvers on 4 December 1979 and 23 January 1996.

    (ii) the 1,216 rounds of 9 mm ammunition held by him on 13 March 1996 can be compared with an authority to hold 1,500 rounds; and the 522 rounds of .357 ammunition may be compared with authority to hold 1,500. It should also be noted that .38 special ammunition could also be used in the revolvers, so that in effect he had authority to hold 3,000 rounds suitable for use with them.

    (iii) Thomas Hamilton had not used the authority to acquire a 7.62 rifle (as from 30 January 1986); and a .22 rifle (as from 31 March 1987). However, since 1986 he had held 100 rounds of 7.62 ammunition.

The system for certification as operated by Central Scotland Police

6.11   Central Scotland Police required to operate a system in accordance with the Firearms Act 1968, as amended, and the Firearms (Scotland) Rules 1989 (which for present purposes can be taken to be in substantially the same terms as the corresponding Firearms Rules of the same year which apply in England). They also were expected to have regard to the advice contained in Firearms Law: Guidance to the Police, issued by the Home Office, the present version of which was published in 1989.

6.12   Section 27(1) of the Firearms Act 1968 provides as follows:

"A firearm certificate shall be granted by the chief officer of police if he is satisfied that the applicant has a good reason for having in his possession, or for purchasing or acquiring, the firearm or ammunition in respect of which the application is made, and can be permitted to have it in his possession without danger to the public safety or to the peace:

Provided that a firearm certificate shall not he granted to a person whom the chief officer of police has reason to believe to be prohibited by this Act from possessing a firearm to which section 1 of this Act applies, or to be of intemperate habits or unsound mind, or to be for any reason unfitted to be entrusted with such a firearm".

6.13   Section 30(1) of the Firearms Act 1968 provides that:

"A firearm certificate may be revoked by the chief officer of police for the area in which the holder resides if -

(a)   the chief officer is satisfied that the holder is prohibited by this Act from possessing a firearm to which section 1 of this Act applies or is of intemperate habits or unsound mind, or is otherwise unfitted to be entrusted with such a firearm; or....."

6.14   The work carried out by the police in regard to firearm applications fell into two main parts, the first being concerned with the carrying out of enquiries; and the second with the carrying out of administration by the firearms department.

6.15   The enquiries were carried out by serving constables, subject to the qualification that as from 1991 renewals in part of the force area were dealt with by a civilian examiner, Mr N J Lynch. For the present I will describe the procedure in cases with which he was not involved.

6.16   The receipt of an application for grant, or, as the case might be, a computer-generated reminder that an existing certificate was due to expire, led to an officer being allocated to the task of enquiry. At a prearranged time he would call on the applicant (or holder) and in the course of a brief visit check the proposed (or current) security; and would check the firearms and ammunition when these were already held. He would also discuss the reason for which they were held or proposed to be acquired. It is likely that he would also see the existing certificate where one was due for renewal.

6.17   The enquiry officer was also expected to check whether there was anything recorded against the applicant (or holder) with the Scottish Criminal Records Office (SCRO) and on the Police National Computer (PNC). The SCRO provides a record of convictions (presently not including road traffic convictions, which may be found through the Driving and Vehicle Licensing Authority (DVLA)): and of pending prosecutions. The PNC provides UK-wide information about persons who are wanted, missing or suspected or are disqualified from driving. In terms of a force memorandum dated 22 October 1990 a check also required to be made on the force's criminal intelligence. The officer was also expected to check that the counter-signatory required by the application form had duly signed it.

6.18   After concluding these enquiries the officer was required to complete a form RL3a. This form was replaced in 1990; and in its latter version it required him to answer yes or no to the question: "Is the applicant a suitable person to hold a firearm certificate?" If he answered no, he had to provide details on a separate sheet. If the SCRO or PNC had provided a trace, a print-out was to be attached to the form. No reference was made on the form to criminal intelligence. The form then asked: "What are the applicant's reasons for requiring the firearm(s) or ammunition for which application is made? If for competition, applicant must be a member of a club. If for sport, applicant must have land permission. Specify reasons for each firearm". Thereafter the form provided for information to be given in regard to the firearms held; the reason for duplicate calibre firearms, if applicable; the suitability of the intended locations for the firearms; and the arrangements for their security.

6.19   The officer's sergeant was expected to review the completed form. Depending upon the experience of the enquiry officer and the trust which was placed in him, the sergeant would ask such questions as he considered necessary in order to satisfy himself that the enquiry had been satisfactorily completed; and would sign the form to signify that he was satisfied. The sergeant was also available to give advice should the enquiry officer encounter a problem.

6.20   The form was then passed up the normal supervisory chain of command with each officer checking that the form had been completed correctly and being able to add any information or intelligence which he considered relevant. In the event that additional information was seen to be required the form would be returned to the sergeant to have this attended to. The form in due course reached the divisional commander who would satisfy himself that all checks had been carried out and all details had been noted correctly, but would not look behind the answers given in the form. Unless there was information indicating to the contrary he would pass on the form with a recommendation to the chief inspector of firearms that the application be granted.

6.21   In the firearms department the application and the form were checked administratively to see that the historical paperwork in the firearms file tallied with their details. The force standing orders relating to firearms and shot guns provided that it was the duty of all officers to bring to the attention of the Chief Constable any information relating to a firearm or shot gun certificate holder which might warrant revocation of that person's certificate(s). Such information was intended to be placed in the firearms file for that person. Up to May 1995 the form RL3a and the firearm file were passed to the chief inspector of firearms. Thereafter they were passed to the inspector in charge only if there was a problem with the application.

6.22   In the cases in which the enquiry officer was Mr Lynch the procedure was the same, save that until May 1992 he reported directly to the chief inspector of firearms; and as from then he passed the form RL3a to the firearms department. The chief inspector of firearms would be available for consultation; and would be involved if the firearms file contained any information which had been placed there during the currency of the certificate or if any trace had been found during the checks referred to in para 6.17.

6.23   If there was no problem with the application the newly completed certificate would be passed, without the firearms file, to the Deputy Chief Constable for signature on behalf of the Chief Constable. If there was a problem the firearms file would also be passed to him.

6.24   It may be noted that the firearms file was not scrutinised prior to the form RL3a reaching the firearms department.

6.25   In the area of Central Scotland Police there are approximately 1,214 firearm certificates and 3,420 shot gun certificates.

Good Reason

6.26   In terms of Section 27(1) of the 1968 Act the chief officer of police requires to be satisfied "that the applicant has a good reason for having in his possession or for purchasing or acquiring, the firearm or ammunition in respect of which the application is made ....". It may be noted that the loss of a "good reason" is not a ground for revocation under Section 30(1). The Guidance to the Police states in para 6.8(e):

> "A certificate for a handgun and ammunition should not be granted (except in very rare cases) unless the applicant has regular and legitimate opportunity of using the weapon, eg for target practice as a member of a pistol shooting club.....".

Para 6.8(i) states that the 'good reason' requirement has to be demonstrated satisfactorily in respect of each firearm. Para 6.8(j) states: "It is not possible to give firm guidance as to the amount of ammunition which may be authorised by a certificate. Each case should be dealt with on its merits....".

6.27   The circumstances of the present case gave rise to discussion in the evidence and in closing submissions on a number of points which had a bearing on Thomas Hamilton's possession of firearms and ammunition, as well as having a wider significance. They were as follows.

More than one handgun of the same calibre   6.28   As I have stated earlier, on 13 March 1996 Thomas Hamilton held more than one firearm of the same calibre, both pistols and revolvers. This did not play any actual part in what happened but it was a potential factor in the event of his not being able to use one of the handguns.

6.29   It is clear from the evidence that an application for more than one handgun of the same calibre is treated by police forces, including the Central Scotland Police, as something for which the applicant has to show "good reason". Two situations were mentioned, the first being where the shooter is seeking a handgun in order to be able to compete on equal terms with other shooters engaged in a particular competition, for example, where it has been modified from the standard specification in regard to sights, barrel length or other features. The second was where in the event of mechanical failure the ability to substitute a back-up gun is seen as an advantage. A random selection of the firearms files of 12 holders of firearm certificates in the area of Central Scotland Police showed that in 10 cases there were 2 firearms of the same calibre and in 7 cases there were more than 2 such firearms.

6.30   While I can understand how positive justification for a second handgun could be provided and accepted in accordance with current practice, the position in regard to Thomas Hamilton is less persuasive. As can be seen from para 6.6, on 30 January 1986 he was given authority for the first time to acquire a second 9 mm pistol. His application for this was referred back to Sergeant Binning for full details of his reasons to be supplied. The reply to this enquiry was that Thomas Hamilton was "active in competition shooting throughout the country". At that stage he was probably a member of the Dunblane Rifle Club and perhaps he was still a member of the Clyde Valley Pistol Club. However, the statement appears to me to be an exaggeration having regard to the scale of his purchases of 9 mm ammunition in the preceding years and the fact that there is no evidence that he was engaged in competition shooting to any significant extent, let alone "throughout the country". On 17 February 1992 he was given authority to acquire not only a 9 mm pistol but also a second .357 revolver. Mr Lynch, who acted as the enquiry officer, said that Thomas Hamilton stated that he wished to buy a revolver with a longer barrel, which would be of use in absorbing recoil and improving accuracy. Mr Lynch understood that this was to enable him to take part in different disciplines. The duplicating of the 9 mm pistols would also be for competitive shooting. However, once again there was no satisfactory evidence that Thomas Hamilton was engaged in competitive shooting. Further, as I have noted in para 6.6, he had purchased no ammunition since 22 October 1987. This does not inspire me with confidence that at least in the case of Thomas Hamilton there was good reason for the authority for additional handguns of the same calibre.

Increase in ammunition

6.31   During the course of the evidence attention was drawn to the fact, as I have already noted in para 6.6, that on 31 March 1987 the certificate was varied so as to make a substantial increase in the amount of ammunition which he was authorised to hold and to purchase or acquire for each of the calibres. However, at that time he was regularly making significant purchases. The then current Guidance to the Police stated that, while each case should be dealt with on its merits, chief officers of police had accepted that for bona fide club members reasonable quantities were 1500 rounds as the maximum to be possessed at any one time; and 1000 as the maximum to be purchased at any one time. However, it is nonetheless strange that Thomas Hamilton was accorded an authorisation which was more in keeping with an allowance for those who were engaged in a substantial amount of competitive shooting.

Renewal where existing authorisation not used

6.32   Thomas Hamilton's authority to hold and acquire or purchase ammunition was renewed in 1992 and 1995 where, according to the purchases recorded on his certificate, he was not shooting to any significant extent. It might be thought that if good reason requires to be shown at the time of renewal the lack of use of what had previously been authorised would at least raise a question as to whether the good reason continued to exist. The current Guidance to the Police implies in para 6.36, as one might expect, that good reason requires to be shown for the number of rounds of ammunition proposed to be held.

6.33   A similar point arises in regard to Thomas Hamilton's lack of use of the authority which he had obtained for the acquisition of a 7.62 rifle and a .22 rifle.

6.34   At this point it is necessary for me to return to the advice given in para 6.8(e) of the Guidance to the Police which I quoted in para 6.26. Mr J Richardson, Deputy Chief Constable of Strathclyde, who prepared a report on firearms certification in respect of Thomas Hamilton from an independent standpoint, argued that this entailed that at the time of renewal enquiries should be made in order to ascertain whether the existing authorisation was being used.

6.35   Mr Taylor on behalf of Central Scotland Police submitted that all the applicant required to show was that he had a regular and legitimate *opportunity* for using the weapon. He did not require to show he had *used* the weapon. He founded on the evidence in the Green Book that the advice contained in para 6.8(e) "makes it clear to the police that membership of a target shooting club at which the applicant *can* (his emphasis) use a particular pistol or revolver can be regarded as a good reason for the issue of a firearm certificate to possess it, and the ammunition for it" (Part I, para 55). In other words "good reason" looked to the future. For the future the applicant might well want to increase his activity. Mr Taylor also pointed out that it would not make sense for Mr Richardson's interpretation to be applied to a situation where an application for the initial grant of a certificate was under consideration. The recording of the use of individual firearms was not provided for in firearm certificates or in the records kept by clubs. Mr Taylor's submission was, he said, consistent with the practice of Central Scotland Police where continuing membership of clubs was checked but where past usage of ammunition was not reviewed when an application for renewal was under consideration. The practice in other forces might not be entirely uniform, but it appeared that there was no general practice of making such a review in order to see whether the "good reason" still held good.

6.36   I agree with Mr Taylor that para 6.8(e) of the Guidance to the Police does not make "good reason" depend on past use. I agree that it looks to the future. However, it does not follow that para 6.8(e) should be read as if it set out the "regular and legitimate opportunity" as the sole test. There is room for the view that it should be regarded as setting out *an* essential condition. It may be maintained that inherent in an applicant having "good reason" is that he had an intention to use or, as the case may be, to purchase or acquire for use. If he has not used a firearm which he was previously given the authority to possess, this may cast doubt on his intention; or there may be a good explanation for it which removes the doubt. If he is able to point to past use it would be a simple and effective way of showing good reason. The same doubt could arise in the case of an authorisation to acquire a firearm which has not been used. It may be noted that para 6.21 of the Guidance to the Police, which is concerned with conditions which the chief officer of police may attach to a firearm certificate, ends with the words: "Conditions setting out arbitrary time limits for acquiring firearms and for ammunition should not be imposed. However, the chief officer may at the time of certificate renewal, enquire why an authorised acquisition has not been completed and consider the renewal in the light of the information received". It may be thought that it is not in the public interest that unused authority should continue on the mere say-so of the applicant, with the risk that acquisition might eventually be made in circumstances very different from those originally envisaged.

6.37   While there is much to be said for this interpretation I realise that, due to the way in which para 6.8(e) has been expressed, police forces have been led into thinking that only "regular and legitimate opportunity" is required. I see no reason to fault Central Scotland Police for the way in which they have interpreted language which, in my view, leaves something to be desired. I am aware from the discussion at the Inquiry that there have been differences of view among police forces throughout the United Kingdom as to the extent to which it is appropriate to take into account past use in dealing with "good reason". This is a matter which will require my attention in Chapter 8.

Unfitness to be entrusted with a firearm

6.38   Section 27(1) of the 1968 Act contains a proviso that a firearm certificate is not to be granted to *inter alios* "a person whom the chief officer has reason to believe ..... to be for any reason unfitted to be entrusted with such a firearm".

Section 30(1) provides that a firearm certificate may be revoked by the chief officer if he is "satisfied that the holder ..... is otherwise unfitted to be entrusted with such a firearm". It may also be noted that, unlike Section 27(1), the latter provision does not include the words "danger to the public safety or to the peace".

6.39 In the case of Thomas Hamilton it was submitted at the Inquiry that his firearm certificate should have been revoked, or at any rate not renewed. I will now set out the background against which that submission was made to me.

6.40 In para 4.69 I explained the circumstances in which DCC McMurdo received information about Thomas Hamilton's display of firearms to a family in Linlithgow towards the end of 1988. In evidence he said that he decided that no action should be taken in regard to this matter. He said that his decision was based on the considerations that Thomas Hamilton's visit was "at the instigation" of the family; that he showed them the firearms and allowed the boys to hold them; that he had been informative in his instruction as to their safe handling; that what was important was that there was no ammunition there and that at no time was the family distressed or concerned by his visit; and that he remained in possession of the firearms. However, Mr McMurdo accepted that with hindsight he could possibly have sent him a warning. It may be noted that a copy of Inspector Nimmo's memorandum in regard to this incident was not put in the firearms file relating to Thomas Hamilton, although it should have been. Further, it was not entered in criminal intelligence.

6.41 On 11 November 1991 DS Hughes addressed a memorandum to the Detective Superintendent, CID, at police headquarters relating to the investigation of the summer camp at Mullarochy Bay in July 1991 (cf para 4.45). This memorandum was written at a stage when his report was before the Procurator Fiscal. In the memorandum DS Hughes referred to the previous investigation into the activities of Thomas Hamilton and his appearance in local criminal intelligence files. He had met him on a number of occasions and recently discovered that he held a firearm certificate. He went on to state:

> "I am firmly of the opinion that Hamilton is an unsavoury character and unstable personality.
>
> It emerged from enquiries that he, during the course of the first week of camp, seemed to become increasingly stressed and had difficulty in managing the group. It was during one such moment that he became extremely angry and assaulted one of the boys. This particular child was in fact assaulted three times by Hamilton during the first few days of the holiday and was eventually removed by his parents.
>
> Furthermore, allegations were made, albeit uncorroborated, by one of the children that Hamilton induced the child to pose in various compromising positions, scantily clad in extremely ill-fitting swimming trunks, for photographs. To date these photographs have not been recovered but neither I nor the officer who interviewed the child have any reason to disbelieve that the allegations are in fact wholly true.
>
> Convincing corroborated evidence was uncovered which confirms that two boxes containing approximately 36 slides each have not been recovered by the police despite Mr Hamilton's claims that he handed over all of the photographs taken. Mr Hamilton has been reported to the Procurator Fiscal in this regard for obstructing the police.
>
> The foregoing report, in part, conveys some of the concerns which I harbour

about this man. I firmly believe that he has an extremely unhealthy interest in young boys which to a degree appears to have been controlled to date. It was his ploy, whenever challenged, to engage in 'smoke screen' tactics which divert attention from the focal issue and this is the purpose for the profusion of correspondence to MPs, Procurators Fiscal, the Chief Constable and the like. I would contend that Mr Hamilton will be a risk to children whenever he has access to them and that he appears to me to be an unsuitable person to possess a firearm certificate in view of the number of occasions he has come to the adverse attention of the police and his apparent instability.

The Procurator Fiscal at Stirling has not yet decided on whether or not he will proceed with the case against Hamilton but at the moment it appears in all likelihood that he will not.

I respectfully request that serious consideration is given to withdrawing this man's firearm certificate as a precautionary measure as it is my opinion that he is a scheming, devious and deceitful individual who is not to be trusted".

6.42 DS Hughes had discussed his report with DCI Holden of the CID Department whose responsibilities included the Child Protection Unit. The latter wrote on the memorandum:

"A difficult situation,—I do agree with DS Hughes' appraisal of Mr Hamilton. Do we have any latitude for progress in respect of the revocation of his certificate".

The memorandum was submitted to his superior, D/Supt Millar (now retired). He wrote on the memorandum the following note to DCC McMurdo:

"While appreciating DS Hughes' concern, I can not recommend the action proposed for obvious reasons, ie Hamilton has not been convicted of any crime and it seems the PF is likely to No Pro the recently reported case".

Mr Millar said in evidence that he passed the memorandum to the Deputy Chief Constable because he knew that he had been engaged in correspondence with Thomas Hamilton and because he was responsible for the issuing of firearm certificates. DCC McMurdo after considering the memorandum marked it "no action" on 11 November 1991 but did not record his reasons for so doing. I will consider later the explanation for this decision which he gave in evidence. Before making this decision he discussed the memorandum with DCI Holden but not with DS Hughes. A copy of the memorandum should have been placed in the firearms file relating to Thomas Hamilton but this was not done. Further, a copy was not entered in criminal intelligence.

6.43 The documentary evidence shows that Mr McMurdo was involved in a considerable amount of correspondence with or concerning Thomas Hamilton during the period 1989-1992. This dealt mainly with his complaint against members of the Central Scotland Police and his persistent complaints about undesirable links between the Scouts and the police. Commenting on a letter from Thomas Hamilton to him dated 8 June 1990 Mr McMurdo agreed in evidence that there was "no love lost between him and the Central Scotland Police Force". When Thomas Hamilton sought to involve The Scottish Office in his complaints about the relationship between the police and the Scouts and the handling of his complaint against the Police Mr McMurdo wrote in strong terms to The Scottish Office in a letter dated 14 January 1992. In the course of that letter he emphatically rejected an implication that police officers' notebooks had been tampered with and the inference which Thomas Hamilton had sought to draw from the fact that many police officers helped voluntary organisations such as the Scouts. He said:

> "How Hamilton can draw a sinister inference from such a healthy and worthwhile pastime is beyond my comprehension. For Mr Hamilton to see his tiny local organisation as a serious rival to the Scouting movement indicates a certain lack of perspective".

Later in the letter he said:

> "In common with most right-minded people I am proud of the connection between Central Scotland Police and all the youth organisations with which we work. Only a bitter and petty minded individual like Thomas Hamilton could pervert such a relationship into something sleazy and dishonourable and imagine some undercurrent of corruption. I am sorry about the length of this letter but, as a comparatively recent beneficiary of Mr Hamilton's vindictive correspondence, you should be aware of the background to almost four years of ever more irrational outpourings. Both I and the two Chief Constables have tried very hard to resolve the matter but, as always when trying to reason with a zealot, each time a point appears to have been settled he re-introduces it in another guise, adjusts the facts selectively to suit his ends and it all begins again".

6.44   When the firearm certificate was renewed as from 17 February 1992 Thomas Hamilton was given authority to purchase or acquire two additional firearms, a .357 revolver and a 9 mm pistol (he having sold the pistol which he had been authorised to purchase in 1986). The renewal was signed by Ch.Supt Adamson, as acting Deputy Chief Constable in the absence of Mr McMurdo. He had before him only the certificate. He had not seen a copy of DS Hughes' memorandum and nobody had discussed its contents with him. However, he said in evidence that at about the time that it had been submitted, DCC McMurdo told him that he had decided that no action should be taken. Nothing was brought to his attention which indicated that this decision should be altered.

6.45   As I have already narrated, a further investigation into complaints about Thomas Hamilton's conduct was carried out in 1993. This led to DC Taylor preparing a memorandum to the Detective Superintendent, Crime Management Services dated 9 June 1993. From an examination of the Scout files he had read a description of Thomas Hamilton's character and Mr Fairgrieve had confirmed to him that he had described him as a bully with grandiose ideas as to his own ability, but not as mentally unbalanced. DC Taylor believed that Thomas Hamilton had been guilty of criminal conduct. However, he did not himself encounter anything which gave him concern as to his fitness to hold a firearm certificate. A copy of his memorandum was not put in the firearms file relating to Thomas Hamilton or in the criminal intelligence.

6.46   In 1995 the certificate was due for renewal once more. DC Anne Anderson was assigned to the role of enquiry officer. It was her one and only firearms enquiry. She carried out the SCRO and PNC checks. When she made a home visit to Thomas Hamilton she experienced, she said, a "strange feeling" about him when he showed her his firearms. She was disturbed by the way in which he looked at her as if he hoped to get some kind of reaction from her. She felt slightly intimidated. She wanted someone to know that she had been in the house and that she was not particularly happy about signing the form. Her own supervisor was not working on the same shift as herself at that time. After consulting a colleague she spoke to Inspector John Anderson. According to her evidence he said that a number of reports had been put in by DS Hughes and other officers about Thomas Hamilton but as there was nothing against him "there is nothing we can do". She felt happier after speaking to Inspector Anderson. She looked at criminal intelligence records in the hope that there was something on him there which would back up her feelings. If so, she would have been able to add her own feelings to that. But there was merely a short note about Thomas Hamilton trying to set up a boys club in the area of Bannockburn. As there was nothing else she felt that perhaps she had misinterpreted his manner. Since she had had merely a feeling about Thomas Hamilton, she did not make an entry about it in criminal intelligence. It should be pointed out that Inspector Anderson's account of this brief conversation was different. According to him, having checked that Thomas Hamilton had no previous convictions she approached him as he had been previously in charge of the Child Protection Unit and she suspected that he knew Thomas Hamilton. He told her to check criminal intelligence; and did not tell her that he did not have any previous convictions or that there was nothing which the police could do. I accept her version. The whole episode made a clear impression on her. Mr R O Campbell, JP, countersigned Thomas Hamilton's applications in 1992 and 1995. He had a general knowledge of his activities and had met his adoptive father but he did not know Thomas Hamilton particularly well. In each case he had received a telephone call from the police and had confirmed that the form bore his signature.

6.47   The 1995 renewal was signed by DCC McMurdo. He said in evidence that he spent a few minutes on it. Only the certificate was before him. He said that he did apply his mind to the question of whether Thomas Hamilton was a fit and proper person. He had to consider whether he had good reason not to sign. He had reservations about the way in which he ran boys clubs but he had no evidence of his being dangerous with a firearm. He knew, he said, that in the event of an appeal against a refusal, he could not justify such a decision before the Sheriff. There were no "contra-indicators". The Procurators Fiscal had decided that there should be no proceedings and not one photograph of an indecent nature had been found. "So over the period, I mean, I have got absolutely nothing at the end of it".

6.48   Mr C M Campbell submitted to me that the certificate should have been revoked, or at any rate not renewed in 1992 or 1995. He founded on the memorandum of 11 November 1991. He also founded on evidence which, he said, indicated that Thomas Hamilton had committed assault, neglect, indecent behaviour and breach of the peace; that he was a scheming, vindictive, deceitful liar who harboured an obsessional grudge against the Scout movement and was hostile to the police; that he was the subject of rumours and gossip; and of frequent complaints by parents due to his abnormal and unhealthy conduct towards young boys, serviced by his obsessional organisation of boys clubs and camps; that he was a misfit, loner, weirdo, oddball who repelled most people; that he had made a habit of unjustified and time-consuming complaints, both formally and informally, about the police; and indulged in a series of false and defamatory accusations of police officers; this was "to tire and eventually deflate his accusers and throw a smoke screen over his own activities". In this he had been remarkably successful. He had also been expelled from the Scouts for reasons which DC Taylor had found in the Scout files in 1993.

6.49   Mr Campbell submitted that an important feature of the approach which had been taken by Central Scotland Police was the extraordinarily narrow interpretation which they had placed on the meaning of "unfitness" in Sections

27(1) and 30(1). He emphasised that this expression was concerned with the trustworthiness of a person's character in regard to the responsibilities which attached to a possessor of firearms. Firearms and especially semi-automatic handguns had a unique ability to kill. No physical contact, strength, prowess or even bravery was required. The chief officer of police had a heavy responsibility to perform in forestalling incidents. Central Scotland Police had concentrated on the need for a serious previous conviction or a strong pending case. They had in effect delegated their responsibility to Procurators Fiscal and were influenced by the risk of failure in an appeal. It was symptomatic of this that the memorandum of DS Hughes had been treated as simply a "gut feeling".

6.50   Mr Campbell was critical of the fact that DCC McMurdo had not made any enquiry of DS Hughes. In evidence the latter said that he considered that Thomas Hamilton had singled out a child for better treatment in order to engage his interest. He strongly suspected that he was a paedophile and that to a degree his tendencies had been controlled. He found him very obstructive; he had no intention of listening to reason; he had very much his own agenda; he firmly believed that he was an outstanding pillar of the community but somewhere within himself he must have recognised that he was not; and he came across as quite calm when he was actually quite angry. By referring to him as "unstable" the witness said that he meant that he was a difficult person to deal with, had very much his own agenda, had an unhealthy interest in children and was an abnormal type of person. As regards the assaults with which he was concerned he did not consider Thomas Hamilton at that time to be a particular threat. He had been more of a bully. However, he thought that he was capable of violence and felt that he tried to be intimidating in a veiled sort of fashion. "Gut feeling" had nothing to do with the charges which he had drafted. He accepted that he was a little aggrieved by the fact that Thomas Hamilton had made a complaint about him but he did not over-react or act unprofessionally.

6.51   Mr Campbell also submitted that Central Scotland Police had failed to take the whole picture together. But for their collective failures the shootings on 13 March 1996 would not have occurred.

6.52   In reply Mr Taylor submitted that Section 27(1) should be treated as posing a composite test which, in his words, was "whether or not the circumstances revealed the likelihood of a disturbance to good order arising out of the possession by the applicant of a firearm". On this approach there was little practical significance in the distinction between the language of Section 27(1) and that of Section 30(1). This was how the matter had been approached in the case of Thomas Hamilton. There always had to be evidence: "gut feeling" was not enough. It was accepted that a previous conviction was not necessary for revocation or refusal to renew. But if any member of the police force did have such a view it would be understandable, in the light of the statement in the Green Book that "unless a certificate holder sustains a criminal conviction during the currency of his certificate, the conditions for revocation may not often apply in practice". (Part I, para 79). Furthermore other passages clearly implied that character should be viewed primarily in terms of criminal conduct (Part I, paras 62 and 65-67).

6.53   Mr Taylor maintained that DS Hughes' memorandum consisted almost entirely of "gut feeling". There was no need for DCC McMurdo to enquire of him. Mr Taylor also suggested that the memorandum was an after-thought on the part of DS Hughes who must have known at the time of his report to the Procurator Fiscal that Thomas Hamilton had a firearm certificate as this would have been shown by the SCRO check which was carried out as a matter of routine. Mr Taylor also emphasised that DC Taylor did not consider that he had revealed any factors which caused concern about the fact that Thomas Hamilton held a firearm certificate. It was of no materiality that details of the Linlithgow and Mullarochy Bay investigations were not included in the firearms file relating to Thomas Hamilton. There was nothing in the firearms file which would have told DCC McMurdo what he did not already know. Even when all the matters were taken together the information available to the police did not show that Thomas Hamilton was predisposed to violence. There was no more than a suspicion of unwholesome activities on his part. When it came to the point of decision DCC McMurdo was in much the same position as others who had difficulty in putting their finger on what was wrong. He would have had no prospect of success in the event of an appeal.

6.54 Before coming to the evidence of Mr McMurdo I should refer to the evidence of the two officers who were involved in the chain of communication between DS Hughes and the Deputy Chief Constable.

6.55 Supt (then DCI) Holden said that he had shared DS Hughes' concerns. He had questioned, and they had discussed, his reference to Thomas Hamilton being "unstable" which he had explained as being based on his inability to cope with a number of boys, resulting in his assaulting one of them. Supt Holden could find no reason why DS Hughes was not right but he could not say whether Thomas Hamilton *was* "unfitted" to be entrusted with a firearm. He felt that they did not have enough at that point. He had never spoken to Thomas Hamilton and relied on second-hand information from DS Hughes. He had agreed that the question as to his fitness should be raised. At the time he had no experience in firearms certification. He accepted that in his police statement for the Inquiry, which he had written himself, he said: "I believed our recommendation was based on Hamilton not being a fit and proper person to hold firearms authority". He did not know whether a person who fitted the description given by DS Hughes in the last paragraph of his memorandum was unfitted to be entrusted with a firearm. If he was unstable he would be. However, he agreed that if a person was a deceitful liar, it would raise a very serious question mark.

6.56 Supt Holden's evidence gave me the strong impression that, without going back on what he had written in the memorandum, he was seeking to dilute the support which he had given to DS Hughes. I am extremely sceptical that at the time he expressed or entertained the qualification which he expressed in his evidence to the Inquiry. As far as DS Hughes was concerned—and I accept him as an honest and well-balanced witness—Superintendent Holden agreed with his appraisal at the time.

6.57 I turn then to Mr Millar, who said that he had handled very many firearms applications and, as a sub-divisional commander, had had to consider whether the applications should be recommended. When he was shown what he had written on the memorandum he said that the word "convicted" had been used by him to cover quite a wide meaning. He was aware that there was no need for a conviction but there had to be evidence of unsuitability and he did not think that on the basis of the information supplied to him there was enough evidence. There were no guns involved. So he recommended that there were no grounds which would stand up in court. Whatever may have been in his mind it is, in my view, quite impossible to read what he wrote referring to anything other than criminal proceedings and a criminal conviction. This was plainly too narrow an approach. A criminal prosecution is concerned with a different question, and is subject to its own peculiar rules of evidence and procedure. When he was asked for examples of persons who would be unfitted to be entrusted with a firearm he mentioned cases of extreme violence (including child assault, depending on the severity); drunkenness; and violence where a firearm was used in the commission of crime. When he was asked about consideration of preventive measures he answered: "In hindsight there possibly should have been. There was not at the time".

6.58   Before leaving Mr Millar I should note in passing that Mr McMurdo seemed to place some reliance on the fact that he had discussed the memorandum with him before deciding to take action; and that the D/Supt agreed with him that there was no evidence to support the conclusion which DS Hughes had reached. However, this was not borne out by Mr Millar who said in evidence that DCC McMurdo had *not* discussed the memorandum with him. He had not seen the witness statements which DS Hughes had obtained but he had received a briefing from DCI Holden. As far as he was concerned DCC McMurdo was *au fait* with the case which had been reported to the Procurator Fiscal. He had been brought up to date by DCI Holden, and knew all about Thomas Hamilton. It seems to me to be more likely DCC McMurdo did not consider it necessary to discuss the memorandum with D/Supt Millar. I prefer Mr Millar's evidence on this point.

6.59   I come now to the evidence of Mr McMurdo. In the course of his evidence it was clear that, so far as he was concerned, the only practical difference between Section 27(1) and Section 30(1) of the 1968 Act was the absence of reference to "good reason" in the latter. He accepted that he was exercising preventive police work; and he asserted that where there was a doubt he would always act positively. But it was clear that great importance was attached by him to convictions. In giving examples of cases which would justify considering someone to be "unfitted" to be entrusted with a firearm he referred to convictions for assault resulting in a 3 months' sentence; a conviction for threatening with a firearm; and three drink-driving convictions. The means of identifying those who were "unfitted" was provided, he said, by the system whereby convictions and pending cases were drawn to the attention of the firearms department along with information which had been entered on criminal intelligence.

6.60   In regard to the memorandum by DS Hughes he did not take it lightly. However, it was a "gut feeling". It did not have the evidence to substantiate it. As regards the "assault" the memorandum was "biased". It was chastisement for bullying involving kicking, punching and throwing stones. The report which DS Hughes had earlier submitted to the Procurator Fiscal was "very mixed". Some parents had supported Thomas Hamilton. He did not accept DS Hughes' description of Thomas Hamilton. He had met and corresponded with him and knew his arguments and personality. In particular he did not consider him to be unstable or irrational. There had been no need for him to enquire of DS Hughes as there was no one in Central Scotland Police who knew him better than himself.

6.61   It seemed clear to me at a number of points that while Mr McMurdo accepted that he was exercising preventive police work he had difficulty in envisaging cases in which a person could be shown to be "unfitted" to be entrusted with a firearm where there was no previous conviction or pending criminal case. When he was asked what would be included in the responsibility to be expected of a holder of a firearm certificate he said that it was "expecting a bit much" for him to be honest in his dealings with the police. These and other passages seem to me to provide support for Mr Campbell's submission that he adopted an unduly narrow approach in which he paid not much more than lip service to the idea that a person could be "unfitted" in the absence of a conviction or pending criminal case. He undervalued the breadth of that expression.

6.62 Much of the criticism of the memorandum which Mr McMurdo expressed was directed at the "assault". However, the main point which DS Hughes was making was that Thomas Hamilton was a scheming, devious and deceitful person who was not to be trusted. This was, of course, within the context of the matters with which DS Hughes had been concerned. It was for Mr McMurdo to see that account was taken of the whole information available to the police and to apply his knowledge and experience of the firearms system. Did DS Hughes' description in the last paragraph of his memorandum indicate someone who should not have a firearm certificate? Mr McMurdo's position on this point underwent a disconcerting shift during the course of his evidence. At one point he made it clear in answer to Mr Bonomy and myself that if the description was correct he was unfitted. His concern had been whether there was evidence to prove it. However, on the following day he explicitly departed from that position on the ground that it did not of itself show unfitness to be entrusted with a firearm.

6.63 At the time when Mr McMurdo received the memorandum he knew that there was evidence that Thomas Hamilton had apparently misled the police in the course of their investigation of his taking of photographs which, to say the least, raised questions as to whether his interest in and behaviour towards boys, and in particular a favourite boy, was healthy and normal. The general context which was already known to him was that there was "no love lost between him and the Central Scotland Police Force" and that Thomas Hamilton would lose no opportunity to find fault with the police in evading questions about his own methods. His letter to The Scottish Office dated 14 January 1992, to which I referred in para 6.43, indicates DCC McMurdo's strongly held views about Thomas Hamilton's character, although I have to point out that when he was giving evidence Mr McMurdo said that he withdrew the word "irrational", explaining that he had "lost his cool" and wanted to put an end to the correspondence. However, it was to the police that Thomas Hamilton was responsible for giving truthful answers as to his reasons for wanting firearms and, when questioned, in regard to his own suitability. DCC McMurdo already knew of at least one instance of a link between Thomas Hamilton's firearms and the boys who attended his clubs. At the house in Linlithgow he had shown firearms to boys—with the parents' consent—after he had offered to do so. On any view it was an inappropriate conduct on the part of a firearm certificate holder and it raised a question as to whether it was serious enough to warrant revocation. Having heard, read and re-read the evidence I consider that these considerations called into question Thomas Hamilton's fitness to be entrusted with a firearm and that DCC McMurdo should have taken the opportunity of making further enquiries, and in particular hearing what DS Hughes had to say. He was after all able to give a first—hand account of Thomas Hamilton's behaviour and reactions when he was questioned at the camp.

6.64 In considering the question whether Thomas Hamilton's firearm certificate should have been revoked in the light of what was known or should have been found out at the time it is, of course, necessary to put aside the effect which hindsight tends to have in colouring the significance of the facts. Bearing in mind the width of the expression "unfitted" it is necessary to look at all the known conduct on the part of Thomas Hamilton which is relevant, whether related to firearms or to any other matter, in order to see whether such an inference should have been drawn. On balance I consider that there was a case for revocation of

Thomas Hamilton's firearm certificate and that it should have been acted upon. However, I do not consider that this would have been the end of the matter. I have no doubt that he would have appealed and argued his case with his accustomed vigour and plausibility. The outcome would have depended very much on the impression which he created with the Sheriff. It is not certain that an appeal would have been unsuccessful.

6.65 The renewal (with a variation) of the certificate in 1992 could quite properly be described as a routine operation. It was abundantly clear that Ch.Supt Adamson was doing no more than giving effect to the decision which he understood DCC McMurdo had taken on 11 November 1991. At no point in the procedure was there any effective assessment of Thomas Hamilton's suitability. I should also point out that those who were dealing with the application for renewal before the new certificate reached Ch.Supt Adamson were provided with no adequate means of carrying out a proper scrutiny of the application as neither a copy of Inspector Nimmo's memorandum nor a copy of DS Hughes' memorandum was recorded in criminal intelligence or in the firearms file. In the result they could not be picked up by either the enquiry officer, in this case Mr N G Lynch, or by the firearms department. DCC McMurdo, who was the repository of knowledge about Thomas Hamilton, was absent. Ch.Supt Adamson assumed that appropriate steps had been taken by others. Thus he accepted in evidence that if, through an administrative error, the firearms file had not been passed to him when this should have been done, it is probable that he would still have signed the new certificate.

6.66 It is clear from his evidence that Mr McMurdo took the view that events between the renewal in 1992 and that in 1995 did not in any way alter his views as to whether Thomas Hamilton should continue to have a firearm certificate. I have already referred at para 6.47 to the evidence which he gave as to the circumstances in which he signed the renewal in 1995. He drew some support from the report which DCI Holden made to him after his interview with Thomas Hamilton in October 1993 (para 4.60). According to Mr McMurdo his view of Thomas Hamilton had changed. He said to Mr McMurdo: "Well, maybe he is a bit of an oddball, but maybe we have misjudged him a bit". However, Mr Holden's evidence was that he would have given the same endorsement to DS Hughes' memorandum if it had been presented to him in 1993 although he would have had to question the word "stable". However, as I have already narrated, he had questioned this expression in 1991; and his endorsement had followed after this had been discussed. In my view Mr McMurdo exaggerated any change in the views of DCI Holden.

6.67 The fate of Police Constable Anne Anderson's impression of Thomas Hamilton is another demonstration of the effect of the failure to enter relevant information in criminal intelligence, in this instance the memoranda of Inspector Nimmo, DS Hughes and DC Taylor. It was clear from her evidence that if she had had any indication of support for a concern as to Thomas Hamilton's fitness to be the holder of a firearm she would have wanted to make known her contribution. As it was, the lack of any other indication of significance led her to treat her impression of an unhealthy attitude to his firearms as being of no account.

6.68 The remarks which I have made in regard to the case for the revocation of Thomas Hamilton's firearm certificate and the outcome of an appeal by him apply also to a decision to refuse the renewal of the certificate.

6.69 If Thomas Hamilton had been finally deprived of his firearm certificate and hence lost his firearms and ammunition, how far would this have altered the course of events? Would he have sought and obtained illegal possession of one or more other firearms and ammunition? Would he have resorted to other means of causing death? Or would the loss of his own firearms and ammunition have forestalled the development of homicidal intentions? The Inquiry heard some evidence that it was unlikely that Thomas Hamilton would have been able to obtain a firearm from members of the criminal fraternity. Even without such evidence it seems to me to be highly improbable that he would have embarked upon, let alone been successful, in such an approach. However, by some means or other he might have purloined a firearm, whether legally or illegally held, from someone known to him. On the other hand it is difficult to envisage that he would have been able to amass a collection of firearms and ammunition similar to that with which he approached the school. This all presupposes that Thomas Hamilton would have had an intention to perpetrate a mass shooting which was independent of the non-availability of his own firearms and ammunition. It is clear that what he did on 13 March 1996 was planned in advance. However, it was planned in the context of the continuing availability of his own firearms and ammunition. Further, his attitude to his own firearms seems to me to be of some importance. They were his "babies": and he gloated over them. He used them as a means of exercising power over his victims and their relatives. It does not appear to me to follow from the evidence that Thomas Hamilton would have sought in any event to perpetrate a mass shooting. It seems to me to be at least as likely that the availability of his own firearms and ammunition influenced him in the way in which he proceeded. Now it is possible that he would have sought out some other means of causing death. In the light of the evidence of Dr Baird it would require to have been a means which encompassed his own death. I am not able to reach any conclusion as to what he would have done in this direction as it is too much a matter for speculation.

Observations on the system

6.70   At this stage I have some comments on the system used by Central Scotland Police. In Chapter 8 I will undertake the more comprehensive task of considering certain aspects of the certification regime which is in force throughout the country.

6.71   Enquiry officers were required by means of form RL3a to provide the answer to a question which is of fundamental importance to a correct decision on the application: "Is the applicant a suitable person to hold a firearm certificate?" If information which was adverse to the applicant emerged from his enquiry he would have to weigh up its significance and seriousness. It might well be thought that the question which was posed should have been a question for the senior police officer who made the decision on behalf of the Chief Constable. The true objective of the enquiry into the question of suitability was surely that the officer should assemble the information which appeared to be of possible relevance to the decision.

6.72   I have referred earlier, and need not repeat here, my remarks about the absence from criminal intelligence of any reference to the previous police investigation of Thomas Hamilton's conduct. The fact that the substance of this information was made known to Mr McMurdo at one stage or another was neither here nor there. It was a glaring deficiency in the operation of the force's information system.

6.73   It was obviously important that an enquiry form should require the enquiry officer to give a positive response in regard to all lines of enquiry which as a matter of routine required to be pursued. Accordingly in the evidence and in the written submission made by the Chief Constable, to which I referred at para 3.28, it was recognised that form RL3a should have referred to a check on criminal intelligence. Such a check was omitted when Thomas Hamilton's certificate was due for renewal in February 1992.

6.74   Any visit by an enquiry officer to the applicant's home was of necessity comparatively brief, but it might well be that during the visit something came to his or her attention which might raise a matter for concern about the suitability of the applicant or holder. The experience of PC Anderson in February 1995 was a striking example of this. There was a danger that some piece of information, even an impression, when seen by itself might appear to be of no account but when considered along with other information not known to the enquiry officer might assume a very different complexion. If an enquiry officer was in effect limited to answering yes or no to the question of whether the applicant or holder was a suitable person, such information might be lost. This suggests that the form should have been worded in such a way as to encourage the enquiry officer to mention any matter which gave rise to any concern in regard to the applicant's suitability and the view which he took of it, whether or not he was asked to, and did, express a view as to the applicant's suitability.

6.75   In the system which I have described earlier it is clear that reference was made to the firearms department only after the enquiry officer had carried out his work. However, it might well be that there were matters which were already known to the department, perhaps in the form of a change of circumstances or some reason for exercising particular caution, which should be looked into. It would have been sensible if such matters had been drawn to the attention of the enquiry officer before he undertook his work.

6.76   I appreciate that I heard evidence which emphasised that a constable who was called upon to be the enquiry officer had the benefit of his sergeant to advise him and to scrutinise his work so far as that is considered necessary. However, it was asking a great deal of a constable who had no previous first-hand experience of firearms or the certification system to undertake enquiries, particularly in regard to the existence of "good reason". The provision of information in response to an enquiry form would not serve the purpose of providing a thorough examination of "good reason" unless full details were set out as a result of the right questions being asked.

6.77   I also note that form RL3a did not specifically require the enquiry officer to name the club or clubs whose membership was relied on in showing "good reason" or the means by which the applicant's current membership was vouched to his satisfaction.

6.78   In the preceding paragraphs I have been principally concerned with the supplying of adequate information to, and by, the enquiry officer. However, the evidence provided a disturbing picture of the operation of the decision-making process. The senior officer who had the responsibility of determining the outcome of Thomas Hamilton's application had nothing put before him but the new firearm certificate to be signed. In the absence of any indication to the contrary he assumed that it was appropriate for him to sign. In such circumstances junior officers made the assessment of the significance of information which was obtained. The senior officer was not placed in the position of making the decision in the light of all the information which was of possible relevance.

Chapter 7 The Control of Firearms and Ammunition

Introduction

7.1   The Firearms Acts provide for the control of firearms and ammunition according to four levels.

7.2   The lowest applies to those for which no certificate is required for their possession, purchase or acquisition. These comprise air weapons other than those declared to be specially dangerous under the Firearms (Dangerous Air Weapons) Rules; shot gun cartridges, subject to certain qualifications; air gun ammunition; and blank cartridges.

7.3   The second level applies to those for which a shot gun certificate is required, namely shot guns provided that they have a smooth bore; have a barrel not less than 24 in. in length and do not have a barrel with a bore exceeding 2 in.; have either no magazine or a non-detachable magazine incapable of holding more than two cartridges; and are not revolver guns as defined in section 1(3)(b) of the 1968 Act.

7.4   The third level applies to those for which a firearm certificate is required, namely revolvers, pistols, rifles; higher-power air weapons, ie those declared to be specially dangerous as above; shot guns other than as described above; any other lethal barrelled weapon; and any "prohibited weapon" as next mentioned.

7.5   The fourth level applies to "prohibited weapons". Section 5 of the 1968 Act, as amended, provides that, except with the authority of the Secretary of State, the possession, purchase, acquisition, sale and transfer (and in many cases manufacture) of a number of specified types of weapons and ammunition is prohibited.

7.6   The methods of control which have been adopted to date thus consist essentially of, firstly, the regulation of the authority to possess, purchase or acquire under one or other of two kinds of certificate; and, secondly, the imposition of restrictions on certain categories of firearms by reference to their relative dangerousness.

7.7   In the aftermath of the shootings at Hungerford on 12 August 1987 it was considered that certain firearms were so highly dangerous as to merit their placing in the class of "prohibited weapons". These included self-loading and pump-action rifles, other than those chambered for .22 rimfire and certain self-loading and pump-action shot guns (see the White Paper *Firearms Act 1968: Proposals for Reform* (1987) Cm 261 and the amendment to the 1968 Act which was effected by section 1 of the Firearms (Amendment) Act 1988). On a similar basis the 1968 Act was also amended so as to elevate certain shot guns to the level of control where a firearm certificate was required. Likewise at the lower end of the scale of control the dangerousness of air weapons is, as I have already noted, the test by reference to which they are or are not assigned to the category for which a firearm certificate is necessary.

7.8   Opinions may vary as to whether the particular types of weapon or firearm have been correctly categorised in the past, but it is clear that the dangerousness of a weapon or firearm is a concept which is fundamental to the system of control which has been in existence for many years.

7.9   In considering what are the lessons of the Inquiry it is plainly unwise for me to look narrowly at the precise events. History is unlikely to repeat itself in the exact detail. The exploration of the background to what happened, which covered a considerable number of years, has brought to light factors which, as matters turned out, did not play a part in the actual result but represented potential dangers. Thus as I turn my attention to what I should recommend for the future I require to take a fairly broad approach, so long as it has some connection with the circumstances with which the Inquiry is concerned.

7.10   The fact that Thomas Hamilton was able to retain his firearms and ammunition, along with authorisation to obtain more, raises questions not merely as to the way in which Central Scotland Police discharged their responsibilities but also as to the system by which firearm certificates are granted, renewed and revoked. Is that certification system in need of alteration? If so, in what respects?

7.11   The scale of the massacre and injuries which Thomas Hamilton was able to perpetrate and the speed with which he accomplished his purpose are such as to raise questions of public concern about the firearms which he used and had with him. Should there be a restriction on the availability of such firearms? If so, what form should it take?

The submission that all guns should be banned

7.12   At this point I turn to consider the submission made by Mr C M Campbell QC who represented the families of the deceased children, the injured children, the children who were absent from class and Mrs Harrild and Mrs Blake. I take this submission first since it would have as its logical consequence the ending of the certification system for any category of firearm. It follows therefore that I should deal with it before going further into the questions which I have posed in the last two paragraphs.

7.13   Mr Campbell emphasised at the outset that Thomas Hamilton's actions had thrown into relief the dangers to society of there being many people armed with "weapons designed to kill" and able to accomplish this with rapid and clinical efficiency. The time had come for radical change. There should be "a complete ban on the civilian ownership, possession and use of all types of gun". In support of that submission he put forward the following. First, even with the most thorough safeguards, the potential for another Dunblane would remain. Mistakes would occur. Second, there was always a conflict or tension between limited resources on the one hand and the need for a rigorous system of control on the other. Third, there was a tension between a police force seeking to regulate the shooting community and a police force which was under pressure to provide a good service to the same people. It could not be ensured that public safety would always be the paramount consideration. Fourth, there was always a potential for an individual's circumstances to change in such a way that danger arose where none existed before. The current firearms laws were not designed to cope with the present relatively large number of urban residents who possessed semi-automatic handguns for no reason other than target shooting. Fifth, the current system and the existence of shooting clubs would continue to introduce many thousands of people to guns over the years—people who otherwise would not be familiar with them. Not all of them were of impeccable character. Some were attracted by the guns themselves, their supposed glamour and their boost to the ego. Sixth, there was, he said, an apparently well-established link between access to guns and the rate of gun-crimes and gun-suicides.

7.14 Mr Campbell added that the debate should not be influenced by any supposed inherent right to hold guns. A safety-first philosophy should be adopted and this pointed to radical change. Any decision to continue to permit lawful possession of firearms necessarily implied a willingness to tolerate an increased rate of gun-crime and gun-suicide. It might be thought that the shooting community "do themselves few favours by their apparent reluctance to countenance any material change".

7.15 The BSSC in their final written submission pointed out that no witness at the Inquiry, with the exception of Mr McMurdo, the former Deputy Chief Constable of Central Scotland Police, suggested such a prohibition. They pointed out that the Dunblane Snowdrop Petition stopped short of such a call, in submitting that all firearms held for recreational purposes for use in authorised sporting clubs should be held securely at such clubs with the firing mechanisms removed; and that the private ownership of handguns be made illegal. The BSSC maintained that there was no convincing evidence that if Thomas Hamilton had been denied lawful access to firearms, he would not have found and used some other means to carry out his premeditated plans, or been able in a relatively short space of time to acquire a firearm and ammunition from the "vast stock of illegally-held guns in circulation". They drew attention to the statement in the Green Book (Part II, paras 4 and 6) that such a prohibition would be unprecedented in a democratic country and would have very serious consequences, including adverse economic impact. Mr Mark Scoggins, who appeared for the BSSC during closing submissions, observed that even if a tension existed between a duty to regulate and a pressure to provide a service it was not in any way unique to target shooting. He instanced the position of other regulators such as the Health and Safety Executive. The general function of the police was to provide a service to the community. Even if there was a potential conflict or tension, the solution was to combine firmness with fairness. It was not correct to depict firearms laws as out of joint with the scale of firearm-ownership in modern times. Evidence had been given as to the large number of guns in private ownership before the first legislation in 1920. The assertion that the shooting community had done itself few favours overlooked the fact that their position was that "at the centre is the individual not guns". In that respect they had made a number of proposals. Sound reasons had been given for not adopting various means of control over guns which had been suggested. Mr C N McEachran QC who appeared for the Scottish Target Shooting Federation drew my attention to submissions which had challenged the assertion that there was a link between the availability of guns and the rate of gun-crime.

7.16 The submission made by Mr Campbell is of such width that it would embrace not merely handguns, with which the Inquiry was directly concerned, but also rifles, shot guns and air weapons; and would admit of no exceptions. It would prevent the use of guns for occupational purposes such as shot guns used for shooting game and vermin; rifles for deer stocking and pest control; and handguns for humane disposal of seriously injured animals, slaughtering of animals and signalling the start of races at athletic meetings. No doubt it would be possible to devise a system of exceptions which could be grafted on to a wholesale prohibition.

However, the more fundamental point is that the range of uses for these types of guns is very different. Thus the considerations relating to the possession and use of shot guns are concerned with very different areas of activity from those relating to handguns. I am not persuaded that it is justifiable to approach all these types in essentially the same manner. That is quite apart from the fact that I do not consider that the availability of shot guns is a matter which has a tenable connection with the circumstances with which this Inquiry is concerned.

7.17   For these reasons I do not recommend that such a wholesale prohibition should be considered. However, that is not to say that I will not have to look at the case for restricting the availability of certain firearms with which the Inquiry is concerned. In doing so I will have to take account of arguments which I have summarised above, as well as many more besides.

The order of discussion

7.18   It follows from the view which I have expressed in the last paragraph that I do not recommend the ending of the certification system.

7.19   In Chapter 8 I will consider the scope for improvement in that system in the first place before returning in Chapter 9 to questions relating to the availability of firearms and ammunition. I say that for the following reasons. Firstly, if there is any lesson which is to be learned from the circumstances with which this Inquiry is concerned it is on any view a lesson relating to the certification system. Secondly, if the correct approach is to tackle the individual rather than the guns, as the BSSC and others submitted, it is only right and fair I should consider first what could be achieved by an improved certification system. If that would be enough, there is no need to look further.

Chapter 8   The Certification System Relating to Section 1 Firearms

Introduction

8.1   In this chapter I will consider a number of aspects of the certification system relating to firearms which fall within section 1 of the Firearms Act 1968 as amended. Except where it is incidental to the discussion I will not be concerned with certification relating to shot guns in accordance with section 2 of the Act. The discussion will deal with:

- the police (paras 8.2-8.23)
- the statutory basis for the granting or refusal of firearm applications and the revocation of firearm certificates (paras 8.24-8.26)
- good reason (paras 8.27-8.55)
- suitability (paras 8.56-8.92)
- prohibited persons (paras 8.93-8.95)
- security (paras 8.96-8.97)
- renewal (paras 8.98-8.102)
- revocation (paras 8.103-8.106)
- decisions and appeals (paras 8.107-8.119)
- concluding observations (para 8.120)

The Police

As the licensing authority   8.2   In March 1992 the Home Office published a consultation paper with proposals for a single national licensing authority for firearms in Great Britain— a firearms control board. This would have been run by civilians and taken over from the police the responsibility for certificates, registration and other licensing work. The Home Office paper together with the conclusions of a feasibility study identified possible advantages, including an improvement in consistency and the release of police officers for policing work. In their Third Annual Report (in 1992) the Firearms Consultative Committee saw the control board as an important first step towards decriminalising the sporting shooter. They pointed out that shooters had long resented the fact that the sport had been governed by an Act the purpose of which was to prevent crime. However, some had commented that the strengths of the current system should not be overlooked. "Although, for instance, the police may lack technical expertise, a reliable and professional assessment of an individual's suitability to possess firearms is more important from the point of view of public safety than detailed technical knowledge. In particular it was felt by some respondents that a centralised firearms board would lose the local knowledge and intelligence available to the police" (3.5). The committee noted on the other hand that it was proposed that the police would retain all their existing powers of enforcement. The committee recommended that the Home Secretary should press ahead with work to establish the board (3.10).

8.3   After examining responses and undertaking a further feasibility study the Government announced in July 1994 that it would not proceed with the proposal. The second feasibility study concluded that it might improve the quality of service to shooters and bring greater consistency to decision-making. But it was clear that the amount and cost of work involved in setting up and running was substantially higher than the levels envisaged in 1992. The running costs would be higher than those of the existing system. In addition there was a need for continuing police involvement in firearms licensing and liaison with the licensing authority. There was a risk of duplication of effort.

8.4   The suggestion of a firearms control board was renewed at the Inquiry. The BSSC maintained that there was a case for taking the administration of licensing procedure, if not also decision-making, away from the police, leaving them to be involved in the supply and interpretation of intelligence about applicants and holders. The Shooters' Rights Association maintained that the Home Office had misrepresented the costs. The Association's proposals were intended to simplify and streamline the licensing system so that it could be used as an intelligence-gathering system. The police would carry out the inspection process in rural areas; and the work would be put out to tender in urban areas.

8.5   I am not in favour of the removal from the police of any of the functions concerned with the operation of the present system. This is not for any reason concerned with cost but on the view that there should be an integration of the carrying out of enquiries and the taking of decisions within a single organisation; that the police are in the best position to collect and assess information bearing on the suitability of applicants or holders, which is at the heart of the certification system; and that there is inevitably a close link between the certification system and questions of enforcement.

8.6   This is not to say that I do not consider there is room for improvement in achieving a standard of expertise and consistency which is worthy of the system.

8.7   During the course of the Inquiry attention was drawn to a number of changes which had been urged upon, and to some extent taken up by, police forces. Examples were the progress in civilianisation, the introduction of postal renewals and moves to end the requirement for counter-signatories. In the report made by Her Majesty's Inspectorate of Constabulary for England and Wales on the Administration of Firearms Licensing in 1993 it was said that it was essential that shooters receive a quality service and value for money. It is no doubt appropriate that efficiency should be an aim but it should not obtain the upper hand over the primary purpose of the system which is the protection and safety of the public. Chief Constable Roy Cameron, who is chairman of the Association of Chief Police Officers in Scotland (ACOPS) said in evidence that while there was a desire to make the system as administratively effective as possible, their concern was that this had to be matched with regulatory effectiveness.

Enquiries   8.8   When examining the organisation and operation of the system used by Central Scotland Police for the carrying out and use of enquiries I expressed a number of criticisms. A number of general lessons can, in my view, be drawn from the circumstances disclosed in the Inquiry.

8.9   It is important for the enquiry officer to be supplied in advance with full information about any known change of circumstances and any reason for exercising particular caution. The need for ensuring that police intelligence is communicated and taken into account is obvious.

8.10 The enquiry officer should not be required merely to give yes or no answers to questions but to provide information on a number of matters which should be investigated as a matter of routine, so as to ensure that not only he or she investigates them but also that his superior officers are made fully aware of what was found. It is, of course, important that attention to routine should not exclude anything else. As I observed in para 6.74 the enquiry officer should be explicitly reminded to be alert to any piece of information, even an impression, which could be relevant to the question of whether an applicant or holder was a suitable person. I am not convinced that there are sound reasons why visits should not be made without prior arrangement, so that any weakness in the applicant's attitude to security can be fully exposed.

8.11 A number of the submissions which were made advocated the use of checklists. Subject to the comment which I have made in the last paragraph, I endorse their use. I note that in their Fifth Annual Report (in 1994) the Firearms Consultative Committee recommended that the police and the Home Office should work with the BSSC to produce a single non-statutory form. This has the support of Her Majesty's Inspectorate of Constabulary for Scotland, according to the terms of the draft report on the Administration of the Firearms Licensing System in 1995.

8.12 Allied to this is the matter of training and guidance. I do not share the suspicion of civilian officers which some have expressed by saying that they might be "soft" on shooters. Chief Constable Cameron observed that in his experience the use of civilians had brought a level of experience and expertise to the process which had not been there before. However, this had to be balanced against a need for adequate police line management and, in regard to the more complex issues, supervision and decision-making. He accepted that police officers who lacked technical knowledge of firearms were at a disadvantage and that this had to be compensated for by sufficient training.

8.13 As long as police officers are used in order to deal with enquiries it is important that they should be given as much training and guidance as is practicable. There is a case for using only members of a group of police officers who have been specifically prepared for the task of carrying out enquiries. However, this may be beyond what is possible in certain police force areas. I have noted with interest the fact that one police force in Scotland uses a pocket guide for beat officers who are used for this purpose. It is important that it should be borne in mind that the way in which enquiries are carried out has a significant influence on perceptions as to the professionalism and efficiency of the police force.

Powers 8.14 It was pointed out in a number of the submissions that the police do not have an explicit statutory power to insist on inspection of security arrangements prior to the grant or renewal of a firearm certificate or at any time during the life of the certificate. They also do not have an explicit power to insist on inspection of the firearms held. I am not persuaded that it is appropriate to go as far as to grant police a statutory power of entry and inspection in connection with the initial grant or subsequent renewal. No doubt the police require to be satisfied in regard to the security arrangements. If the police cannot obtain satisfactory information about the security arrangements, or for that matter the firearms held, the remedy should be the refusal of the application. If necessary, legislative provision for this can be made. As regards the position during the currency of the certificate I do not consider that there are sufficient grounds to arm the police with a general right to insist on entry and inspection regardless of whether there is any apprehension of danger to the public.

8.15   The Association of Chief Police Officers for England and Wales (ACPO) submitted that police officers should be given the power to enter premises and seize firearms without warrant on refusal, revocation or suspension of a firearm certificate. The Association of Chief Police Officers in Scotland (ACOPS) submitted that police officers should be given a power to seize certificates, firearms and ammunition prior to any revocation. It may be noted that where a firearm certificate is revoked under section 30(1)(a) or (2) of the 1968 Act the chief officer of police may require the certificate holder by notice in writing to surrender the certificate and any firearms and ammunition which are in his possession by virtue of it. Failure to comply is an offence (section 12(1) and (2) of the Firearms (Amendment) Act 1988). This would justify an application for a warrant to search premises and seize firearms and ammunition under section 46 of the 1968 Act which applies where there is reasonable grounds for suspecting that a relevant offence has been, is being or is about to be committed. However, leaving that particular case to one side, there do not appear to me to be explicit powers enabling police officers to seize certificates, firearms and ammunition where there is no question of an offence but where there is reasonable ground for suspecting that there is a substantial risk to the safety of the public. At present the police have to rely on the co-operation of the holder. I consider that provision should be made for such a power to be granted by a justice of the peace or, in Scotland, the sheriff, on the same lines as section 46. The powers under section 46 should also be extended to any civilian licensing and enquiry officer who is authorised in writing by the Chief Constable for that purpose.

8.16   I have also noted that while such civilian officers now have the right to possess firearms in the course of their duty without the need to hold a firearm certificate covering them, they do not have the same powers as police officers to inspect dealers' registers and premises and approved clubs. I agree with the view that this is an area which needs to be dealt with in the process of making civilianisation effective.

Database   8.17   As regards firearms, ACOPS take the view that a central firearms register would bring clear benefits in crime detection and prevention. They submitted that it should be the subject of a feasibility study. At present, it was said, there is no way of charting the route of firearms. They do not have unique serial numbers. Those which are acquired by dealers "disappear", in respect that dealers are not required to report such transactions but merely to log them. The SCRO maintain a database of firearms which have been lost or stolen but the police have no way of knowing how many firearms in total are in circulation.

8.18   It is clear that at present there are considerable practical difficulties in creating a central firearms register, of which the absence of unique serial numbers for firearms and their components is a primary one. In his evidence Mr D J Penn, who is the chairman of the technical and research committee of the BSSC, explained that in some instances firearms bore no serial number and in many other cases what appeared on them were merely batch numbers. He also questioned whether a significant contribution to public safety could be achieved through the creation of a central firearms register.

8.19   It is clear that the proposal of a central firearms register raises considerable questions as to its practicability and value which extend far beyond the scope of the present Inquiry. I do not consider that I am in a position to make any form of recommendation as to whether this should be pursued.

8.20   As regards firearm certificates, I understand that most police forces hold information on computer as to the individuals who hold them and the particular firearms to which each certificate relates. It is unclear whether the information which is held also includes particulars as to the individuals whose applications have been refused or whose certificates have been revoked. I note in passing that advances in the use of technology have not been as great as they should have been because a number of police forces held back during the period when a diversion was created by the proposal for a firearms control board.

8.21   In his evidence Chief Constable Cameron explained that there was a strategy in Scotland for police forces to work towards interaction. The computer systems used by the police forces in Scotland were not yet compatible. At present there was no standard approach as to the information which should be held. It was the policy of ACOPS to advance a strategy of uniformity and commonality.

8.22   Chief Constable Cameron added that the SCRO, like its equivalent in England, provided a flagging of individuals who held firearm and shot gun certificates or whose applications had been refused or certificates revoked. It also enabled an individual to be flagged in order to show to an enquirer that another force was interested in him and might hold information about him. When road traffic convictions were entered in the SCRO, as was intended, the same would apply. The PNC presently showed such convictions but did not necessarily indicate anything about the firearm certificate or firearm application.

8.23   I note with approval the steps which are being taken in order to enable each police force to hold information on computer as to the individuals who hold firearm certificates, along with information as to the firearms held, and those individuals whose firearm applications have been refused or certificates revoked; and the moves which are being made to enable such information to be standardised and readily exchangeable between police forces.

The statutory basis for the granting or refusal of firearm applications and the revocation of firearm certificates

8.24   There are, in brief, four main considerations which feature in the language of sections 27(1) and 30(1) of the 1968 Act:

  (i) "good reason" for the possession, or for the purchase or acquisition, of the relevant firearm or ammunition;

  (ii) "danger to the public safety or to the peace";

  (iii) prohibition by the 1968 Act from possessing a section 1 firearm; and

  (iv) being of intemperate habits or unsound mind, or for any reason unfitted to be entrusted with such a firearm.

8.25   I do not consider that it is necessary for me to recommend any alteration in or addition to these concepts which have formed part of firearms legislation for many years. However, I am in no doubt that the way in which they are used and interpreted is in need of examination and revision.

8.26   I will now consider each of these concepts—in so far as relevant to the Inquiry.

Good Reason

Scope   8.27   A number of the submissions to the Inquiry proposed that there should be a definition of what classes of activity can constitute "good reason". I do not consider that it is wise for me to recommend the laying down of any rigid definition as to what can constitute good reason. New or unforeseen situations may arise and should be dealt with on their merits, in the light of the current Guidance to the Police and, where appropriate, after the advice of the Firearms Consultative Committee has been obtained. It is right that room for discretion should be left and that this discretion should be exercised by the chief officer of police. He would require to consider not simply whether the applicant has put forward a reason (which is not the same thing as a need) but also, more importantly, whether it is a "good" reason.

8.28   Other submissions have maintained that "good reason" should be defined in such a way as to exclude the possession, purchase or acquisition of certain firearms, such as the second handgun of the same calibre, or firearms intended for use in certain shooting disciplines. As regards such exclusions it seems to me that they would more appropriately be considered as proposals for restricting the availability of certain firearms, and accordingly I postpone a discussion of them to Chapter 9.

The relevance of the use of firearms and ammunition; and the use of authorisation to purchase or acquire them   8.29   Here I refer to my discussion in Chapter 6. Since "good reason" looks to the future it is not appropriate that it should depend exclusively on whether an applicant has made adequate use of what he already possesses or whether he has purchased or acquired what he was authorised to do. On the other hand "good reason" implies intention, by which I mean genuine intention (para 6.36). It is appropriate that lack of use should be taken as indicating *prima facie* the lack of such an intention; and giving cause for enquiry as to whether the applicant does in fact have good reason to possess or, as the case may be, to purchase or acquire.

8.30   This point may not require legislation. However, it does require that the existing Guidance to the Police is altered in order to make it clear that "good reason" implies intention; and that lack of past use *prima facie* indicates the lack of it. Para 6.8(e) of the Guidance should be amended accordingly.

Revocation   8.31   In the course of Chapter 6 I adverted to the point that section 30 makes no provision for the revocation of a firearm certificate due to the loss of a "good reason". This is an anomaly of long standing which should be corrected, so that those who no longer have a "good reason" for possession or, as the case may be, purchase or acquisition should be deprived of the authority for it.

8.32   It should, of course be borne in mind that since at the outset "good reason" requires to be shown in respect of each of the firearms to which the application related (see the Guidance to the Police at para 6.8(i)). It follows that provision should be made for partial revocation where that is appropriate.

8.33   Since questions may arise as to whether the holder still has a "good reason" in respect of the amount of ammunition to which the certificate relates, provision should also be made for combining revocation with the substitution of different quantities.

Target shooting   8.34   While making these recommendations in regard to revocation I am conscious that, within the field of target shooting, such a reform will not be fully effective unless there are adequate measures for ascertaining that the holder has ceased to have a good reason and this information is communicated to the police so that they can act upon it.

8.35   Under the current Guidance the police are advised that firearm certificates should not be granted for target shooting unless the applicant is a member of a shooting club. In practice this means that at least in respect of the initial grant of a certificate the applicant requires to be a full member of a club approved by the Secretary of State for the purposes of section 15 of the Firearms (Amendment) Act 1988. The basic purpose of such clubs is to enable members to carry on target shooting without the necessity of holding a firearm certificate. For that purpose such clubs require to meet certain criteria, including formal requirements as to their management structure and constitution.

8.36   At present there are 2,118 rifle and pistol clubs throughout Great Britain which have been approved by the Secretary of State. 247 of them are in Scotland. There are four categories of approval—for full and small-bore rifle and for full and small-bore pistols (including revolvers). Full-bore and small-bore are otherwise known as centrefire and rimfire. 1049 clubs have approval to offer centrefire pistol as a discipline and 1395 to offer rimfire pistol. The approval of a club lasts for 6 years. Approved clubs are subject to inspection by the police under section 15(5) of the 1988 Act. The inspection of the club in connection with renewal provides the police with an opportunity to inform the Home Office or The Scottish Office about how a club is run and whether they support the application. The criteria for approval are set out in a leaflet which was recently revised as from the beginning of 1996. An approved club must generally have at least 10 members. Such clubs vary greatly in size and there are different estimates of the total membership. It should, of course, be understood that the fact that a club is approved does not mean that it is better or safer than one which is not, but that it has been recognised as one having the appropriate arrangements for management and supervision.

8.37   A member of such a club may possess (but not purchase or acquire) a rifle or pistol without a certificate while engaged as a member of that club in, or in connection with, target practice. The firearms and ammunition used by members may be provided by the club under a firearm certificate issued to an office bearer without charge or by a club member who holds a firearm certificate in respect of them. A member may also bring his own firearm and ammunition for which he holds a certificate. The current criteria require that all new members should be sponsored by at least one existing club member; and, unless this is waived by the club in respect of persons in certain categories, he or she requires to go through a period of probation lasting for at least 3 months during which he or she must be given a course in the safe handling and use of firearms on a one-to-one basis by someone who is either a full member of the club or who is a coach with a qualification recognised by the Great Britain Target Shooting Federation and governing bodies. After satisfactory conclusion of the course he or she requires to be supervised at all times when in possession of firearms or ammunition either by the range officer or a full member of the club or someone who is a coach with the qualification already referred to.

8.38   It may be noted that a person who is a member of an approved club does not *require* to apply for a firearm certificate but may continue to use the club's facilities indefinitely in reliance on section 15. Mr Scoggins who appeared for the BSSC informed me that at least several tens of thousands of club shooters fall into that category. Approved clubs are permitted to hold a limited number of guest days in the year. Guest members must be either members of a recognised outside organisation or individuals who are known personally to at least one full member of the club. They require to be supervised on a one-to-one basis at all times when handling firearms and ammunition, by either a full club member or a qualified coach. It appears that such guests are treated as members of the club *pro tempore* in order to ensure that they are covered by section 15 of the 1988 Act.

8.39   At the same time it has to be borne in mind that some rifle and pistol clubs, the exact number of which is not known, operate without the need for approval under section 15. In such clubs the participants should all have their own firearm certificates and are expected individually to abide by their terms and conditions. Such clubs are in themselves not subject to legislation, and are not subject to any form of statutory inspection. Mr D J Penn pointed out that some of these "clubs" amount to no more than a means by which a group of people who share an interest in a certain type of firearm or competition get together on an informal basis on certain occasions during the year.

8.40   If the police are to have the opportunity to consider the revocation of a firearm certificate in whole or in part in respect of lack of use it is essential, in the first place, that there should be some means by which the use of firearms and ammunition can be ascertained; and in the second place, that the police are made aware of circumstances indicating lack of use.

8.41   As regards the first of these objects, it is, in my view, necessary to have a system by which the particular "good reason" put forward by the applicant or holder can be compared with a record of use.

8.42   Most shooters are members of at least one approved club. On the evidence it appears that an approved club would have little difficulty in keeping a record of the attendance of its members including those who were holders of a firearm certificate, together with details as to the particular firearms which were used and the competitions in which they participated. Some clubs already keep registers for this purpose. An alternative might be for such information to be recorded by a club official on an appropriate part of a redesigned firearm certificate. However, I am inclined to think that this would be somewhat impractical, especially in the case of those who hold a large number of firearms on the same certificate; and I do not consider that overall there is a case for having separate certificates in respect of each firearm. Accordingly I have in mind that each approved club should maintain a register of this information. The register would be open to inspection by the police if after making enquiries of the holder they wished to check the use which he had been making of one or more of his firearms. In the case of a shooter who was a member of more than one club it might, of course, be necessary for more than one register to be consulted.

8.43   Such a system would require to provide an adequate indication of the certificate holder's activity. For this purpose it has been suggested that all clubs would require to be approved. However, one difficulty about such a proposal is that in the case of the informal type of arrangement which was described by Mr Penn it may not be easy to determine whether there is a true club, let alone one which could conceivably meet the criteria for approval. Such a proposal seems to me to be impractical as well as excessive and accordingly I do not recommend it.

8.44   It seems to me that the matter may be tackled in a different way by requiring that every certificate holder should be a member of at least one approved club. The approved club or clubs should be specified in the firearm application and on the firearm certificate and in each case by reference to the individual firearms. This would provide the normal source of information for the police if they seek to check up on the use of individual firearms. I should add that the enquiry officer should be expected to ascertain from the applicant and to record all other clubs or more informal arrangements in connection with which the applicant intended to use his individual firearms.

8.45   There may be circumstances which require to be differentiated. During the currency of his certificate the holder may move to a different district and join a new approved club in place of the old. There will be nothing to prevent him doing so and, if necessary, the police can consult the register of the new club when dealing with renewal of his certificate. There may be shooters whose use of particular firearms takes place mainly in non-approved clubs. Such shooters should be alert to the need to ensure that, if the police want to make an enquiry as to the use of these firearms, evidence as to such use should is readily obtainable.

8.46   I should add that I have not considered it necessary to recommend a separate recording of information as to the use of ammunition, on the view that this would adequately be indicated by inference from the other information which is to be recorded. However, the present situation in regard to the recording of the purchase of ammunition is somewhat unsatisfactory. The firearm certificate requires to show only commercial purchases and purchases from clubs which are taken away from the range where they were purchased. Shooters are not at present required to keep a record of their reloading of ammunition or of the purchase of materials for this purpose. Stirling Rifle and Pistol Club submitted that home-loaders should keep a ledger of all ammunition produced and provided a possible format for such a ledger in Appendix VI to their submission. I do not consider that such a ledger should be mandatory. However, it would be in the best interests of shooters who reload to maintain such a record.

8.47   I have considered whether the law should go further and require that the continued holding of a firearm certificate or the continued holding of membership of an approved club should depend on the holder maintaining a minimum number of attendances at club meetings or competitions. I am aware that some clubs have rules as to attendance but this is not required by the current criteria for approval.

8.48   There are a number of practical difficulties about such a proposal. If this was to be a condition of a firearm certificate it is not easy to see how it would be applied where the holder was a member of more than one approved club. In the event whether this is considered as a condition of the certificate or as a condition of membership I am very doubtful whether it would be possible to arrive at a number of attendances which was appropriate for clubs at large. During the evidence it was pointed out that it might be difficult for some clubs to meet such a requirement where they had no ranges of their own and their range bookings were subject to cancellation. Further, what should constitute attendance? In their final submission to the Inquiry the Scottish Target Shooting Federation stated (at page 6) that they were conscious that there might be persons who became members of clubs in order to maintain the validity of their certificate and to hold firearms for reasons other than competition. So how is adequate attendance to be determined? Is it to depend on whether the holder takes part in a number of competitions or merely on whether he fires a certain number of shots? It may be that this subject would require further study by the Firearms Consultative Committee but for my part I do not consider that I can identify a measure which would be both practicable and effective.

8.49   As regards the second of the objects which I mentioned in paragraph 8.40 it is clearly necessary that there should be adequate communication between approved clubs and the police.

8.50   I consider that approved clubs should be put under a duty of informing the police when the membership of the club by a firearm certificate holder comes to an end for whatever reason; and to do so within a given period of that termination, so that the police may be able to determine promptly whether there is any occasion for revocation.

8.51   While I have decided, for the reasons given above, not to make any recommendation as to minimum attendance I consider that there is a case for an approved club being put under a duty to notify the police if for a substantial period the holder has not, as far as the club is concerned, attended a meeting of the club. I have in mind a period of one year. While the club would be under a duty to report this automatically, it would obviously be open to it to draw the attention of the police to any matter, such as temporary illness, which could account for a whole or substantial part of the absence. It would then be for the police to decide whether the matter required to be pursued.

8.52   I agree with the view expressed by the BSSC that there is room for improvement in the flow of information between clubs and the police. This is a subject to which I will require to return later in this chapter. In the meantime I accept that the maintaining of liaison would be most useful not only in monitoring the operation of the clubs but also in dealing with any concern which is expressed about the intentions or attitude of individual shooters. I agree with their suggestion that clubs should appoint liaison officers for this purpose. During the course of the Inquiry I encountered the suggestion that some police officers had been slow to act on information provided to them by club officials. It is important that there should be confidence on each side of the relationship.

8.53   Before leaving the subject of the criteria for approved clubs I should add that at a late stage of the Inquiry a question was raised as to the power which the Home Office has to lay down criteria for the approval of rifle and pistol clubs as it has done for many years. Mr Scoggins informed me that the view of the Home Office is that the current source of the power is sub-section (2) of section 15. I do not propose to make any comment on this point except to say that it would be preferable if explicit statutory provision were made for this purpose.

Time limits   8.54   It was submitted on behalf of ACPO, on the ground that good reason to possess a firearm fell to be strictly interpreted, that it was reasonable to expect that a certificate holder would purchase a firearm within 6 months of obtaining authority to do so; and would not require the variation of a certificate within 12 months of a grant. They accordingly submitted that an open authority to purchase a firearm should be valid for 6 months only and that no variations on a certificate could be made within the first 12 months.

8.55   I do not consider that either of these proposals flows from an interpretation of the legislation. The first amounts to a reversal of the current Guidance to the Police (at 6.21 and 6.36) and would require legislation. It is not inconsistent with a genuine intention that some shooters find that it is some years before they can make a suitable purchase or acquisition. As regards the suggestion that a variation could not be sought within the first year, it appears that what underlies the submission is that certificate holders are currently allowed to change their firearms on a one-to-one basis as often as they like and at no cost to themselves. If this is the problem then it could be tackled by introducing charges.

Suitability

Sections 27(1) and 30(1) 8.56   I use the term "suitability" as a convenient expression to cover the provision in section 27(1) that a firearm certificate is to be granted by the chief officer of police if he is satisfied that the applicant "can be permitted to have it (the relevant firearm or ammunition) in his possession without danger to the public safety or to the peace" (in so far as this turns on the personal suitability of the applicant); and the provision that the certificate is not to be granted to a person whom the chief officer of police "has reason to believe .... to be of intemperate habits or unsound mind, or to be for any reason unfitted to be entrusted with such a firearm". Section 30(1) enables the chief officer to revoke if he is "satisfied that the holder ... is of intemperate habits or unsound mind, or is otherwise unfitted to be entrusted with such a firearm".

8.57   This language is substantially the same as that contained in the Firearms Act 1920, which was the first legislation for regulating the possession of firearms. Although the language is of long-standing it contains a number of difficulties which were discussed at the Inquiry. These may be summarised as follows.

8.58   The intention behind the proviso to section 27(1) seems to have been to prohibit the granting of a certificate in certain definite situations; whereas under the leading provision of that sub-section the chief officer of police was to have some discretion in deciding whether the applicant could be permitted to have the relevant firearm or ammunition in his possession. If he was so satisfied he was bound to grant the certificate.

8.59   However, the matter is not as simple as that. It is not difficult to understand why "unsound mind" should appear in the proviso. Even if it is wider than insanity and encompasses any degree of mental instability, it will be normal for it to be presumed that a person is of sound mind until the contrary appears. It is also a matter which can be reasonably closely defined. The same perhaps may be said of "intemperate habits" which appears to embrace not merely lack of temperance in regard to alcohol or drugs but also immoderate conduct whatever be the cause (*see P J Clarke and J W Ellis, The Law relating to Firearms* (1981) at pages 96-97). Thus far the terms of the proviso appear to deal with cases which are irrespective of whether there is danger to the public safety or to the peace in the applicant being permitted to have possession of the firearm or ammunition in question. However, there is already an overlap between cases which fall foul of the proviso and those which do not meet the leading provision. When one comes to the expression "unfitted to be entrusted with such a firearm" it is clear that there is a substantial overlap, and it is in regard to a matter which appears to be primarily a question of judgment. It suggests that the arrangement of concepts with which the sub-section deals is not of the happiest.

8.60   The meaning of "unfitted ...." has been little discussed in decisions and text books. It is clearly a neglected corner in firearms legislation. When one looks at the Guidance to the Police one finds that after para 6.6 which recites the terms of the proviso the text concentrates on the question of danger to public safety and to the peace (6.9). This seems to overlook the point that the phrase "unfitted ...." is of wide import.

8.61   When one turns to section 30(1) one finds not merely that there is no provision for revocation where the good reason has ceased but also that the power to revoke is limited to a situation in which the proviso in section 27(1) would have applied; with the two additional peculiarities, that section 30(1) uses "is satisfied that" rather than the somewhat weaker expression "has reason to believe"; and that the word "otherwise" now appears in front of the word "unfitted". The mismatching between sections 30(1) and section 27(1) is highlighted by the fact that in the case of shot guns the same test of danger is used both in regard to the granting of the application (section 28(1)) and in regard to the question of revocation (section 30(2)).

8.62   I am bound to say that I consider that it is high time that the language of sections 27 and 30 is revised in order to achieve a logical and consistent arrangement.

8.63   However, there is at this point a consideration which is of greater moment in regard to the protection and safety of the public which lies at the heart of the legislation. The circumstances of the present case seem to me to demonstrate the need for a positive requirement that the applicant should be a person who is fit to be entrusted with the relevant firearm and ammunition, so that where the information on this is not seen as persuasive the certificate should be withheld. This entails some reorientation of section 27(1) with the result that the matters as to which the chief officer of police is to be positively satisfied would include the fitness of the applicant.

8.64   At the same time I am conscious that, without prejudice to what a court may decide are the limits of "fitness", it would be desirable if some guidance could be given to the police and to applicants. I am aware that a number of police forces provide leaflets for the guidance of shooters but, so far as I have been able to discover, there is no national guidance on the subject. The expression "unfitted", in the context in which it is used, seems to me to be capable of embracing deficiencies not merely in physical or mental ability but also in a responsible attitude to such matters as compliance with the legislation, the safe keeping and handling of firearms and elementary co-operation with the licensing authority.

8.65   As regards section 30(1) I consider that it should be brought into full correspondence with section 27(1) with the result that a certificate may be revoked also when the chief officer of police is satisfied that the holder cannot be permitted to possess the firearm or ammunition without danger to the public safety or to the peace.

8.66   I do not think it is necessary for me to recommend that a statutory definition should be given to any of the phrases with which I have been concerned.

Probationary membership of an approved club

8.67   I have already mentioned that the criteria for such a club provides for the probationary member being given a course in the safe handling and use of firearms; and that after its satisfactory completion he or she is to be supervised under certain conditions. Stirling Rifle and Pistol Club submitted that such a course should be organised from a national syllabus, but I do not consider that this is an area which calls for any recommendation on my part.

8.68   The recent reduction in the mandatory probationary period from 6 months to 3 months has attracted some criticism and I understand that a large number of clubs continue to require a period of 6 months as they are fully entitled to do. The

Scottish Target Shooting Federation submitted that the restoration of the original requirement would not add a material safeguard since in practice clubs will extend the period when they consider that more examination of a potential member is required. I consider that it should be left to each club to decide whether the normal period should be 6 months; and, if it is to be 3 months, whether in a particular case it should be extended.

8.69   Under the criteria for approved clubs the members must be "of good character". Clubs naturally wish to ensure that they do not admit as a probationary member someone who is not of that character, not only because of the criteria but also out of concern for their own reputation. Plainly there are difficulties facing clubs who wish to vet their probationary members. The police do not become officially aware of the identity of the new member until full membership is obtained and the firearm application is presented. It has been suggested that a prospective member should be required to obtain a copy of any records held about him or her by the police on computer—which they are entitled to do under the Data Protection Act 1984 at a cost of £10. This proposal was rejected by the Home Office Working Group on the Criteria for the Approval of Rifle and Pistol Clubs which reported in 1995. They considered that it would be wrong to require individuals to do this as a prerequisite of joining a club. Whilst appreciating the difficulties faced by clubs in ensuring that members were of "good character", the Working Group were against routine police involvement and considered that vetting of members was a responsibility for the clubs by whatever method they saw fit. The Working Group went on to state that it was not good practice for clubs to use the firearm or shot gun certificate procedure to vet members. However, they recommended a requirement upon clubs to ask a prospective member or guest to declare that he or she was not a prohibited person under the 1968 Act (paras 15-17). This requirement is now part of the criteria. Note 2 on the criteria states also: "Clubs should make their own arrangements for assessing whether members or prospective members are of good character. Police firearms licensing departments should not be asked to disclose whether someone has a criminal record or not".

8.70   In the Inquiry it was also submitted that a person who wished to use a firearm as a member or probationary member but who did not produce a firearm certificate should be requested to provide a certificate issued by the police confirming that he or she was not a prohibited person. The BSSC maintained that this would be a simple document to issue and would not require to list any particular convictions. It could take the form of a simple confirmation that there was nothing in the police records to disqualify the would-be member.

8.71   I do not see any good reason to differ from the Working Group in regard to the proposal that a prospective member should be required to obtain a copy of any records held about him or her. I am not persuaded that it would be appropriate to set up a system for the granting of certificates as the BSSC have proposed. However, I consider that each approved club should be required to inform the police of the receipt of an application for membership. This would enable the police to take prompt action where the applicant was found to be a prohibited person or where his criminal record was such as to give cause for concern. Clubs should also be required to inform the police of the outcome of each application. Each of these duties should fall to be performed within a given period of the event to which it relates.

8.72   I have also considered whether it is necessary to go further and to require that clubs should be under a duty to inform the police as to the reasons for any refusal of membership. As the Green Book points out there is nothing to prevent clubs from doing this at present, but there could be a disadvantage in making it a requirement. It might lead the club in marginal cases to decide that the less embarrassing course was not to refuse the application. The same considerations could apply in cases of expulsion (Part II, paras 119-122). It has also been claimed that clubs should enjoy immunity from liability for any statements of this kind. I consider that on balance it is better to let matters take their course on the present informal basis.

8.73   It would be of assistance if each applicant were required to state whether he or she had submitted any prior application for a firearm or shot gun certificate which had been refused; and whether he or she had previously held such a certificate which had been revoked; and in either event to supply details.

Counter-signatories   8.74   Rule 5 of the Firearms (Scotland) Rules, and the corresponding rule in England and Wales, introduced the requirement that a firearm application should be countersigned. This followed an amendment of section 26 of the 1968 Act by section 10 of the 1988 Act. It is required that the counter-signatory should not be a member of the applicant's family and must—(a) be resident in Great Britain; (b) have known the applicant personally for 2 years, and (c) be a Member of Parliament, justice of the peace, minister of religion, lawyer, established civil servant, bank officer "or person of similar standing". The counter-signatory is required to verify certain information given by the applicant on the application form and to declare that "he knows of no reason why the applicant should not be permitted to possess a firearm". Counter-signatories are asked to bear in mind the character, conduct and mental condition of the applicant "in so far as they are relevant to these matters".

8.75   The purpose of counter-signature is evidently to assist the police in their consideration of the application. However, the system has attracted considerable criticism.

8.76   Difficulty has been experienced with the application of the words "or person of similar standing". The Guidance to the Police states that this category might have to be extended fairly widely where an applicant had few contacts in the community (6.5); and the Firearms Consultative Committee advocated flexibility in their First Annual Report (in 1990)(4.8). However, this very flexibility tends to devalue the worth of the counter-signatory's declaration.

8.77   The declaration itself is essentially negative. In one sense the less that a counter-signatory knows about the applicant the less likely would he be to have any difficulty in providing his support to the application.

8.78   A further particular difficulty is encountered by medical practitioners. While the form asks the same of them as for any other counter-signatory they have two concerns, firstly, that their signature might be taken as implying that they were endorsing the applicant as medically fit to be entrusted with a firearm; and, secondly, that any reservation on their part about signing the certificate might impair their relationship with their patient. The interim firearms guidance note issued by the BMA, revised in April 1996, states: "Where the applicant is a patient, doctors are advised not to support firearm applications unless they believe that they have sufficient knowledge about an individual to justify a judgment that the individual could safely possess and control such a firearm. The occasions when this is so will be rare". At the annual meeting of BMA representatives on 27 June

1996 it was resolved, although by a small majority, "that doctors should not endorse gun licence applications".

8.79   The abolition of the requirement for counter-signature was called for in a number of reports, starting with the Multi-Force Firearm Scrutiny by Devon and Cornwall Constabulary in 1991 (8.2). I note that in the latest draft of the report of Her Majesty's Inspector of Constabulary for Scotland on the Administration of the Firearms Licensing System in 1995 there is a call for a "review" of the current requirement. An earlier draft had called for its discontinuance.

8.80   One way in which to proceed would be to require the counter-signatory to state specifically that the applicant was considered to be a fit person to be entrusted with a firearm. I do not support such a proposal. It would impose a burden which few would be prepared to undertake; and would merely serve to detract from the primary responsibilities of the police to reach a view on that question.

8.81   I consider that the current requirement for a counter-signatory should be abolished and should be replaced by a system for the obtaining of references as one source of information for the police. The object of such a system would be to provide the police not with negative but with positive statements about the applicant without imposing on referees the burden of declaring that the applicant was a fit person to the best of their knowledge and belief. I consider that there should be two referees, neither of whom should be a member of the applicant's family. They should both be persons of good character. One of them should be an official of an approved shooting club of which the applicant is a member. The other should be a person who is not a member of any shooting club. The latter should have known the applicant personally for at least 2 years. Each of the referees should be expected to supply a reference to the police in the form of answers to a questionnaire designed to bring out the extent and nature of their knowledge of the applicant, with particular reference to his character, conduct and mental condition. It would be open to the police to reject a referee who did not appear to have adequate knowledge of the applicant. A reference would normally be treated as confidential but might require to be made available to the applicant in the event of an appeal.

8.82   I do not support the submission that such referees should be made responsible for reporting any subsequent material change of circumstances or be subject to prosecution for failing to do so. It would, in my view, impose such a burden as to be counter-productive.

8.83   If a system of referees were introduced it would be for the police to decide in the particular case whether and to what extent a reference should be followed up by further enquiry of the referees.

Medical and psychological information   8.84   It was submitted that a significant improvement in the elimination of the unsuitable applicants could be achieved by the following as a matter of routine:

(i)   a report on the applicant by his general practitioner, with or without the disclosure of his or her medical records; and

(ii)   the carrying out of a psychiatric examination or a psychological test of the applicant.

8.85   I am entirely satisfied that general practitioners cannot reliably assist in the identification of those who pose a risk of violence and those who do not. There is at present no scientific evidence which would allow this to be determined. It is clear that forensic psychiatrists and clinical psychologists doubt their own ability to predict violent behaviour. A generalist such as the applicant's doctor, who lacks specialist expertise, is even less able to reach soundly-based judgment as to his potential for violence. As regards mental illness, it was pointed out by the Royal College of Psychiatrists in their submission that this of itself does not indicate the risk of violence since only a small proportion of those who suffer from such illness commit such offences. Severe mood disturbance or instability or alcohol abuse or a history of violence might suggest that the patient should not be permitted to possess a firearm, but this is based on common sense rather than on scientific grounds. Quite apart from these considerations there are cases, of which Thomas Hamilton is an example, where the general practitioner has no adequate personal knowledge of the individual patient. There may, of course, be cases in which a doctor is under the duty of disclosure in the interests of others. Such cases are covered by paragraph 18 of the Guidance on Confidentiality issued by the General Medical Council which states: "Disclosures may be necessary in the public interest where a failure to disclose information may expose the patient, or others, to risk of death of serious harm. In such circumstances you should disclose information promptly to an appropriate person or authority". For such cases a confidential telephone advice and information service is offered to doctors by the DVLA. In his letter to the Home Affairs Committee dated 24 May 1996, which formed part of the BMA evidence to the Inquiry, the Secretary, Dr E M Armstrong, stated: "Our conclusion, sadly, is that until such time as methods are developed to provide reliable predictions, firearms policy needs to be based on the understanding that, from time to time, unpredictable behaviour will occur".

8.86   As regards carrying out of a special examination or test, essentially the same considerations apply. The carrying out of risk assessments by psychiatrists and clinical psychologists who were trained for this type of work would involve considerable expense, and the use of resources which are in short supply. Such assessments would require to be carried out at least annually. On the basis that firearm certificates have a life of 5 years approximately 35,000 applications require to be dealt with each year. The corresponding figure for shot gun applications is 145,000. Professor Cooke in his evidence said that it would be possible to identify individuals who had a propensity to violence but that this would require 2 days' work interviewing the applicant, seeking to build up rapport and trust and using collateral information. However, there would always be errors, which would tend to be errors on the side of regarding the person as unsuitable rather than the other way round. Extreme violence was very rare and was virtually impossible to predict. Mental illness, as distinct from traits of personality, could come about rapidly and unexpectedly; and accordingly it could not be taken that this would be picked up in an examination. The remarks which Professor Cooke made about a psychological examination applied also to psychometric testing. In any event there is a danger that applicants would discover what were the "right" answers.

8.87   In the light of the above I am satisfied that neither of these approaches is practicable. In each case there are grounds for considerable reservations as to its effectiveness.

8.88   The Inquiry heard the evidence of Dr H D Davies who has had many years of experience as a police surgeon and is the immediate past president of the Association of Police Surgeons. He outlined a possible system by which the applicant's medical practitioner would on request from a selected police surgeon (now referred to as a forensic medical examiner) supply information as to the applicant's medical history. For this purpose forms similar to those used for the purpose of obtaining life assurance would be used. The medical practitioner would be able, but not bound, to add comment of his own as to the suitability of the applicant. The forensic medical examiner would make an assessment as to whether there was any point in the applicant being interviewed by him or examined by a psychiatrist or psychologist. The forensic medical examiner would make a formal and confidential recommendation to the Chief Constable as to whether the applicant was or was not suitable from a medical point of view. The final decision would, as at present, rest with the Chief Constable. It was also suggested that medical practitioners would be under a duty to advise the police or the forensic medical examiner if the holder of the firearm certificate became mentally unwell or if there was some other change of circumstances which raised a question as to whether he was still suitable.

8.89   The advantage of such a proposal is that it could be of some benefit in screening out at least some of the applicants which are unsuitable on medical grounds. It would relieve the medical practitioner of the difficulty of being asked to give what he regards as an assurance as to the medical suitability of the applicant; and it would enable him to exchange information with a fellow-professional who would have the responsibility of deciding whether the information provided called for further action. In cases in which the medical practitioner knew so little of his patient that he was unable personally to give details of the applicant's medical history it might prove necessary for a medical examination to precede any further consideration of the application by the forensic medical examiner. The proposal would also provide a means by which a medical practitioner could discharge his duty to provide information in accordance with paragraph 18 of the Guidance on Confidentiality.

8.90   I consider that there is some merit in the proposal which has been put forward on behalf of the Association of Police Surgeons. However, as it raises questions on which there should be full consultation with the professional bodies, I consider that the best course for me is to recommend that the Home Office and The Scottish Office institute a process of consultation in order to see whether such a system is feasible. It would, of course, on any view involve the need to make it an essential part of the procedure for applying for a firearm certificate that the applicant consented to the disclosure of details of his medical history and was subject to being required to undertake an interview, examination or test. I have some reservations about the proposal that medical practitioners should be under a duty to report changes relating to the holder of the firearm certificate, in respect that it might well be very difficult for them to know when such a duty arose.

Advertisement   8.91   It was suggested that each firearm application should be advertised locally so that members of the public could express any objection to or reservation about the applicant while the application is under consideration by the police.

8.92   I do not favour this proposal in the case of those who already hold firearms. It would serve to draw attention to the fact that they possessed firearms and would tend to increase any risk of their homes being broken into and the firearms stolen. As regards the application of such a proposal to those who are applying for a firearm certificate for the first time, I do not consider there is sufficient reason for making advertisement obligatory only in the case of such applicants.

Prohibited persons

8.93   Here I am concerned with the categories of person whom the 1968 Act treats as prohibited persons. A number of suggestions were made for additional categories. The only proposal which appeared to me to have any tenable connection with the Inquiry was that those who have been detained under the Mental Health Acts, whether or not as a result of an order made by a criminal court, would incur prohibition. As is pointed out at para 80 of Part II of the Green Book any such change in the law would need to make provision for a right of appeal.

8.94   This matter was considered by the Firearms Consultative Committee in Chapter 9 of their Third Annual Report (in 1992). They regarded the issue, especially in the case of non-offenders, as raising formidable legal, medical and enforcement difficulties. They recommended to the Home Secretary that he should look closely again at the whole issue in consultation with his ministerial colleagues in other interested departments to see whether a solution was possible.

8.95   Up to a point the need for depriving a person of firearms could be met by the system for communication of medical information with which I have been concerned above. It seems to me that it may well be preferable that such cases should be handled through the process of revocation rather than by the creation of an additional prohibited category. In the circumstances I have no particular recommendation to make.

Security

8.96   The question of whether an applicant can be permitted to have a firearm or ammunition in his possession includes the question of the security in which they are held. Standard condition 4 of the firearm certificate places holders under a duty to take all "reasonable" security precautions, both when the firearms and ammunition are in store at home or elsewhere and when they are in use or transit.

8.97   It was suggested—as it has been before—that it should be a mandatory requirement for a particular means of security to be provided. I can see that this would have the advantage of certainty, mainly for the police. On the other hand on the limited submissions made to me I am not convinced that it would be right to recommend such a change. The greater advantage seems to lie with the present system in which what is required is intended to be proportionate to the circumstances of the case.

Renewal

8.98   Here I am concerned with two inter-related matters, firstly, the period after which firearm certificates fall to be renewed; and, secondly, the manner in which the renewal enquiry should be conducted, and in particular whether it should be by visit or by post.

8.99   Firearm certificates issued on or after 1 January 1995 are valid for 5 years. Certificates issued before that date are valid for 3 years. There is no legal requirement that applicants for the initial grant or renewal of a firearm certificate should be visited. Police forces have been encouraged to carry out a thorough investigation of all initial applications so that a postal system, supplemented by home visits only where strictly necessary, could be introduced—thereby reducing the time, workload and cost of renewal process. A number of Scottish police forces have introduced a postal renewal system for shot gun certificates but only one has introduced such a system for firearm certificates. Chief Constable Cameron said in evidence that most forces were reluctant to introduce postal renewal because they considered that it was essential to continue to have as many home visits as possible in order to maintain the quality of the enquiry in the interests of public safety and the application of the regulatory aspects of firearms law, especially in view of the extension of the life of the certificate from 3 to 5 years. He added that it was anomalous to have enquiries into the renewal of shot gun certificates carried out to a different standard.

8.100   The practice of carrying out a postal renewal represents a shift away from the advice given in the Guidance to the Police at a time when the life of the firearm certificate was 3 years. The advice was that it was helpful to combine a personal visit with the inspection of firearms and the interview; and that applications for renewal gave an opportunity for reviewing the circumstances of each case and the extent to which the provisions of the Act had been complied with by the holder of the certificate and by persons supplying him with firearms or ammunition (6.29).

8.101   It is my understanding that it was intended that postal renewal would be used only where there had been no change of circumstances and no reason to do otherwise. However, it seems to me that even with an improvement in the level of police criminal intelligence, it may well be that a change of circumstances or a cause for concern will not be known *unless* a home visit takes place.

8.102   I do not consider that the life of the firearm certificate which has been so recently extended to 5 years should revert to 3 years. However, in the light of the evidence which I have heard and read I consider that this calls for greater emphasis on the quality of work which is done by the police gathering and utilising intelligence. I do not favour postal renewals as the general rule.

Revocation

8.103   I have discussed above the enlargement of the scope for revocation under section 30(1) of the 1968 Act (paras 8.31-8.33); and an extension of the powers to enter and seize firearms (para 8.15).

8.104   It was submitted that in addition to the power of revocation the police should also have the power to suspend the certificate pending a decision as to revocation. I do not consider that this is necessary, having regard to my recommendation in para 8.15.

8.105   It was also submitted that certain consequences should follow from revocation, in particular that a period of time should elapse before the former certificate holder would be able to reapply for a certificate. I am not convinced that it would be appropriate to enact a rule which would apply to every case irrespective of its circumstances. Accordingly I do not favour such a proposal.

8.106   I noted that it was also submitted that a person whose firearm certificate had been revoked should be unable to take advantage of any of the special exemptions from section 1 of the 1968 Act. While I see some force in this proposal it seems to me to lead into a consideration of matters which are too far removed from the scope of this Inquiry, and accordingly I have not given it further consideration.

Decisions and Appeals

Decisions   8.107   It is essential that the officer to whom the duty of making a decision to grant or refuse an application for a firearm certificate or a variation or a decision as to revocation of a firearm certificate is placed in the position of being able to make that decision in the light of all the information which is of possible relevance (cf para 6.78).

8.108   It was submitted that the chief officer of police or the officer acting on his behalf should be given a discretion to decide which was subject only to the process of judicial review and hence that the present appeal system should be abolished. I do not recommend such a course. Apart from any other consideration it would mean the loss of access to a local independent forum.

8.109   It was also submitted that the chief officer of police should be subject to a general duty to hear the applicant or holder prior to making his decision. The purpose of this would be to give the applicant or holder an opportunity to respond to the case against him. At present the Firearms Acts make no provision for any form of procedure. It seems to me to be inappropriate to introduce such a formal requirement regardless of the circumstances. That is not to say that there may not be circumstances, especially in regard to revocation, where it is arguable that considerations of natural justice indicate that the holder should be given the opportunity to respond. However, that is a matter to be determined according to the circumstances of the case.

8.110   Another duty which, it was submitted, should be imposed on the chief officer of police was to give reasons for his decision. This is already advised as a matter of good practice (see the Guidance to the Police, paras 6.7 and 6.39). In their Fifth Annual Report (in 1994) the Firearms Consultative Committee did not support such a proposal. I do not consider that I should differ from them.

8.111   It was pointed out by the BSSC that there is no mechanism by which the chief officer of police may refer his doubts or concerns about a particular applicant to an independent review outwith the court system and his own police force. They submitted that there was merit in the introduction of an "intermediate" tribunal comprising suitable experts to which cases could be referred. This would enable him to express his concerns without having to commit his force to the expensive option of defending an appeal. No such suggestion has come from any of the bodies which represent police officers of whatever rank. I consider that it would tend to detract from the responsibility attaching to the chief officer of police as well as delaying the prompt disposal of what he has to decide. I do not favour this proposal.

Appeals   8.112   Under section 44 of the 1968 Act an applicant or holder has a right of appeal in Scotland to the Sheriff; and in England and Wales to the Crown Court. A study of a number of decisions—to which my attention was drawn in a note by Mr Bonomy and Mr Lake in regard to Scotland and an opinion by Mr Jeremy Carter-Manning QC in regard to England and Wales—shows that there is a considerable variation of approach.

8.113   In England and Wales the appeal is treated as if it was a re-hearing. While the decision of the chief officer is of considerable importance the Crown Court substitutes its own decision for his, taking into account not only matters considered by him but also any other matters brought to its notice (see *Kavanagh v Chief Constable of Devon and Cornwall* [1974] QB 624 and *R v Acton Crown Court ex parte Varney* [1984] Crim LR 783).

8.114 In Scotland it was thought for many years, in the light of the decision in *Kaye v Hunter* 1958 SC 208, that the sheriff was performing not a judicial but an administrative function; and in that capacity he could only interfere with the decision of the chief officer of police if he was persuaded that it was a capricious or arbitrary exercise of his discretion. However, in *Rodenhurst v Chief Constable of Grampian Police* 1992 SC 1 it was held that *Kaye v Hunter* was wrongly decided; that the sheriff was acting in a judicial capacity; and accordingly that an appeal to the Court of Session was competent. On the other hand the court did not express a view as to the scope of the appeal to the sheriff. It was sufficient for the outcome in that case that it was common ground that the chief officer's decision was based on materially incorrect information and accordingly could not stand.

8.115 Against that background it will be understood that until the decision in *Rodenhurst* there was a dearth of authoritative decisions as to the scope of an appeal to the sheriff. Since *Rodenhurst* sheriffs have disposed of appeals to them on a variety of bases. In some cases the sheriff has proceeded to reconsider the subject of the chief officer's decision in much the same way as it would have been reconsidered in England and Wales. In some the sheriff's decision has turned on whether the chief officer's decision was "justified and reasonable". In others the sheriff has considered whether the decision was based on an error of fact or law, oppressive, unjust or malicious or unreasonable. A recurring theme in many of the decisions is that the chief officer's discretion should be recognised and respected. The only case which has come before the Court of Session since *Rodenhurst* was *Howson v Chief Constable of Fife* 5 November 1993, unreported, in which the court said in the course of its opinion: "The essential matter that the chief constable had to decide, that the sheriff had to decide or that we should have to decide if we were considering the matter afresh, is whether or not the circumstances revealed a danger to the public". This may suggest that the sheriff was in the position of being able to exercise an independent decision *de novo*.

8.116 It is clearly unsatisfactory that in Scotland there should be uncertainty as to the correct approach to be adopted. In the ordinary way it might well be appropriate, if one was concerned only with the ascertainment of the law as it stands, to await a suitable opportunity for the Court of Session to clarify the position in Scotland. However, the existence of diverging approaches as between Scotland and England and Wales serves to highlight certain questions which may be pertinent in the present Inquiry where the scope for an appeal is an element in the strictness of the certification regime.

8.117 It is, in my view, open to question whether an appeal should be as wide as to amount to a re-hearing of the application or the matter of revocation. It is to my mind strange that, when so much importance attaches—and rightly so—to the responsibility of the police and in particular the decision-maker, that a court of law should take on the responsibility of discharging that function in deciding an application or a question of revocation, all within the comparatively narrow range of the information which is provided by the evidence before it. While cases may occur in which a chief officer of police proceeds on what turns out to be incorrect information or mistaken view of the law, the core of his function is the exercise of his judgment. Although the decision in *Kaye v Hunter* is no longer of any authority one of the remarks by Lord President Clyde at page 211 is apposite: "He is probably in a far better position than any other official to know or to be able to ascertain whether the granting of the certificate is in the public interest ....". As I have already noted, in a number of cases in Scotland sheriffs have reiterated the importance of the discretion which is entrusted to the chief officer.

8.118   These considerations lead me to question whether it is appropriate that a court of law should approach the question as if it was for itself to decide in place of the chief officer. For the same reasons I also question the submission which was made for the BSSC that the appeal function should be transferred to a specialist tribunal on the ground that "one of the fundamental problems of the current appeal system is the unfamiliarity of some courts with the sport of shooting, with firearms law and its application, and with the practical side of firearms licensing".

8.119   I consider that the more appropriate approach is to recognise the discretion of the chief officer of police, retain the courts as the avenue for appeal, and limit the scope of appeal to enumerated grounds which between them should cover the areas in which there should be room left for appeal. Purely by way of illustration I would draw attention to the fact that under the Licensing (Scotland) Act 1976 and the Civic Government (Scotland) Act 1982 the scope for appeal to the sheriff against a decision of the licensing board or, as the case may be, the local authority, is limited to cases in which the decision-makers (i) have erred in law; (ii) have based their decision on an incorrect material fact; (iii) have acted in a manner contrary to the requirements of natural justice; or (iv) have exercised their discretion in an unreasonable manner. I recommend that consideration be given to reforming the scope for appeal on these lines, although I appreciate that the exact terms in which it should be cast is a matter for further study and consultation.

Conclusions

8.120   From the discussion in this chapter I draw a number of conclusions. It would be practicable to supplement existing measures with a view to ensuring that no holder of a firearm certificate remained in possession of a firearm unless he continued to have good reason to do so. However, as regards ensuring the suitability of the applicant or holder—the aspect which is of greater importance for public safety—there would still be significant limitations. The provision of medical information can provide warning signs in some cases but there is no certain means of excluding the onset of a mental illness which poses danger or of identifying those whose personalities harbour dangerous propensities. These limitations would be inherent in the system itself, quite apart from any failure to operate it adequately.

Chapter 9　The Availability of Section 1 Firearms

Introduction

9.1　In the light of my conclusions in the last chapter I require to consider whether there should be a restriction on the availability of firearms which fall within section 1 of the 1968 Act, and in particular handguns; and, if so, what form that restriction should take.

9.2　I will begin with the general question whether there is a relationship between the legal availability of firearms and the incidence of crime and suicide (paras 9.3-9.32). I will then consider:

- handguns and their use in target shooting (paras 9.33-9.44)
- the dangers posed by the misuse of handguns (paras 9.45-9.53)
- the assessment of risk (paras 9.54-9.62)
- measures for restricting the availability of handguns (paras 9.63-9.98)
- the implications of restricting the availability of handguns (paras 9.99-9.105)
- what should be done (paras 9.106-9.113)

The chapter ends with some observations on other matters (paras 9.114-9.119).

Is there a relationship between the legal availability of firearms and the incidence of crimes and suicide?

Crime　9.3　Two points are in controversy both in this country and abroad, especially in the United States of America. Firstly, is there a relationship between the legal availability of firearms and the level of firearm-crime? Secondly, even if there is such a relationship, would restriction on the legal availability of firearms affect the overall level of crime?

9.4　As regards the first of these points, there is unfortunately no systematic recording as to the extent to which legal, as distinct from illegal, firearms are used in the commission of crime in Great Britain; and there is no routine research into this subject. Firearms used in crime are generally not recovered after they have been so used and, when they are, they are usually found to have been tampered with so as to obscure their origin. However, as the Research and Statistics Directorate of the Home Office (RSD) observed in its note, to which I referred in para 2.23: "It would be naive to think that the majority (perhaps the vast majority) of offences did not involve illegal firearms, albeit noting that some of the most notorious murders have involved lawfully held ones". Mr Colin Greenwood, a firearms consultant, used the estimate that "something like 96% of the firearms used in crime had never formed part of a licensed pool". This appears to have been based on a study by Inspector A Maybanks of the Metropolitan Police in 1992. He concluded that in only 3.6% of the cases in which firearms were used in robberies in London were the firearms known to have been previously licensed. However, this is not the only source of such evidence; and in any event it takes account only of theft as the route by which legal firearms come to be used in the commission of crime, and a particular type of crime.

9.5   A number of commentators, including not only Mr Greenwood but also Mr Michael Yardley and Mr Jan Stevenson, maintained that in the light of the large number of illegal firearms in Great Britain a restriction on legally-held firearms would not place criminals in any difficulty in arming themselves. Mr Greenwood emphasised that there was nothing which the Inquiry could recommend which would do more than was being done in order to deal with illegal firearms. Over the last decade various estimates have been made of the pool of illegal firearms. Mr Stevenson and Mr Yardley cited estimates of 4 million or more. Mr Greenwood suggested that, on the basis that there were 2.7 million firearms which were legally held in Great Britain, the illegal pool was at least equal to that figure. His estimate of the number of legally held firearms appears to me to be distinctly on the high side. I note that on the basis of data provided by police forces the Home Office in recent years estimated the total at 1.7 million. Further, there is no definite factual basis for the view that the number of illegally held guns is at least as large. It is also important to distinguish (i) the number of firearms which are used by professional criminals; and (ii) the much larger number of firearms which lie in the hands of the public. Many in the latter group, such as inherited guns and war souvenirs, are "benign" in the sense that they have been largely forgotten about and would be difficult to supply with suitable ammunition. In his evidence Mr D J Penn estimated the first of these pools at 2,000-4,000 firearms; and the latter at probably "around the million mark". Mr Yardley in his submission said that the latter pool was shrinking due to (a) changing attitudes to firearms in society; (b) a greater threat of prosecution; and (c) amnesties. The wide range of these estimates demonstrates that there is no certainty as to the size of the total number of firearms which are illegally held. The number of firearms which are used in practice by professional criminals may well be relatively small.

9.6   Mr Greenwood placed some reliance on trends over time. He pointed out that despite the fact that the number of firearm certificates had been declining since the middle 1960s and that the number of shot gun certificates had declined since the coming into force of the Firearms (Amendment) Act 1988, the rate of armed crime in Great Britain had undergone a considerable increase. Homicides and robberies involving the use of firearms in England and Wales had risen from 26 and 464 respectively in 1969 to 66 and 4,104 in 1994. In his book on the subject he explained that this was due to a greater willingness on the part of criminals to resort to violence, including the use of firearms. Robberies with firearms were generally committed by those who by reason of their record could never hold firearms legally. Mr Stevenson emphasised repeatedly in his submission that firearm-crime formed an integral part of total crime and could not be "peeled off" by restricting the number of firearms.

9.7   There appears to be no doubt that the proportion of crime which involves the use of firearms has risen along with the general increase in crime since 1969, and indeed has shown a small upward trend relative to the general increase; and that illegal firearms have been used increasingly since that time. However, there is no way in which this can be measured. Likewise the extent to which what are thought to be firearms are in fact imitations is not known with any degree of certainty.

9.8   As I have already noted, one of the ways in which firearms can find their way into use in the commission of crime is following their theft. In 1994 there were just under 3,000 offences in England, Wales and Scotland in which one or more firearms were stolen, most often from residential property, although it should be noted that the principal weapon which was stolen was an air weapon in more than 50% of cases, whereas it was a shot gun in 19.5% of cases and a pistol in only 9.6%. It should not, of course, be assumed (i) that firearms were the main object of the crime; or (ii) that the firearms stolen were in fact legally held.

9.9   In addition to the conclusion of Inspector Maybanks to which I referred in para 9.4 I noted that a study by Morrison and O'Donnell in 1994 showed that 6% of the armed robbers who were interviewed for the purposes of that study (5 out of 84) knew that the gun which they had used had come from a residential burglary. The robbers stated that their main sources of firearms were burglaries, the army and illegal imports from Europe. Again it may be unwise to assume that the firearms in question had all been held legally by the victims of the burglaries but it seems reasonable to take it that a substantial proportion of them were so held. A study for the Home Office, *Theft of Firearms* by Martin Corkery in 1994 showed that at least 9% of the firearms recovered had, since being stolen, been used in crime, mostly robberies. Virtually all the firearms had been licensed.

9.10   In addition, in an examination of 152 out of the 196 cases of firearm homicides in England and Wales in the years 1992-94 it was found that in 5% of the cases in which firearms were not legally held at the time of the crime (7 out of 130) the firearm was "believed to have been stolen". There were 88 homicides where the police did not know whether the firearms had been stolen or not. An examination of 34 cases in Scotland in 1993 where a firearm was used in connection with murder, attempted murder, culpable homicide, and assault and robbery showed that in 20% of the instances in which the source of the firearm was identified (4 out of 20) the firearm was said to have been stolen.

9.11   Another way in which legally held firearms could be involved is through the perpetration of serious crime by their legal owners. The shootings at Hungerford and Dunblane provide stark examples. However, Mr Greenwood claimed that it was generally accepted that, save in a small number of cases of domestic violence, legally held firearms were not used in crime by their original owners. The study of homicides in England and Wales to which I referred in the last paragraph showed that the firearm was lawfully held by the perpetrator in 14% of the cases in which it was known whether the firearm was legally held or not (22 out of 152, mostly domestic homicides). In one additional case it was held by a member of his family. No firearm which was lawfully held was used in a robbery. According to information provided by The Scottish Office, in 12.5% of the firearm-homicides in Scotland in the years 1990-94 (3 out of 24) the firearm was lawfully held by the perpetrator. In the study for 1993 to which I referred in the last paragraph it was shown that 7.3% of the firearms which featured in the crimes (3 out of 41) were legally held.

9.12   The statistical evidence to which I have referred in the last four paragraphs is of limited value. It is based on comparatively small numbers over only a few years. However, it does show that while illegal firearms are used in the great majority of firearm-related crimes, and especially robberies, the existence of legally held firearms leads to their use in crime in a significant, thought relatively small, number of cases.

9.13   In Annex G to the Green Book the RSD discussed certain recent research into the relationship between firearm-ownership and firearm-homicide. This material was strongly criticised by a number of commentators, in particular Mr Greenwood, Mr Stevenson, Mr R A I Munday and Mr Steven W Kendrick. The RSD provided a further note, prepared by Ms Pat Mayhew, which was followed by further submissions from the four commentators. In his closing submissions at the end of the Inquiry Mr C M Campbell founded on the written evidence of Professor Thomas Gabor which had been submitted on behalf of his clients. Professor Gabor is Professor of Criminology in the University of Ottawa and has made a study of criminal violence for almost 20 years.

9.14   The main research to which the RSD referred was certain of the work of Professor Martin Killias of the University of Lausanne which was published in 1993. He sought to use the results from the International Crime (Victimisation) Surveys of firearm ownership in eighteen countries in 1989 and 1992; and to compare the results with the levels of firearm- homicide in those countries. Previously the lack of measurement of the availability of firearms across a wide range of countries on the same basis presented a major difficulty in investigating the link between ownership and homicides. In these surveys the measure used was not the number of firearms but the number of households in which a firearm was owned.

9.15   The RSD considered that the comparison of firearm homicide per million of population with the percentage of households in which a firearm was owned, as set out in Annex G, did not show an exact relationship, but that the overall picture indicated a strong statistical relationship. That relationship was taken to be of some value in ascertaining whether there was a relationship between the legal ownership of firearms and the incidence of firearm-homicide.

9.16   There is no doubt that the work of Professor Killias attracted criticism in some academic quarters. Its use by the RSD drew scornful observations from the commentators to whom I have referred. Some said that resulting levels of firearm-ownership in certain countries or the apparent relationship of one country to another lacked credibility. It was maintained there were differences of definition and recording of crime as between one country and another which made comparison unreliable. It was also suggested that the picture could be much affected by the inclusion or exclusion of particular countries. But the aspect of the exercise to which the most trenchant criticisms were directed was the method by which the researchers had sought to find out whether anyone in a household had a firearm. This was done by random survey by telephone call. 47% of those who responded to the call refused to answer the question or terminated the interview. The commentators maintained that this could not give realistic results.

9.17   The RSD accepted that there was force in some of the criticisms to which I have referred but maintained that their strength was exaggerated. The point was that there was a strong overall association between firearm-homicides and firearm-ownership. The fact that the survey was conducted by telephone did not invalidate the figures. It might indeed lead to a more reliable result than face-to-face interviewing. In any event it did not show that there was a difference in preparedness to admit ownership as between one country and another. The fact that the response rate was lower in some countries and higher in others (47% being the average) did not of itself affect the reliability of the measurement.

9.18   I should add at this point that in their submission to the Inquiry, which is reproduced in their Seventh Annual Report (for 1995), the Firearms Consultative

Committee noted that Annex G had rightly drawn attention to the ideological and partisan nature of the academic debate on gun control. However, Professor Killias' study had been strongly criticised for its factual inaccuracy and its methodology. They then referred to a footnote to page 74 of Annex G which stated that in Switzerland where gun availability was relatively high because of the reserve militia, ammunition was kept in sealed boxes which were checked every year and was not available for sale. This was said to be based on Professor Killias and to be incorrect. The Firearms Consultative Committee then stated: "The validity of Killias' exclusion of military arms from his Swiss gun ownership rates is therefore seriously open to doubt, as the arm is in the home and ammunition is readily available". In its note the RSD accepted that the statement in the footnote was probably incorrect but they pointed out that in the particular study from which the results were shown in Annex G military weapons in Switzerland were taken into account.

9.19   It is possible that an apparent relationship between the level of firearm-ownership and firearm-homicide in a particular country could be due to some factor which operated within its society and culture as distinct from those of other countries. For example, reference was made to the possible significance of poverty, alcohol abuse and violence on television. More directly still it could be due to a pervading "violent culture". However, the view of Professor Killias was, as I understand it, that if this were so higher firearm-ownership would also need to be related to higher non-firearm homicides.

9.20   In order to test such a hypothesis in the case of the United States of America, which was one of the countries covered by the study and has a much higher level of firearm ownership than this country, the RSD made a comparison of the firearm and non-firearm homicides as between England and Wales and the United States for the period 1985-90. This comparison was similar to a study which had been carried out by Clarke and Mayhew in 1988. The comparison, as set out in Annex G, showed that the average annual rate of firearm-homicide per million of population in the United States was 51 times that in England and Wales; and the handgun-homicide rate 150 times. On the other hand non-firearm homicide was only 3 times; and the overall homicide rate was 8 times. In its note the RSD extended the exercise to the years 1990-94 and to a larger range of crimes. The resulting figures showed that the picture of a more violent culture in the United States was to a degree suggested by the fact that non-firearm robberies and homicides were 70% and 140% higher than in England and Wales. On the other hand firearm-related robberies and homicides were 11 and 50 times higher. The conclusion of the RSD was: "These results strongly suggest that the availability of guns increases both fatal and non-fatal gun-related crimes considerably in excess of what might be expected from differences in recorded crime levels for other offences".

9.21   The criticisms of the work of Professor Killias, and in particular the methodology used, leads me to treat the results with considerable caution but I am not persuaded that it should be wholly rejected as unreliable. It shows that there is *a* relationship between firearm- ownership and firearm-homicide when considered overall. The material provided by the RSD tends to show that while different cultures may explain differing levels of firearm-homicide to some extent it is probably not the whole explanation.

9.22   The RSD also placed some reliance on a study carried out in 1995 by the Canadian Department of Justice which collated information from agencies in 8 countries as to the levels of legally held firearms and the rates of homicide. The figures for the latter as set out in Annex G unfortunately suffer from a misplaced decimal point; and a comparison with the study of Professor Killias is hampered by the fact that they relate to different periods. The RSD stated that the results showed a fairly suggestive relationship between firearm-ownership and firearm-homicide, although it was weaker than in Professor Killias' study. The Canadian work was also criticised by commentators who challenged the accuracy or comparability of the figures used. It is sufficient for my purposes to say that even if the material was accurate and comparable, the fact that it related to a much smaller group of countries makes it less persuasive. For that reason I attach little importance to it. The remaining research on which the RSD relied was a comparison between homicide rates for Seattle and Vancouver. However, this limited comparison has been strongly criticised in academic circles. It is a comparison between only two locations and there is at least a likelihood that patterns of crime, including armed crime, were affected by demographic and other local conditions.

9.23   Attention is often directed to the case of Switzerland as having a low rate of firearm-related homicide but high firearm ownership even apart from the firearms held by the reserve militia. Comparing Switzerland with this country is difficult since Swiss police figures do not distinguish between homicides and attempted homicides. Further, it has been estimated that the rate of firearm homicide in Switzerland is rather more than 4 times higher than in England and Wales. This has to be taken with some caution because of the relatively low figures. It is true that the level of firearm-related assaults is less than in Great Britain. This is consistent with a much lower rate of violent crime in Switzerland generally. The RSD stated in its note that the reason why this is not reflected in firearm-related homicides may be because very many of such homicides are domestic incidents, where the presence of a firearm at home, including military firearms, may turn conflict into a fatal event.

"Weapon substitution"   9.24   So far I have attempted to assess evidence with which I was presented in regard to the first of the questions which I set out in paragraph 9.3. As regards the second of these questions I have to turn to "weapon substitution". This refers to the theory propounded in 1958 by Professor Martin E Wolfgang "according to which it is not the weapon that dictates the crime, but the gravity of the crime that dictates the weapon". Thus the most significant factor in determining the outcome of a crime of violence is the intent or attitude of the assailant. Compared with this the availability of one type of weapon or another has little significance in the end. The use of a firearm implies a more deadly intent. If offenders are denied access to firearms or a particular type of firearm they would resort to other methods to achieve the same effect. The opposing argument is that the lethal effect of firearms reflects their properties rather than the determination of the users.

9.25   Thus in commenting on the comparison between England and Wales and the United States to which I referred in para 9.20 Mr Munday pointed out while the number of handguns in the United States had doubled since 1974 the rate of handgun homicide was now lower than it was. This showed that the overall homicide rate was not explicable in terms of gun availability. If guns had not been available the offenders would have resorted to other means. He and Mr Stevenson cited the conclusions of researchers that violent acts almost always formed part of a pattern of behaviour. From this they drew the lesson that the objective should be to identify those who posed a threat before it became a reality. Mr Stevenson in particular maintained that this was true not only of the "professional" criminal but also of the "domestic" criminal. Murderers, he wrote, were "real criminals, not good citizens who happened to have a loaded gun in a moment of anger". So robbers who carry a firearm show that they are prepared to use it if the need arises. Banning a certain type of firearm would, as Mr Munday contended, leave children helpless before a man with an axe, a bill hook, a machete or a flame-thrower. Mr Stevenson warned that some criminals would "trade up" to a more dangerous firearm if they were denied access to a particular weapon.

9.26   In my view while there may be many cases in which an assailant's attitude to his victim will be the main determining factor in the result, the proponents of this approach overstate their case. I do not accept that the proposition that many serious crimes and in particular firearm crimes are committed spontaneously can be so lightly dismissed. This seems to me to run counter to general experience. In that connection I note that Professor Gabor observed: "Many people who kill do so out of momentary anger, rather than as a result of an unchangeable determination to kill. The anger often dissipates quickly, but if firearms have been used it is too late for the victim. The fact that a high proportion of those who have killed their spouses attempt or commit suicide afterward attests to the spontaneity of many homicides and the regret that may follow. Many homicides stem from spontaneous altercations and it is especially in these cases that the type of weapon used is instrumental in terms of the outcome". It does not follow from the fact that a domestic homicide is preceded by a history of violence or abuse that there was a determination to kill which was irrespective of the presence or absence of a firearm.

9.27   I also noted that Professor Gabor is in agreement with the RSD in noting that firearms research has shown consistently that assaults and robberies in which firearms are involved are much more likely to result in death or serious injury than incidents in which other weapons or no weapons at all are involved. The RSD also point out that firearms have certain "advantages", providing (i) a relatively impersonal means of killing at a distance; (ii) a method for those who are physically less powerful than their victims to inflict serious damage; and (iii) a means of attacking heavily armed targets.

The net benefit argument

9.28   In the United States of America there are and have been strongly opposed views on either side of the debate concerning gun control. According to the submission of Mr Stevenson many criminologists in the United States had reached the position that they believed that the possession of firearms had a positive effect in discouraging crime and limiting its adverse effect—either through the victim being able to defend himself or through the assailant achieving early control. Mr Stevenson sought to point out that a number of countries had enjoyed advantages from such an approach to gun availability. Thus in the United States burglars were reluctant to break into occupied domestic property. However, in Great Britain there had been no acceptance of this approach, although it was notable that in rural areas where farmers are known to possess shot guns there was a lower level of housebreaking.

9.29   In this country the possession of firearms for self-defence has not, except in special cases, been regarded for many years as a "good reason" for their possession and there never has been a policy of facilitating, let alone encouraging, the acquisition of firearms to discourage crime or limit its effects. Different countries may require to tackle their problems in different ways. In Great Britain the level of firearm ownership is relatively low. I do not see anything in the net benefit argument which is relevant to this country.

Suicide　9.30　Gun availability has implications beyond crime. According to Professor Gabor a number of studies had been to the same effect in finding that countries with higher levels of firearm ownership tended to have higher rates of firearm suicide than those with lower ownership levels; and many of those studies also showed that where ownership levels are lower there was no compensating increase in suicides by other means. Such studies showed that people who had limited access to firearms did not always switch to other suicide methods or that the methods to which they switched were less lethal. Several studies had also shown that the lowering of accessibility of firearms by enhancing safe storage might also lower the number of both attempted and completed suicides.

9.31　The RSD also pointed out that in the United States the rate of firearm suicides was nearly 20 times that in England and Wales, whereas the overall suicide rate was only 40% higher. In the United States nearly 60% of all suicides were by firearm; whereas in England and Wales it was only 4%.

9.32　The importance of the availability and accessibility of firearms seems to be due to the transitory nature of suicidal motivation in many cases. No doubt people who are set on killing themselves can and do find the means where firearms are absent. Professor Gabor pointed out that many suicides, especially those of adolescents are not premeditated. "They are often precipitated by interpersonal crises and facilitated by the consumption of intoxicants. Many survivors of serious attempts by firearms have confirmed the transitory nature of suicidal thoughts and have adjusted well after their attempts".

Handguns and their use in target shooting

9.33　This Inquiry has been directly concerned with handguns, that is to say firearms which are designed to be held and fired using one hand. Whether they are revolvers or pistols they are generally used only for target shooting, either at traditional bulls eye targets or in "practical shooting" which involves firing at multiple and possibly moving targets to time limits. However, as I indicated in Chapter 7, they may also have a number of occupational uses.

9.34　At the end of 1995 there were a total of 32,000 firearm certificates in Scotland and 142,000 firearm certificates in England and Wales. According to Table 7 of Annex A to the Green Book, in 1995 in England, Wales and Scotland there were a total of about 200,490 hand-guns permitted on firearm certificates. The average amount of ammunition permitted ranged between 500 and 1,000 rounds per calibre. The table also shows that there were about 57,510 firearm certificates on issue allowing the holder to possess a handgun; and about 45,540 allowed the holder to possess more than one handgun.

9.35　Handguns may be either multi-shot (self-loading pistols or revolvers) or single shot. I will take each type in turn and then deal with comparisons between them.

9.36　A self-loading pistol (otherwise known as a semi-automatic) operates on the principle that after the pistol and its magazine have been charged it will continue to fire one cartridge every time the trigger is pulled until the magazine is empty. The fired cartridges are automatically ejected by the recoil action. Such pistols range in calibre from .22 rimfire up to .50 magnum, but, apart from the high power rifle cartridge, the most common is the 9 mm x 19. The barrel length can be between

2 and 14 inches but commonly is 4-5 inches. The magazine may be integral (8-10 rounds) or removable (commonly 6-10 rounds, but can be increased to 20 or more, according to the make and model). A few magazines are interchangeable between makes. It is common for military-style pistols to be used with magazines which can contain 13-17 rounds. Self-loading pistols are extensively advertised. Additional magazines can be purchased by mail order or over the counter without the need to produce any legal authorisation. A magazine which has been removed from a firearm which has been deactivated in accordance with section 8 of the 1988 Act can be used with a compatible design of non-deactivated pistol.

9.37 In a revolver the cylinder, which commonly contains 5 or 6 chambers, is revolved as the hammer is cocked and fired. The particular manner of operation depends on whether the action is single or double. Revolvers range in calibre from .22 rimfire to .50 Action Express. The barrel length is most commonly 2-6 inches. Revolvers which have a cylinder which can be swung out can be very quickly emptied of their spent cartridges and reloaded by means of a speedloader. Such devices can be bought without production of any legal authorisation. Like self-loading pistols revolvers are extensively advertised.

9.38 In the case of a single shot pistol one cartridge has to be manually loaded and extracted each time the pistol is fired. Such pistols range in calibre from .22 rimfire to high power centrefire rifle cartridges such as the .308 Winchester. This type of handgun can be used with the most extensive range of ammunition. The barrel length ranges from 2 to 16 inches. According to table 7 in Annex A to the Green Book under 5% of licensed handguns are single shot pistols. In his evidence Mr Alastair Paton, a firearms expert, observed that there was a fairly limited market for them, especially where they had short barrel lengths. According to Mr D J Penn, who has extensive knowledge of firearms, single shot pistols fell principally into one or other of the following types: (i) a very evolved, high precision gun for shooting at 50 metre distances in the Free Pistol competition, which was for .22 rimfire; (ii) a club-owned gun usually .22 calibre, for introducing newcomers to the sport of target shooting; and (iii) a very highly evolved and specialist gun for long distance shooting at distances between 300 metres and 1000 yards. Single shot pistols accounted for well under 5% of rimfire shooting: in centrefire they were very little used.

9.39 As regards the comparison between single shot and multi-shot competitive shooting Mr Penn provided the Inquiry with the following description: "Competition discipline with a single shot pistol is restricted to slow, deliberate, precision target shooting pure and simple, making no significant use of other skills such as overall physical fitness, decision-making and speed of response which all come into play with the availability of multi-shot pistols and for which the great majority of competitions are designed. Very few competition disciplines are available for single shot pistols, reflecting the now large interest in other more physically and mentally demanding disciplines. Shooting as a sport thrives on the variety of skills which can be brought to bear, and which convert shooting from what may traditionally have seemed a passive sport into one which requires and develops considerable agility and fitness of mind and body".

9.40 Mr Penn described self-loading pistols as having a distinct advantage over revolvers in those competitions which required fairly rapid firing of a series of shots. In particular pistols which were designed for competitions were almost exclusively of the "single action" type so that less effort was required to pull the trigger and the pistol was easier to control in a consistent fashion. As a result such pistols were dominant. In revolvers "double action" was an inevitable feature of contemporary designs and the forces involved tended to disturb accurate aim. For recreational shooting or shooting at a lower level revolvers would suffice.

9.41   In differentiating between rimfire and centrefire shooting Mr Penn estimated that at least 50% of club activity was concerned with the latter. Within centrefire shooting the trend was towards self-loading pistols and away from revolvers. Centrefire handguns whether revolvers or self-loading guns, were, apart from the highly-tuned and expensive single shot long-range pistols and a small number of expensive multi-shot guns, neither designed nor intended to have inherent "one-hole-group" accuracy as their sole or even principal attribute. They were designed to combine and balance a number of different features, principally reliability of operation, ease of cleaning and maintenance, accuracy, robustness in widely varying conditions of climate and use, weight, force of recoil and capacity of cartridges. In the many competitive disciplines which required centrefire handguns, inherent pinpoint accuracy of the gun was almost always less important than reliability and ease of control.

9.42   Mr Penn added that in terms of pure precision the .22 calibre was capable of levels of inherent accuracy beyond the skill of the shooter. Whether high accuracy was obtained depended on the quality of the particular gun, the quality of the ammunition and the skill of the shooter. The .22 rimfire represented the highest precision cartridge which was available. It was highly evolved. It was not possible to make a significant improvement on its performance. This was because the cartridge case had to be made of a light metal so that the rim would be crushed by the firing pin. However, in the case of .22 centrefire, which was mainly used in rifles for the destruction of medium-sized vermin, and was little used in this country at present, it was possible to use a very strong brass cartridge case with a large amount of powder hence giving much higher velocities than the rimfire. Such velocities would be in excess of 3,000 feet per second, as compared with a velocity of 1,100 feet per second for the rimfire.

9.43   Appendix 6 contains a brief description of the categories of competitions which are shot with different types of handgun.

9.44   Over the last 20 years there has been a considerable expansion in the use of larger calibre and high capacity handguns. These are based on military and police models. These are not target guns in the true and original sense, but courses of fire have been evolved for them which make use of their greater power and other characteristics, as well as calling for agility and quick thinking on the part of the shooter. This has led to the growth of combat shooting. It has led some shooters to don the trappings of combat, such as holsters and camouflage clothing. It has caused others to feel uneasy about what appears to be the use of guns as symbols of personal power.

The dangers posed by the misuse of handguns

Crime 9.45   It is clear that the proportion of offences in this country in which handguns were involved has been rising. Thus in England and Wales the number of offences in which handguns were reported to have been used rose from 1,232 in 1984 to 2,981 in 1994. This increase of 142% may be compared with an increase of 17% for shot guns. In each year the handgun was the single most common firearm used in robberies. Taking the longer period from 1974 to 1994 in England and Wales the proportion of all offences in which handguns were involved rose from 36% to 51%, whereas shot guns and rifles declined from 50% to 22%. As regards robberies the proportion in which handguns were used rose from 45% to 60%, whereas shot guns and rifles declined from 37% to 17%.

9.46   The study of homicides in England and Wales during the years 1992-94, to which I referred in para 9.10, showed that two-thirds of the firearms which were used in homicides connected with organised crime, drug related crime, contract killing and similar offences were handguns, but none of them were known to be legally held. In domestic homicides shot guns were used more than twice as frequently as handguns. Of the 15 handguns used in domestic homicides 6 were legally held by the perpetrator. These figures should, of course, be seen in their overall context. In the study period there were 196 cases of firearm-homicide: and such cases represented about 9% of all homicides. Thus handgun-homicides comprised a very small part of the whole.

9.47   Table 5 in Annex A to the Green Book shows the principal weapon involved in notifiable offences recorded by the police in England, Wales and Scotland in 1994. When handguns were involved they were proportionately less often fired than shot guns. However, in instances where handguns were fired they caused fatal results and injury in 11.7% and 52.3% of cases respectively; whereas, in instances where shot guns were fired, they caused fatal results and injury in 11.6% and 37% of cases respectively. The same general picture is provided by statistics relating to the use of firearms in incidents in England and Wales during the years 1992-94. In the study of serious crime in Scotland to which I referred in para 9.10, although handguns featured in only 26% of the incidents (9 out of 34), shots were fired from them proportionately more often, and they were responsible for more injuries and deaths, than any other type of firearm. However it may be noted that none of them were legally held. Although the numbers are comparatively small it is perhaps worth noting that out of 16 instances when handguns were fired in notifiable offences in Scotland in 1995 a fatal result occurred in one case and injury in 10 others. In the United States of America where approximately one third of all guns owned are handguns, they account for over 85% of gun-homicides for which the type of weapon is known, as against 8% for shot guns and 5% for rifles.

Lethality   9.48   All firearms are by definition lethal weapons. However, it is possible to give some comparison between single shots from different types of firearm.

9.49   Mr Paton pointed out that the amount of kinetic energy at the muzzle had been used in the Firearms (Dangerous Air Weapons) (Scotland) Rules 1969 as the means of discriminating between those air weapons which did and those which did not require to be licensed. Kinetic energy depended on the velocity of the projectile and its weight. The velocity depended on the amount of powder which was used. He provided the following as a general example, while recognising that the exact figure in a particular case would depend on the cartridge which was used:

.22 long rifle rimfire (revolver/pistol) -	90 foot lbs
.357 Magnum revolver -	530 foot lbs
9 mm pistol -	340 foot lbs
.45 Colt revolver -	420 foot lbs
.45 ACP pistol -	400 foot lbs
5.56 mm rifle (NATO calibre) -	1,280 foot lbs
.303 rifle -	2,400 foot lbs

Mr Paton gave evidence that the velocity of the bullet once it left the firearm would be affected by the extent to which its shape was aerodynamically efficient. The "stopping power" of the bullet would depend on whether it expended most of its energy on the victim. This was affected by the shape of the nose of the bullet and the part of the body which it struck. Thus a soft lead bullet would deform easily on impact and have less penetrative power than a bullet which had a copper/nickel jacket. A bullet with a hollow point in the nose would tend to deform into a mushroom shape; and the consequent enlargement of its nose diameter would cause it to stop more quickly. For the same velocity a larger bullet would cause more damage. It should not be supposed that .22 rimfire cannot be as lethal as other ammunition. The BSSC pointed out that at point-blank range and aimed at vital parts of the body .22 cartridges would be as lethal as 9 mm. In their submissions Mr Greenwood and Mr Stevenson emphasised that at close range a shot from a shot gun was more lethal than a shot from a rifle; and a shot from a rifle was more lethal than a shot from a handgun. Mr Greenwood pointed out that a normal shot gun cartridge would fire 1 ounce of shot with a muzzle energy of 1,600 foot lbs. At a distance of 15 feet the 270 lead pellets in ordinary game shot would cause, in his words, "an enormous impact" covering a circle of about 5 inches. If large "buckshot" loads were used, the charge might well consist of 9 lead pellets each 9 mm in diameter.

Ease of Use 9.50   However, these are not the only considerations which should be taken into account in making a comparison between different types of firearm. A handgun is comparatively light, weighing approximately 2 lbs, as compared with 8 lbs for a rifle. It is plainly easier to carry and to conceal by reason of its size and shape. It fits into a range of holsters or other accessories which allow it to be attached to a belt under a jacket or strapped to a leg. It is easy to aim and fire. According to Mr Paton a handgun was a better firearm to have in a close encounter as it was easier to use and to move from target to target. No doubt it is for such reasons that it is attractive for use in robberies, although the sawn-off shot gun is often encountered. The BSSC submitted that there was no evidence that Thomas Hamilton would not have been able to enter Dunblane Primary School just as easily with a larger firearm, such as a 7.62 mm rifle which he held the authority to acquire. I am sceptical of that proposition. In any event the advantages of handguns are plain.

Rapidity of fire 9.51   The particular feature of handguns which the shootings at Dunblane Primary School demonstrated with appalling results was the capability which semi-automatic pistols have for rapid fire. Earlier in this report I referred to the evidence given by Mr Malcolm Chisholm that when the 9 mm Browning pistol used by Thomas Hamilton at the school was tested it was found that if it was used to fire off a full magazine of 20 shots as quickly as possible the time taken for this was 5.46 seconds; and that Mr Paton gave evidence that it was consistent with his experience for this to take 5 or 6 seconds with some degree of accuracy, although this depended on the expertise and physical make-up of the person firing. At the same time I noted the reservation expressed by Mr Penn (para 3.40). The replacement of a spent magazine with a fresh one would take at most a few seconds. Mr Penn said that with practice the time could be reduced to less than 2 seconds. With .22 rimfire a higher rate may be achievable. The BSSC pointed out that due to the lower recoil forces involved in .22 rimfire it was possible to fire a greater number of controlled and carefully aimed shots in a given space of time than was possible with centrefire. This factor was of particular significance at shooting distances of 5-10 metres. I also noted that with a revolver it is possible to maintain a speed of firing which approaches that of the self-loading pistol. Further, as I stated earlier, the use of a speedloader in conjunction with a revolver which had a cylinder which could be swung out would enable a whole set of cartridges to be removed and replaced very quickly.

9.52 Mr Paton gave evidence that it would probably take longer than 5 or 6 seconds to fire a round with a single shot pistol because after firing one shot, the shooter had to lower his aim, break open the pistol, extract the spent cartridge case, pick out a fresh cartridge, put it in the chamber, close the pistol and resume his aim. It would take "10, probably 15 seconds" but this depended on the position of the shooter relative to his ammunition. Mr Penn said in evidence that he did not agree with this estimate. He said that most single shot pistols were very similar to a conventional shot gun in that when the barrel dropped the spent cartridge case could be ejected. It was possible to reload quite quickly so long as there was access to additional rounds. He recounted that he had used a .22 single shot pistol for vermin destruction with a wrist bandolier some 4 or 5 inches from the breech. With reasonable practice a shooter could get the reloading time down to about 5 seconds. I am content to accept that this could be achieved.

9.53 I should also refer to the evidence given by Mr Greenwood in a supplementary submission which was directed to showing how quickly shots could be discharged from a double-barrelled shot gun. He said that he had carried out tests using standard 12 bore cartridges with one ounce shot and a device for holding 40 cartridges head forward. Without bringing the shot gun fully to the shoulder he hit a rectangular target, measuring 2 feet x 1 foot at a distance of 15 feet, with 36 cartridges in 1 minute 56 seconds (4 cartridges fell to the ground as a result of fumbling). Bringing the shot gun to the shoulder for each shot he hit a 5 inch square target with all 40 shots in 2 minutes 40 seconds. Without the device and taking the cartridges from his pocket he hit the rectangular target with 30 cartridges in 2 minutes 30 seconds. He suggested that with practice someone like Thomas Hamilton could have improved on such times. With two or more such devices it would have been possible to fire 105 shots (the number discharged by Thomas Hamilton) within 5 minutes if the shots were directed rather than aimed. If the shots were aimed it would be possible to fire up to 75 shots in that time. If "buckshot" loads had been used, between 675 and 1,000 missiles would have been discharged, depending on whether the shots were aimed. Mr Greenwood evidently used the period of 5 minutes on the understanding that the shootings took place within that space of time.

The assessment of risk

9.54 If there is a case for placing a restriction on the availability of any particular type of firearm the starting point should be an assessment of the risk which is associated with it. It has often been said that it is not the gun that kills but the man that fires it. No doubt a gun cannot kill if someone does not pull the trigger, but it is right to regard a gun as dangerous and to treat some guns as more dangerous than others. As I observed in Chapter 7 this is one of the principal features of the policy of firearms legislation in this country.

9.55 An assessment of risk involves an examination of two elements in combination—(i) the chances of harm happening; and (ii) the nature and extent of the harm. Drawing on what I have written above I will indicate what seem to me to be the salient considerations.

9.56 As regards the first of these elements, the evidence shows that firearms which are or have been lawfully held are used to a significant but relatively small extent in the commission of crime. Handguns are being used to an ever increasing extent in crime in general. In the case of robberies the increase is greatest but it is unlikely that the handguns used in this category of crime are owned by their perpetrators. It appears that handgun-homicides comprise a very small part of the total of homicides. Handguns are attractive in the ease with which they can be carried and concealed and in the speed with which they can be aimed.

9.57   I have already indicated that there are significant limitations in the extent to which the certification system can be relied upon to exclude persons who are unsuitable. In this connection I note that Mr Michael Yardley in his submission drew attention to what he described as a fundamental problem in modern times—the problem of personal empowerment in mass society. According to him the average person today felt more isolated and alienated than ever before as society became more centralised and less personal. Thus one might expect a shift in the whole normal distribution of human behaviour with, at one side of the curve, ever more bizarre and aggressive behaviour. Unless this problem was addressed, he said, more Dunblanes and Hungerfords were not only possible but likely.

9.58   As regards the second of these elements, the evidence shows that where handguns are fired in the commission of crime there is as great a proportion of fatal results and an even greater proportion of injuries than is the case with shot guns.

9.59   While all firearms are by definition lethal an individual shot from a handgun, depending on the distance and calibre, may well be less lethal than a shot from a shot gun or a rifle. However, the multi-shot handgun, whether it is a self-loading pistol or a revolver, has the capacity by reason of its high rate of fire and speed of aim to kill or injure a greater number of people within a given short space of time than would be possible with any other type of firearm which is legally available; and likewise it provides a greater number of instant opportunities to kill a particular victim. The evidence provided by Mr Penn and Mr Greenwood about the rate of fire of other firearms still leaves a substantial difference.

9.60   I noted that the BSSC in their final submission maintained that the evidence which was given as to an unaimed rate of fire bore no relation to actual events at the school. However, in the light of the evidence it is likely that Thomas Hamilton's shots were to some extent indiscriminate. In any event the point of the evidence as to the rate of fire which a Browning 9 mm semi-automatic pistol was capable of delivering, whether in aimed or unaimed fire, was to demonstrate what was possible. I have no doubt that if Thomas Hamilton had chosen to do so he could have killed every person in the gym. If he had entered on the stage of the Assembly Hall while assembly was in progress (which may have been his original intention) he could have killed and injured far more by indiscriminate shooting. On the other hand Mr Greenwood claimed that few armed criminals fired more than one or two shots. He also stated in his submission that in the other "amok killings", including those at Hungerford, which he listed the rate of fire was not a significant factor. He defined an "amok killing" as being "one in which an unstable individual for no discernible or logical reason kills a number of people who were not known to him".

9.61   There is no way in which the risk of homicide or serious injury through the misuse of legal firearms can be calculated, let alone the risk associated with one particular type of firearm as against another. The instances in which legally held handguns are misused are relatively infrequent. On the other hand the harm which results can be very great, as the shootings at Dunblane Primary School demonstrated, perhaps in a unique manner. Both factors have to be borne in mind. Having considered the evidence I have reached the view that the dangers which are inherent in the availability of self-loading pistols and revolvers which are held for target shooting are so great that there is a case for restricting that availability. I distinguish them from other types of firearm, including rifles, by reason of their combination of ease of carrying and concealment, ease of aim and rapidity of fire. In the light of the evidence I see no good reason for making an exception in the case of any particular calibre of multi-shot handguns.

9.62   If there is a case for restricting the availability of multi-shot handguns, what form could that restriction take? I will now examine a number of possible measures which were discussed in the Inquiry, seeking answers to these questions:

would the measure be practicable?

would it be effective, and, if so, to what extent?

Thereafter I will consider the implications of implementing the different measures before coming to my recommendation.

Measures for restricting the availability of handguns in target shooting

Limiting the number of handguns, or the number of a particular calibre, which may be held

9.63   In the White Paper *Firearms Act 1968 : Proposals for Reform* (1987) Cm 261 the Government commented that the imposition of arbitrary limits on the number of weapons which an individual might possess or a prohibition on the possession of more than one weapon of the same calibre, whilst superficially attractive, would have little significant benefit in terms of control. I agree with that view, which has been supported by the Firearms Consultative Committee and is in line with the current Guidance to the Police in regard to "good reason".

9.64   While Thomas Hamilton took all four of his handguns to the school he used only one in order to fire all the shots at his victims. I see no reason to disagree with the point made by the BSSC that there is nothing to indicate that a shooter would be able to achieve a materially higher rate of fire by changing guns rather than by changing magazines as Thomas Hamilton did.

9.65   If individuals are to continue to be authorised to possess or acquire firearms I consider that it is acceptable that they should be able to justify the holding of more than one, or more than one of the same calibre, on the same basis as at present (cf para 6.29).

Separating handguns from their ammunition

9.66   There is an attraction in the idea that handguns should be in separate hands from their ammunition, except during such time as they are used together on a range. However, whichever way the matter is approached there are substantial problems.

9.67   I consider first the suggestion that handguns should be kept by shooting clubs. While there are some clubs which have the premises and the security which would enable them to keep their members' guns, a large number of clubs do not have any premises at all and are dependent on the Ministry of Defence or other owners for access to shooting ranges. Stirling Rifle and Pistol Club is one example. For such clubs the responsibility for safe storage would fall upon club officials who would have to use their homes. This would involve them accommodating a considerable number of guns, with attendant risks to safety and security. Where clubs have their own premises the concentration of a large number of guns in a single place, often in a remote location, would present an obvious target for organised theft. Upgrading the security of such premises would not necessarily discourage, and might even encourage, attack. In his evidence Mr Penn cited the case in about 1995 in which thieves carried out a highly organised raid on a pistol club in South West London in which they removed the clubhouse roof and used a crane to lift through it a safe weighing some 2.5 tonnes containing a large number of guns. Further, if handguns were kept at club premises or by club officials shooters would no longer be able to practice dry-firing at home.

9.68 It is clear from the evidence that it is common for shooters to travel to clubs or ranges other than their own in order to compete either in teams or as individuals. Where teams are shooting at other clubs or ranges it might be possible to provide some form of arrangements by which a gun was transported to and back from the other location without being in the possession of the individual shooter. But if an individual shooter was to compete elsewhere it appears that it would be necessary to release the handgun to him at some point. I noted that while the Dunblane Snowdrop Petition suggested that, on the basis that the private ownership of handguns should be made illegal and that all firearms held for recreational purposes for use at approved shooting clubs should be held there with the firing mechanisms removed, there should be a pass system to deal with cases where shooters wanted to attend organised shoots at other locations. According to that system, confirmation from the shoot organisers would need to be sent to the individual's club that he was booked on the shoot and payment had been received. A pass for the main body of the firearm would be issued to allow it to be transported to a fixed location. Pass details would include the travel-out date, period at other location and travel-back date as well as the serial number and description of the firearm. Any firearm not returned to the original club by the pass expiry date would be notified immediately to the police, and non-compliance with the authority given by the pass would lead to various possible sanctions. However, the position adopted by the BSSC was that "no matter what system of checks and paperwork is maintained in such circumstances, it would be a simple matter indeed for a shooter intent in recovering his guns to enter a competition, provide evidence to his club secretary that he had done so, recover possession of the complete gun together with ammunition for it, and perpetrate an outrage" and for this reason they regarded such a system as containing a fundamental flaw.

9.69 I noted that ACPO took the view that, despite the inherent risks, storage at the certificate holder's premises was still preferable, while the Police Superintendents' Association of England and Wales and ACOPS took a different view. It is pointed out in the Green Book (Part II, para 103) that an arrangement for the storage of firearms operates in Hong Kong where all handguns must be kept at shooting ranges or at gun dealers. This may, of course, be easier to arrange within a relatively small territory.

9.70 Many of the same points apply to the suggestion that handguns should require to be stored in a central location, such as the premises of dealers or at police stations.

9.71 While the police at present require dealers to comply with conditions as to security in connection with their registration under section 36 of the 1968 Act, it might well be that additional measures would be required if they were expected to look after the handguns of club members. In the case of many shooters access to a dealer's premises would be difficult. In any event it may be questioned whether any such responsibility should be imposed on dealers whether they like it or not.

9.72   The storage of handguns at police stations would raise similar problems in regard to the provision of secure accommodation and reasonable accessibility. It would also involve the police in what might well be thought to be an inappropriate role in being responsible for looking after shooters' handguns. This suggestion was not supported by ACPO or ACOPS.

9.73   The converse of the above is that the desired separation should be achieved by the ammunition being stored away from shooters' homes. I note that the White Paper of 1987 concluded (at para 29) that there were serious obstacles to such storage and recommended against it. It was pointed out that many clubs did not have secure facilities and that many serious competitive shooters loaded their own ammunition (ie centrefire ammunition) at home for reasons of economy. It was quite common for shooters to belong to several different clubs and to shoot at a number of ranges and it would be inconvenient and uneconomic for them to store ammunition at each of those premises or to buy a new supply each time they shot. Above all the Government felt that such an approach would be irresponsible in providing large and readily identifiable stores of ammunition which might attract the criminal or the terrorist.

9.74   In their final submissions the BSSC added to such objections. As regards rimfire cartridges, which were not reloaded at home, it might be possible for clubs to provide a reasonable range for purchase. However, a very significant number of shooters, including all serious competitive shooters, would be at a disadvantage as visitors to clubs where they could not count on being able to use the same batch as that for which their gun had been "zeroed". (A gun is "zeroed" when its sight is adjusted for the individual shooter and the ammunition which he is using so that if a known point of aim is taken the bullet should hit the centre of the target.) To have to "re-zero" the gun before starting the competition would be distracting and give an edge to the home team. As regards centrefire cartridges, there could be a similar problem due to variation in factory-made ammunition. Since there was a wider range of brands in the case of centrefire the club might not even be able to stock the same brand as that which the shooter was accustomed to using, let alone the same type and weight of bullet. In any event about 70% of shooters who shot competitively loaded their own ammunition at home according to their own specifications. Reloading in the club was not practicable where the club did not have any premises. In any event it raised questions of safety. Such an operation was best and safest done under conditions of privacy and without distraction. It might well not be practicable to provide a check to prevent shooters removing rounds from the club premises if they were of a mind to do so. Where clubs had no secure storage ammunition would require to be kept at the homes of club officials or elsewhere. This would raise further problems of security, accessibility and accounting.

9.75   I consider that the objections expressed by the Government in the White Paper in 1987 remain valid. As regards the additional points made by the BSSC, which were supported by Mr Penn, unsuitability or lack of club premises provide additional and important grounds for ruling out the suggestion that ammunition should be kept elsewhere than in the homes of shooters.

9.76   It is sufficient for me to say, without having to go further into the question of effectiveness, that I am not satisfied that the proposal for the separation of handguns from their ammunition, whichever method is adopted, is a practical proposition.

Restricting the capacity of multi-shot handguns

9.77   Evidence was given as to how to achieve *restriction to single shot*. Mr Paton and Mr Alexander W Dalgleish, a registered firearms dealer and gunsmith, gave evidence as to the practicability of this operation. They described a number of techniques which could be used in order to deal with pistols, depending on whether the magazine was detachable or integral. However, they considered that there was no method which would prevent a pistol from being re-converted with relative ease. Mr Paton added that the handling and in particular the loading of a pistol which had been converted to single shot might also be difficult, if not dangerous. The conversion of a revolver could be accomplished by blocking all but one of the chambers or by removing the dividing walls until only one complete chamber was left. Mr Paton said that the latter course was probably more secure against re-conversion but repeated firing in one chamber might create such stresses within the remaining sections as to make it a dangerous practice. Mr Dalgleish added that with the former method it would be necessary to ensure that the single chamber was strong enough as the welding could result in the annealing of the steel, even if it was carefully carried out. I consider that the permanent restriction of multi-shot handguns is impracticable and in any event it would in certain cases be ineffective.

9.78   Another approach is to consider *restricting the capacity of magazines* of self-loading pistols. Almost all pistols which are in private ownership and available for purchase have magazines which will hold a larger number of rounds than is required for a particular course of fire in competitions. Such a course commonly involves 5 or 6 rounds. As I mentioned earlier they may be used with magazines which hold up to 20 or more rounds. It would therefore be necessary to consider dealing with those already in use as well as those that may be sold in the future.

9.79   As regards those in use, the alternatives are confiscation or modification to a smaller capacity. One immediate problem is the fact that probably there are several hundred thousand in circulation. They do not have serial numbers. They are not recorded on firearm certificates. There is and has been no limit to the number which may be purchased at any time. Deactivated firearms are an additional source of them. The opportunities for evasion would be considerable. Mr Penn said that it would be possible to restrict the capacity of individual magazines by crimping their sides or inserting a pillar. However, neither method was irreversible. As regards new magazines, the fact that they were freely available on the continent of Europe meant that a shooter who was determined to acquire large-capacity magazines would have no difficulty in so doing.

9.80   However, all these considerations are subject to the important point, which I noted earlier, that it takes only a few seconds for a shooter to change a magazine. Thus reducing the capacity of magazines or making illegal the sale of magazines which were greater than a certain capacity would have little overall effect on the speed with which a large number of shots could be fired.

Temporarily disabling multi-shot handguns

9.81   With a view to making handguns less readily usable by their owners and potential thieves it was suggested that they should be temporarily disabled by the *removal of magazines*, where they were detachable, when the shooter left the club range. The magazines would be retained by club officials and restored to the owner when he next wanted to shoot. This would have the effect that for the time being the handguns would be inoperable, with the exception of those pistols which were so designed that the absence of the magazine did not prevent them being used as single shot pistols. The fact that a huge number of magazines are already in existence and unrecorded leaves ample scope for evasion even if new legislation required that magazines should be entered on firearm certificates. This would not be an effective method of restricting availability.

9.82   Another possibility which was canvassed was the *removal of the firing pins*. However, this is essentially unsuitable for routine dismantling. Removal can be technically difficult. In the case of pistols the pins consist of small pieces of machined metal. They are liable to fracture and replacements can be obtained without a firearm certificate. In the case of revolvers the pin is often an integral part of the hammer or may be riveted to it. Removal of the pin carries with it the risk of damaging the gun or losing a small component from the mechanism. A gun owner who was bent on mischief could keep a spare firing pin at home and, if he was technically confident, he could use it to reactivate his gun when he wanted.

9.83   I next consider the *removal of major components* of multi-shot handguns, and in particular the slides of pistols and the cylinders of revolvers. These components require the production of a firearm certificate for their replacement. This was advocated in a subsidiary submission by Mr Andrew Gibb, who represented the family of Mrs Mayor and members of the teaching staff of Dunblane Primary School, although his primary submission was in support of the Dunblane Snowdrop Petition.

9.84   Mr Paton and Mr Penn were in agreement that the generality of pistols were designed to be field stripped, ie broken down into separate components, for cleaning purposes; and that the generality of revolvers were capable of being easily dismantled. In each case the handgun would be rendered inoperable.

9.85   In his evidence Mr Paton explained that self-loading pistols were so designed that their dismantling did not require specialist assistance. In most cases this involved the removal of the slide assembly without the use of special tools. He demonstrated at the Inquiry how the removal of the slide on a 9 mm Browning pistol took 2 or 3 seconds. He said that the majority of pistols would not take much longer than that. The user who knew what he was doing would be able to dismantle a pistol. However, care had to be taken not to dislodge small parts lest they be lost. There would be no risk of degradation with repeated dismantling.

9.86   Mr Penn said that he agreed broadly with the evidence of Mr Paton. There were very few pistols which did not have a slide. One exception was the Luger .22 pistol which had a bolt instead of a slide. This pistol was not well designed for the easy removal of the bolt. It was a difficult operation but its repeated removal should not cause damage to the gun. Mr Penn pointed out that some pistols had the barrel permanently attached to the frame but the detaching of the slide would be sufficient to disable them. However, in the case particularly of many high precision .22 pistols the removal of the slide was not recommended unless the gun malfunctioned and required disassembly for cleaning. Repeated disassembly involved disruption of carefully tuned components and would very quickly impair the accuracy for which they were designed. Such pistols were not developed for military service and ease of dismantling played little if any part as a consideration in their design.

9.87   As regards revolvers Mr Paton demonstrated at the Inquiry that the cylinder in a solid frame revolver could be easily removed and replaced in a matter of seconds by withdrawing the axis pin and lifting out the cylinder. In the case of the "break action" revolver the operation was slightly more complicated and required the use of a screwdriver. The safety or accuracy of the revolver would not be affected if this was done regularly. Revolvers which had a "swing out" cylinder also required the removal of a screw, in this case a fairly small one.

9.88 As I have already said Mr Penn expressed general agreement with Mr Paton. However, he pointed out that some revolvers of the "break action" were not designed to allow easy removal of the cylinder. Small parts, especially springs, could easily be lost. The majority of revolvers in current production had a "swing out" cylinder which, together with the arm on which the cylinder rotated, could be removed by undoing a screw set in the frame although it was not intended (for reasons of maintaining accuracy and avoiding undue wear and tear) that such removal be at all frequent.

9.89 At this point I should add that in their final submission the BSSC drew my attention to evidence which was given to the Home Affairs Committee at its hearing on 8 May 1996 on the subject of the dismantling of "guns". At that hearing Mr Jim Sharples, Chief Constable of Merseyside Constabulary and President of ACPO said that, as he understood it, there could be problems with dismantling guns. They could be damaged very easily. A lot of those weapons were expensive and he thought that there were some practical difficulties with dismantling weapons and keeping different components in different places. Inspector Brian Tolley, Firearms and Explosives Officer with West Mercia Constabulary, agreed and said that it was not advisable to pull guns backwards and forwards. They wore, they became loose and it would cause a few serious problems with target weapons. They could become a danger by becoming loose and worn very quickly, other than the bolts from rifles which could be stored elsewhere. Chief Superintendent Brian Mackenzie agreed and said that he thought that it was easy to separate them from the ammunition (Q37-38).

9.90 Whatever may have been covered by the expression "guns" I can find no suggestion in the evidence of Mr Paton or Mr Penn that dismantling and re-assembling self-loading pistols and revolvers could give rise to danger. Neither was any suggestion of possible danger mentioned in the relevant part of the Green Book (Part II, paras 109-115). Mr Paton and Mr Penn are both highly experienced firearms experts and I fully accept their evidence. I do not have the slightest doubt that if Mr Penn had considered that there could be danger he would have said so. I do not overlook the fact that in his written statement Mr Terry McCarthy, who gave evidence about shooting clubs and competition disciplines, stated that while many guns could be dismantled into separate major components, there were also many guns constructed in such a way as to make separation into components difficult, if not impossible, for anyone except a skilled gunsmith. He added that constant disassembly/reassembly would have an adverse effect on the durability and accuracy of the firearm and could present serious safety hazards if not carried out with exemplary skill and care. The guns to which this comment refers were not further specified and it may be that his statement referred to single shot handguns, to which different considerations may apply. In any event I prefer the evidence of Mr Paton and Mr Penn.

9.91 However, Mr Penn went on to observe that if it was accepted that there should be circumstances in which a shooter should be allowed to recover the "missing" component and take it away so that he or she could compete elsewhere there would have to be a system by which club officials or other responsible persons would check that he or she had indeed entered into the competition in question. However, it would be a simple matter for a shooter who was planning to kill to use his or her entry into a competition as an excuse for reassembling the handgun and thus circumvent the checks. Thus a requirement for separate storage of component parts—without an absolute and effective ban on their removal from the place of storage, which could not be justified—would never prevent a scheming, cunning and premeditating killer such as Thomas Hamilton from acquiring the component he needed to fulfil his purpose. Such a person could acquire the necessary component from the stock of illegally held firearms or from abroad. In the latter connection he mentioned the obtaining of components in the United States, Finland and certain cantons in Switzerland.

9.92   In their Report the Home Affairs Committee dealt with the dismantling of weapons as follows:

> "Another possibility raised in evidence would be to ban the possession of assembled handguns at anywhere other than licensed premises (such as shooting ranges). Some parts of each firearm would have to be stored centrally, to prevent owners from re-assembling firearms illegally. This suggestion received little support. ACPO recognised that there was a danger of damage being done to weapons if they were to be constantly dismantled and re-assembled; weapons could become loose and worn, possibly becoming dangerous. Some types of firearm are almost impossible for anyone but a gunsmith or a very experienced owner to strip. Shooters would still carry assembled weapons when travelling to shoot elsewhere. We do not favour the proposal for possession of assembled handguns to be banned other than at licensed premises".

9.93   In the light of the evidence of Mr Paton and Mr Penn I am satisfied that the dismantling of self-loading pistols and revolvers would in general be practicable. The exceptions would be for those cases, which appear to be relatively few, in which the operation was either too difficult or would tend to impair the accuracy of the handgun. On the other hand, if shooters were still to retain the ability to use their handguns at other ranges, this would make it difficult to exclude all possibility of the misuse of the handgun by its owner.

9.94   Evidence was also given by Mr Paton about *fitting barrel blocks* which would fit and be locked within the barrels of self-loading pistols and revolvers. There was little doubt that it would be possible for them to be manufactured. Such blocks were already available for shot guns to prevent third parties using the gun. He had been unable to find anyone who manufactured blocks for pistols or revolvers but he was in no doubt that it would be simple for them to be made. One part of the device would fit into the chamber and the other into the front of the barrel with a locking device at the muzzle end. This would prevent ammunition from being placed in the chamber or fired. The design and tamper-resistance of such a device would be a matter of some importance. In addition there would require to be adequate provision of padding in order to limit any damage to the rifling inside the barrel which would impair the accuracy of the handgun.

The banning of the possession by individuals of multi-shot handguns

9.95   This is the course of action which is advocated by ACOPS in the form of a recommendation that "all multi-shot pistols be raised to the prohibited category", ie so that they would fall within section 5 of the 1968 Act. However, as Chief Constable Cameron explained in evidence, ACOPS envisaged that the Secretary of State would authorise such handguns to be possessed by shooting clubs where they would be stored. Both ACOPS and ACPO recommend that the handguns in respect of which firearm certificates may be granted for target shooting should be restricted to a single shot and to .22 calibre. The Police Federation of England and Wales advocate that the private possession of all handguns should be banned. It may be noted that the position of ACPO has changed since the hearing before the Home Affairs Committee on 8 May. At that time their position was that a prohibition on the licensed possession of hand guns was impracticable. Giving ACPO's views to the Committee Mr Sharples acknowledged that Great Britain featured in national/international, European and Olympic events and that the use of handguns in connection with that sporting interest was extensive. A complete ban of handguns would cause significant difficulties for a very substantial law-abiding element in the country who pursued quite proper sporting activities (Q19).

9.96   The practicability of such a measure was not questioned save in one respect. It was suggested that the EC Weapons Directive (91/447/EEC) would prevent the implementation of such a ban. This Directive provided for the partial harmonisation of Member States' domestic firearms controls in order to reach consistency in regard to minimum standards. However, it allows Member States to maintain or introduce domestic controls which are more stringent than those standards, provided that the European Commission and other Member States are advised accordingly. Thus, as I understand the position, the Directive does not prevent this country from introducing such a ban. The Directive is due to be reviewed by the European Commission by the end of 1997. This will provide an opportunity for the Government to put its case for altering any of the prohibitions which apply to all Member States if it sees a case for so doing.

9.97   As I have already indicated in the first part of the chapter it was questioned whether any restriction on the legal availability of firearms would be effective. It was suggested that the owners of handguns which were currently in lawful possession might avoid confiscation by causing them to "disappear". Examples of this phenomenon were drawn by some commentators from the past history of firearms control in this country and in Germany. Even if the withdrawal of lawfully held handguns was achieved, professional criminals and others who were bent on mischief could obtain illegal handguns. Further there was a risk that by process of "displacement" they might resort to the use of other types of firearm, such as shot guns, which were capable of delivering shots which were more devastating; or to other methods of destruction such as bombs. There was nothing to suggest that the banning of self-loading rifles under the 1988 Act (which had led to the confiscation of Thomas Hamilton's rifle) had prevented the happening of anything that was worse than occurred. The same points also apply to the proposal that the handguns in respect of which firearm certificates may be granted for target shooting should be restricted to .22 calibre.

9.98   None of these points can be dismissed from consideration. However given that lawfully held handguns are identified in firearm certificates, the opportunity for them to "disappear" is much less than if they were not identified at all. I have already rejected the contention that legally held firearms are of no significance in regard to the commission of crime; and expressed the view that the arguments in support of weapon substitution are overstated. I am not convinced that a restriction on the availability of handguns would actually lead to an increase in injury. I am satisfied that a ban on the possession of multi-shot handguns would have some effect on the incidence of serious crime.

The implications of restricting the availability of handguns

9.99   So far I have concentrated on the practicability and effectiveness of various measures. However, it is necessary now to consider the implications.

9.100   The various measures which stop short of a ban would obviously cause varying degrees of inconvenience to shooters. They would impose heavier responsibilities on club officials: and they would entail additional work on the part of the police. On the other hand the banning of handguns of one type or another would have very serious implications for the future of the sport of target shooting.

9.101   In his evidence Mr Penn said that restriction to single shot would rule British shooters out of serious competition in a wide range of international events. More importantly it would, he said, destroy the variety of shooting disciplines which required multi-shot pistols and provided the principal reason for the popularity of the sport. It would virtually eliminate pistol shooting in its present form in this country. As I understand the position, clubs own a certain number of handguns which are primarily intended for the use of those who are not yet ready to apply for a firearm certificate or who have no intention of applying for one. However, the sport of target shooting depends essentially on the activity of those who possess their own handguns under their own firearm certificates. As I have already noted Table 7 Annex A to the Green Book states that under 5% of licensed handguns are single shot pistols.

9.102   In their submission the BSSC emphasised that one of the principal attractions of target shooting, and the reasons for its continuing popularity, was the variety of competitions and the demands made on physical and mental fitness—variety and demands which have grown and developed as the handgun has evolved, particularly over the past 20 years or so.

9.103   By way of comparison, what would be the effect of banning of handguns with calibres greater than .22 but leaving .22 multi-shot handguns unaffected? Mr Penn said that this would have a very major effect on the sport. It would for practical purposes remove this country from international target shooting as a sport. It would substantially reduce the range of interests which were available to shooters, and in particular the challenge of improving accuracy which was a strong attraction. He accepted that there would still be many shooters who would go on with the sport. He envisaged that centrefire events might be redesigned for the use of .22 handguns. A combination of this ban with a restriction to single shot would have more or less the same effect. It may be noted that such a combination would affect all Olympic events for handguns except the Free Pistol, which, according to Mr Greenwood, is probably the least popular event in pistol shooting on account of the cost of the pistol and the demands of the event. The BSSC pointed out in their final submission that a ban on calibres greater than .22 would reduce the physical skills required in competition and therefore reduce both the attraction and level of achievement gained through practice and competition. In international competitions the number of events for centrefire pistols far outnumbered those for .22. Such a ban would involve the expropriation of some 50% or more of all handguns.

9.104   The expropriation of handguns would give rise to claims for compensation. Mr Paton provided evidence as to their cost. He stated that prices for new self-loading pistols ranged from £200 to £2,000 or more; with second-hand handguns ranging from £150 to £1,500 or more. The most common price range for both new and second-handguns was from £300 to £600. The cost of new revolvers ranged from £200 to £1,000 or more; with second-hand ranging from £100 to £500 or more. The average range for new and second-hand revolvers was between £150 and £500. By way of comparison, a single shot pistol ranged in price between £200 and £2,000 or more; and second-hand from £50 upwards. Due to the limited market for such guns it was not possible for him to estimate an average cost. It is also right to take account of the money invested in accessories such as optical sights, holsters, carrying boxes and security cabinets. In his submission Mr Colin Greenwood stated that in Great Britain the annual sales of ammunition and related accessories approached £20 m: and that a considerable number of jobs - such as in clubs, manufacturing and supplying, the gun trade and the work of gunsmiths - were dependent on pistol shooting.

9.105   It has been said that as a sport target shooting has a good record for safety. The evidence at the Inquiry did not give me any reason to doubt the accuracy of that claim, but what matters is what may be done with the guns when they are not being used in target shooting. I have no doubt that the great majority of those who participate in target shooting are law-abiding and sensible people who are highly committed to the sport and derive great satisfaction from what they do. Mr Penn and the BSSC set out what they maintained were the benefits of target shooting. In brief, they were that it was a very social sport; it was classless; did not discriminate according to gender; competition was on equal terms; physical disability was no barrier to success; it brought a sense of achievement and progress through improving scores and success in competitions; it developed mental skills, self-discipline and clear thinking; it developed physical skills and in particular manual dexterity and co-ordination; it offered both team and individual participation; it could be carried on indoors or outdoors; it instilled a disciplined sense of responsibility, particularly for safety; it provided a significant opportunity for distinction at national, international and Olympic levels; and it could provide a lifetime's enjoyment and challenge.

What should be done

9.106   I will now review what I have set out above. I am satisfied that of all the measures which stop short of a ban the one which is open to the least objection on the ground of practicability is the temporary dismantling of self-loading pistols and revolvers by the removal of major components (para 9.83-9.93). It has the merit that it does not require clubs to accommodate the handguns, with the various accommodation and security problems which I have already mentioned. In each case the component which is removed could be kept by a club official or on the club premises, where there was adequate space and security for the purpose, while the remainder of the handgun would be kept by the shooter at home. In exceptional cases it would not be practicable for some pistols and some revolvers. The exact extent to which that would be the case is a matter of detail. The solution to it, short of banning such handguns, would be to require barrel blocks of the type which Mr Paton envisaged (para 9.94). The barrel block would require to be fitted and locked to the satisfaction of a club official. He would keep the key while the shooter would keep the handgun in its blocked state until it was to be used again. Where the club had premises with adequate security to accommodate members' handguns, there would be no need for either of these expedients. If the shooter is to be able to shoot elsewhere there would be a limit on the effectiveness of such measures. However, a pass system of the type which, as I have explained in para 9.68, was outlined by the Dunblane Snowdrop Petition would be worthy of consideration. I appreciate all that has been said about what a calculating would-be killer could do but it does seem to me that such a system would effect a substantial reduction in the opportunity for misuse of lawfully held handguns.

9.107 A ban on multi-shot handguns on the other hand would be clear cut and would effect some reduction in the incidence of serious crime. However, the appalling result of the actions of Thomas Hamilton should not obscure the fact that such outrages are comparatively rare; and that the number of crimes which are committed by means of firearms which are or have been in lawful ownership is relatively small, especially so in the case of handguns. A ban on multi-shot handguns would to a very large extent destroy the sport of target shooting and have significant effects on the economy.

9.108 It is not enough to consider what would be practicable and effective. No assessment of what should be done would be complete without considering what would be proportionate and just, having regard on the one hand to the scale of risk and on the other the implications of one course of action or another.

9.109 It has seemed to me that if there was a case for restricting the availability of multi-shot handguns, as I have held there to be, it would be a proportionate and just result if a practicable and sufficiently effective way could be found to minimise the opportunity for such handguns to be used except on the ranges without in effect destroying the sport in the process. If such means could not be found, there would then be a case for banning them. That remains my view.

9.110 At this point I should observe that throughout the Inquiry the BSSC who acted as the umbrella body representing the interests of the shooting community at large were opposed in principle to any restriction on the availability of handguns; and objected not merely to the suggestion of one kind of ban or another but also, as I have explained above, to various measures which stopped short of a ban. This entrenched attitude meant that as each measure was supposedly discredited what was at stake became the greater. That has not, of course, prevented me from making my own assessment as to the merits of any particular measure but it did mean that so long as the principle of there being any restriction was in dispute there was no incentive for them to see how a measure less drastic than a ban could be made to work.

9.111 At the same time I am very conscious that proposals such as a ban on the possession of a certain type of firearm raise questions which are peculiarly within the province of the Government and Parliament to decide. Thus after the shootings at Hungerford in August 1987, the Government decided how far there should be, in the words of the White Paper, a shift in the balance of controls "between safeguarding the public at large and protecting the interests of the legitimate shooting community" (*Firearms Act 1968: Proposals for Reform, para 4.*) Michael Ryan had killed half of his victims with shots from a self-loading pistol and the fact that handguns posed particular dangers was recognised (*Green Book* Part II, para 11). However, the Government did not propose that handguns should be banned. The proposal of such a ban after the shootings at Dunblane once more raises a question of policy. It is necessary to decide what risk is acceptable, bearing in mind that some risk is an inevitable feature of daily life. Against the risk to society has to be balanced the loss of freedom of the individual and the other implications which I mentioned earlier (paras 9.100-9.105). There may also be competing claims on the use of resources. In the light of these points it is clear to me that in stating my own conclusions I should confine myself to what I recommend should be *considered*.

9.112 Following out the approach which I have explained I recommend that consideration should be given to restricting the availability of self-loading pistols and revolvers of any calibre which are held by individuals for target shooting. Preferably this should be done by their disablement while they are not in use, by either (i) the removal of the slide assembly/cylinder, which is to be kept securely on the premises of an approved club of which the owner is a member or by a club official: or (ii) the fitting of a locked barrel block by a club official. As I stated in para 9.106 where the club has premises with adequate security to accommodate members handguns there would be no need for either of these expedients. There would require to be a system which would enable the handguns to be used elsewhere for target shooting, but subject to the strictest controls which are practicable. I regard this as the preferable course having regard to the scale of risk, the practicability of disabling handguns and the extent to which such a system would be effective in reducing the opportunity for the misuse of such firearms.

9.113 If for any reason that course is not to be followed I see no alternative to considering the more draconian alternative of a ban on multi-shot handguns. However, in such circumstances I would suggest that the ban should be directed to the possession of such handguns by individual owners rather than the possession of handguns by shooting clubs, since it is through possession by individuals that the risk, in so far as there is a risk, of homicide or serious injury arises. Thus I do not consider that the banning of handguns for target shooting or the banning of shooting clubs would be justified. I have no particular recommendation as to the legislative means by which effect would be given to such a ban.

Other matters

9.114 Before leaving this chapter I should make some reference to a number of other matters on which I was invited to make recommendations but have not done so.

9.115 During the course of the Inquiry there was some controversy as to the status and acceptability of hollow-point ammunition which is commonly used in target shooting in Great Britain. The object of such a bullet is to maximise the transmission of energy to achieve "stopping power" and minimise over-penetration. As part of his evidence to the Inquiry Mr Penn explained that it was undesirable in police or self-defence use that a bullet should exit from its target, or exit with any significant residual energy, since this placed innocent third parties at risk. It was also desirable that bullets that miss their intended targets should penetrate wood, brick, etc fully so that risks to third parties were reduced. As I recorded in chapter 3 of this report this type of ammunition formed part of what Thomas Hamilton brought with him to the school. On balance I am not satisfied that I should make any recommendation in regard to the availability of such ammunition.

9.116 Some of those who presented submissions to the Inquiry sought to have me entertain a large number of proposals relating to firearms which had no connection with the circumstances which were my concern. It may be of some assistance if I give a brief summary of the main ones which I have declined to entertain. It should, of course, not be taken as indicating that I formed any view adverse to them.

9.117 As regards weapons I was invited to recommend the prohibition of the sale of deactivated weapons; and in any event the further tightening of the specification for deactivation. I was asked to enter into the question of whether certain weapons should be classed as "carbines"; and to recommend a restriction in the scope of the expression "antiques". I was also asked to recommend the prohibition of the sale of replica firearms; and restrictions on the advertising and sale of firearms by mail order.

9.118   As regards the certification regime I was asked to recommend, on the one hand, that there should be a single type of certificate for all firearms; and, on the other hand, that there should be different types of certificate for different users. It was also suggested that there should be separate certificates for each firearm and for the ammunition. As regards shot guns it was proposed that "good reason" should require to be shown; and that multiple ownership should be discouraged. In regard to the use of firearms for shooting over land it was proposed that there should be a means of restricting the number of persons who were authorised to do so. It was also proposed that the minimum age for the possession of firearms should be raised; and that young shooters should be subject to a greater degree of supervision.

9.119   There are two matters which I have not so far mentioned. They caused me some concern and, while they do not properly arise out of the circumstances of the Inquiry, I would like to draw particular attention to them. The first relates to the dangers posed by the use of air weapons at large, along with the question of whether they should be subject to certification and unavailable until a later age than at present. The second relates to the fact that at present the components for reloading ammunition may be obtained without production of a firearm certificate. In that connection it was suggested, with a view to preventing the reloading of ammunition for illegal purposes, that the purchase of primers and propellants should be subject to the production of a firearm certificate by the purchaser. There was widespread agreement in the written and oral evidence before the Inquiry that the current position was anomalous when compared with the requirement to produce a firearm certificate for the purchase of factory-made ammunition, and that this loophole should be closed by legislation. I make no recommendation on these matters but would draw them to the attention of the Home Office and The Scottish Office.

Chapter 10   School Security

Introduction

10.1   This chapter is concerned with the safety of staff and pupils in schools, and in particular with their protection against violence. It is written primarily from a Scottish standpoint. In some cases violence may take the form of an attack by an unauthorised intruder, such as Thomas Hamilton. In other cases a person who has gained access to the school on some basis, such as being a parent or having some work to perform, becomes violent when he is there. Not all attacks are premeditated. Some might arise spontaneously, when the aggressor is, for example, under the influence of drink or drugs, suffers from some form of mental instability or simply loses self-control in an excess of anger.

10.2   The subject of violence to staff, and in particular staff in the education sector, has attracted a significant amount of interest in the last 10 years. I would refer in particular to the report *Preventing Violence to Staff* by B Pointer and C Warne of the Tavistock Institute of Human Relations which was published by the Health and Safety Executive (HSE) in 1988 and the guidance contained in *Violence to Staff in the Education Sector* which was prepared by the Education Service Advisory Committee (ESAC) and published by the Health and Safety Commission (HSC) in 1990. The ESAC advises the HSC on the health and safety at work of employees in the education sector and on the protection of pupils, students and others on directly related hazards arising from work activities. The ESAC's working definition of violence is: "Any incident in which an employee is abused, threatened or assaulted by a student, pupil or member of the public in circumstances arising out of the course of his or her employment". I am also aware of the work of the Suzy Lamplugh Trust which includes a comprehensive guide to personal safety for education staff.

10.3   There has been a clear recognition of the potential dangers to pupils arising from the state of school premises, machinery and equipment and from the processes and substances which are used in the course of school work. It is also recognised that there should be arrangements for security to prevent unauthorised access to the school. However, so far as I have been able to determine, there has been little, if any, published guidance on tackling the dangers which an unauthorised intruder could pose to the school population at large, and in particular its pupils.

10.4   It is, of course, possible for action to be taken against intruders by the police and the criminal justice system. In the report of the Working Group on School Security which was presented to the DfEE in May 1996 reference was made to certain statutory offences in England and Wales (para 7); and in its commentary The Scottish Office Education and Industry Department mentioned the equivalent powers in Scotland. No doubt the existence and use of the law will have some deterrent effect. However, in this chapter I am concentrating on a proactive approach to the subject.

Factors for consideration

10.5   It is understandable that in the aftermath of what happened at Dunblane Primary School there should be calls for additional measures to protect the school population, either in the form of physical alterations to schools or an increase in the extent to which access to them is supervised. However, it is plain that schools vary greatly across the country in regard to their nature, size, layout and age. What would be appropriate for an inner city school of 700 pupils would be unlikely to be suitable for an isolated rural school. Some older schools may be housed in accommodation originally designed for a different purpose. Some schools may operate on split sites. Some methods of opening locked doors could be operated by older children but would be impracticable for younger or disabled children.

10.6   The protection of the school population needs to be carefully distinguished from the related problem of providing protection to school buildings and equipment which may be at risk of vandalism, theft or fire-raising. Some measures may be of greater significance for the latter than for the former. In allocating scarce resources it is necessary to be clear as to the object of what is proposed and the value of what it can achieve.

10.7   In considering any particular measure it is clearly necessary to consider not merely whether and to what extent it would be practicable and effective but also whether it would be acceptable. The point has often been made that schools should be welcoming places. Many schools represent a community facility, receiving adults for evening classes and recreation. It would be unacceptable to carry measures to the point where schools were turned into fortresses. At some point a balance has to be struck.

10.8   Whatever measures are to be taken it is unrealistic to expect that the risk of a violent intruder gaining access to a school can be eliminated. All that can be done is to take whatever measures are reasonably practicable.

Protection from violence through the management of safety

10.9   I am in no doubt that a solution to the problem of protection should be tackled through the application of sound principles of safety management.

10.10   The principal legal basis for the responsibility for the protection of staff against violence which they encounter in the course of their work lies in section 2 of the Health and Safety at Work Act 1974, under which every employer has "to ensure, so far as is reasonably practicable, the health, safety and welfare at work of all his employees". This duty is not confined to the physical working environment but covers also the provision of information, training and supervision. Subsection (3) of section 2 supports the main provision by imposing a duty to prepare and issue a statement of policy and the organisation and arrangements for carrying it out.

10.11   At the same time every employer has a duty under section 3 "to conduct his undertaking in such a way as to ensure, so far is reasonably practicable, that persons not in his employment who may be affected thereby are not exposed to risk to their health and safety".

10.12 Section 4(2) of the Act also imposes a similar duty on every person who has to any extent control of premises in connection with his carrying on an undertaking, the means of access thereto or egress therefrom or of any plant or substance in such premises.

10.13 I do not intend to embark on an exposition of how the duties imposed under the health and safety legislation should be complied with or to attempt to improve on the guidance which the HSE and the ESAC have issued from time to time in their various publications relating to statements of policy or successful health and safety management. However, I propose to highlight a number of aspects which appear to me to be pertinent to the subject of this chapter in the light of the evidence which I heard.

Legal responsibility 10.14 Firstly, it is important that there should be no misunderstanding as to the persons on whom the legal responsibility for safety, and hence the responsibility for seeing that action is taken, lies. An employer may delegate the performance of various functions to others but he cannot delegate his responsibility under the Act. Thus, purely by way of example, recent decisions have shown that employers cannot avoid their duty under section 3 by pointing to the extent to which they have delegated their functions to an independent contractor or by showing that senior management were not involved in the breach *(R v Associated Octel Co Ltd* [1994] IRLR 540; and *R v British Steel plc* [1995] ICR587).

10.15 In Scotland the employer in regard to schools is the local authority, except in the case of self-governing schools where the employer is the board of management: and in the case of independent schools where it is the proprietor. In England and Wales the position in regard to legal responsibility is different.

Functions 10.16 Secondly, it is important that there should be no uncertainty as to the allocation of health and safety functions. I would draw particular attention to the advice about the organisation for safety which is set out in paras 10-14 of *Safety Policies in the Education Sector,*(revised 1994) which was prepared by the ESAC. This includes the point that key personnel in the line management structure should be identified and their health and safety roles clearly defined. I mention this aspect particularly in view of the fact Mr G D Jeyes, Director of Education for Stirling Council, who attended as a witness in regard to school security and who spoke of the desirability of making risk assessments, appeared to be unsure as to whether the 1974 Act applied to schools.

Safeguarding against violence 10.17 Thirdly, the duty which an employer of teaching staff has under section 3 plainly covers the safeguarding of pupils against violence associated with the running of the school. The expression "risk" in section 3 conveys simply the idea of the possibility of danger *(R v Board of Trustees of the Science Museum* [1993] I WLR 1171); and there can be no doubt that an attack by an intruder is a possibility, as the events at Dunblane Primary School and other schools in this country have demonstrated. This is not an aspect of health and safety which has been specifically recognised in the past, at least in the case of some education authorities. Mr B W Pill, Health and Safety Adviser to Stirling Council, and formerly to Central Regional Council, frankly accepted that in the formulation of the safety policy for the Regional Council the idea that anyone might enter school premises to commit assault "never crossed our minds". However, he accepted that intruders would now require to be considered.

Preventive strategy　10.18　Fourthly, the existence of that risk calls for the working out of a preventive strategy, at the heart of which is risk assessment. Such an assessment is implicit in the test of reasonable practicability, by means of which those who have duties under the 1974 Act can demonstrate that they have fulfilled their responsibilities. However, it came to be explicitly required by the Management of Health and Safety at Work Regulations 1992, which provide by regulation 3(1):

> "Every employer shall make a suitable and sufficient assessment of:
>
> (a) the risks to the health and safety of his employees to which they are exposed whilst they are at work; and
>
> (b) the risks to the health and safety of persons not in his employment arising out of or in connection with the conduct by him of his undertaking,
>
> for the purposes of identifying the measures which he needs to take to comply with the requirements and prohibitions imposed upon him by or under the relevant statutory provisions".

For this purpose previous incidents, which should be recorded in a systematic fashion, may on analysis yield useful information in identifying and evaluating risk. However, the exercise of assessment covers any significant risk whether or not it has yet been realised. To assist the employer in undertaking the measures he needs to take to comply with the requirements and prohibitions imposed upon him, regulation 6 requires him to appoint one or more "competent persons". On the basis of the risk assessment and its regular review decisions have to be made as to what should be given priority, which of a number of alternative courses should be adopted and how the effectiveness of these measures should be monitored.

Individual schools　10.19　Fifthly, the differences between individual schools indicate that each is likely to pose its own particular set of strengths and weaknesses; and that the assessment of risk should take account of each situation. If a blanket approach to the installation of measures is adopted this may involve unnecessary or inappropriate expenditure. If, on the other hand, each school is left to proceed with what it can do in a piecemeal fashion this may lead to a risk being overlooked or under-appreciated. What seems to me to be needed is a safety strategy and action plan for each school which would be based on a risk assessment relating to its particular features.

Possible measures

10.20　What approach should be adopted in the action plan for a particular school and what measures the plan should include must, of course, depend upon the particular case. However, I will set out an outline of the main points which were put to me in the helpful submissions which I received. At the risk of being thought to be providing a glimpse of the obvious I will consider the protection of the school population in two phases, first, restricting or regulating access to the school; and second, dealing with emergencies within the school.

Access to the school　10.21　It may be of value to consider whether the school should have one or more than one line of defence. Should the first line of defence be the boundary which defines the grounds of the school. Should attention be given to walls, fences or gates? Should steps be taken in other ways to restrict public access to or through the grounds?

10.22 Next, turning to the playground, should it be lit in the evenings and in winter? Are there any special risks associated with outlying buildings, courtyards or the school car park? Is there a need for surveillance by closed circuit television?

10.23 As regards the means of entry to the school buildings, there may be scope for restricting access by reducing the number of doors or by modifying them. However, that may have to be balanced against a number of other factors. Should some subsidiary doors be altered so as to operate as fire doors, opening outwards only? Should there be some form of special entry system? Should this require locks which can be operated by means of a code? Or should it be an entryphone system, which may involve additional manning? Is some form of surveillance of the entry points required? Each of these methods may involve significant drawbacks, such as presenting a forbidding aspect or creating difficulty for children to understand and use. Should any of the windows be modified so as to prevent them being used as a means of entry?

10.24 Taking next the reception of those who visit the school, should parents and others be required to give advance notice of their intention to visit? Should some form of surveillance be installed at subsidiary points of entry? Are the signs in the school adequate to provide clear directions to a reception point? What staff, such as a janitor or a secretary, should be on hand to speak to those entering the school? What training should they have for dealing with aggressive visitors? What backup should they have? Should there be a system whereby all visitors sign in and sign out? Should there be badges to indicate who are members of staff and who are visitors?

Dealing with emergencies 10.25 Let me suppose a situation in which some untoward incident is imminent or is already in progress. The object will be to contain and defuse the situation on the one hand; and on the other make sure that staff have immediate support and can call for assistance. The first points to the need for staff to receive regular training in dealing with aggression, acquiring knowledge of security procedures and equipment and in general cultivating a sense of safety awareness. The latter involves a consideration of physical measures which will depend very much on the school layout. It may be appropriate to consider panic buttons or telephones, especially in regard to outlying buildings. Personal alarms for teachers may be required. Closed circuit television may be of some assistance but if it is to help in averting or minimising the effect of incidents it will require to be monitored. Pupils can be encouraged to play their part by being alert to the presence of strangers and aware of security and evacuation procedures.

Further guidance

10.26 I have noted that the ESAC is updating its guidance in regard to violence to staff in the education sector. It would, in my view, be of significant assistance to the efforts of those with legal responsibilities in that sector if that guidance could be extended to encompass the safety and protection of the school population as a whole, particularly in view of the problems which this presents in reconciling conflicting objectives and in striking the right balance in the use of limited resources.

10.27 The safety of the school population should be a consideration during the designing of new school buildings and significant alterations to existing buildings, when the opportunity can be taken to apply lessons derived from the weaknesses of the past. I note that according to paragraph 19 of the Report of the Working Group on School Security, to which I referred above, that *Crime Prevention in Schools: Practical Guidance* which was published by the Department of Education and Science in 1987 is due to be replaced by the DfEE in the coming year. Since The Scottish Office Education and Industry Department has generally withdrawn from the practice of issuing guidance to local authorities on matters relating to school buildings there are no plans in Scotland for the issuing of separate guidance equivalent to what the DfEE produce. However, I understand that The Scottish Office Education and Industry Department intends to draw the DfEE's guidance on school security to the attention of education authorities and any other relevant interests in Scotland.

Chapter 11   The Vetting and Supervision of Adults Working with Children and Young People

Introduction

11.1   This chapter is concerned with the means of protecting children and young people who attend clubs or other groups against abuse by leaders or others who have regular contact with them; and in particular with the steps which can and should be taken to vet such persons and to supervise their conduct. I will be considering this subject from a Scottish standpoint, but I will require for certain purposes to refer to practice in England and Wales.

11.2   The evidence in the Inquiry showed the relative ease with which Thomas Hamilton over many years was able to open a succession of clubs in a number of local authority areas despite persistent complaints and concerns about his behaviour. There was no system in general use for the vetting of persons who operated such clubs or for monitoring their conduct. No doubt such systems could be introduced for dealing with the premises of local authorities. During the course of his evidence Mr G D Jeyes, Director of Education of Stirling Council, spoke to the adoption of vetting procedures by the Community Committee of the Council on 8 May 1996. However, this does not achieve the dissemination of information about those persons who are regarded as potentially unsuitable, nor does it deal with those who use premises other than those owned by a local authority.

11.3   The opportunities which adults have for coming into direct contact with children and young people in clubs or other groups are very many. The form of contact can vary from activities where a group of adults are involved, such as in the Scouts or Guides, to cases where a single adult may be involved with a single child, eg in personal tuition. It can range from well-regulated statutory relationships, such as those between teachers and pupils, to informal activities which may be based on personal friendship or family contacts. Membership of a club or group may be free of charge or in return for payment. The payment could be a small subscription to cover costs or a fee which would also provide a return. The adults may or may not be personally known to the parents. The venue for club activities may be a public building, a private building or simply somewhere out of doors. The activities cover arts, music and drama tuition as well as coaching and training in a variety of sports and practical skills.

11.4   At present there is nothing to prevent an individual declaring himself or herself a "youth leader", renting premises and starting a youth club or some other similar kind of activity for children over 8 years of age.

11.5   The number of those involved in working with children and young people on a paid or voluntary basis is very large. According to The Scottish Office paper of June 1996 on the recruitment and supervision of adults, between 70,000 and 100,000 adults are associated with recognised voluntary youth organisations, which number around 11,000. In addition, there may be the same number of adults involved with young people outwith the ambit of recognised youth work organisations; and many volunteers working within organisations concerned with child care, such as befrienders, home visitors and playgroup workers. There is also an unknown number of individuals working alone outwith any organisation, often in very informal arrangements. A youth club may be set up on a trial basis, either to explore the demand for such an activity, meet a short-term need or for the individual to assess his or her aptitude to undertake youth work. Such clubs may continue, become affiliated to a larger organisation or simply cease to operate. Another situation is where a parent or interested individual assists in the absence of a recognised leader.

Existing controls and advice

11.6   In general the existing levels of control are greatest in the case of statutory bodies; and with organisations working with the youngest children, as I will explain in the following three paragraphs.

11.7   It is common practice for statutory bodies to require references at the time of recruitment and to ensure that they are of the right kind. A check with the Scottish Criminal Records Office (SCRO) is mandatory in the case of a person who applies for admission to the register held by the General Teaching Council for Scotland. Statutory bodies which are involved in the provision of health, social work and educational services may require an SCRO check in the case of a wide range of posts, depending on the access which the applicant would have to children. Such a check would include any convictions which are "spent" for the purposes of the Rehabilitation of Offenders Act 1974. In England and Wales employers in the statutory sector may, depending on the policy of the particular police force, obtain additional information about offenders from local police records.

11.8   In addition local authorities hold lists of those who have been struck off the register of the General Teaching Council and of those who have been banned from employment as teachers in England and Wales (the latter being referred to as list 99 of the DfEE).

11.9   Voluntary organisations which provide "day care" (which includes "supervised activity") for children under 8 years of age for 2 hours or more in a day and on more than 6 days in any one year have to register and be inspected under Part X of the Children's Act 1989, which applies to Scotland, England and Wales. In connection with this legislation local authorities require two references and may require an SCRO check to be made. There is a current proposal to amend the legislation to exclude "supervised activities", the prime purpose of which is to develop skills rather than provide care; and to extend the exemption for occasional day care facilities from 6 days to 60 days in any one year.

11.10   There appear to be greater controls within large well-organised voluntary organisations than within small voluntary or private organisations. Many of the former adopt practices which are in line with the advice contained in the code of practice *Protecting Children* which was produced by Volunteer Development Scotland. The aim of this code of practice is to encourage voluntary organisations to make the protection of children from physical, sexual and emotional abuse an integral part of their policy and practice. To that end the recommendations in the code are directed essentially to three matters: (i) procedures for the selection of suitable staff and volunteers, including using references, interviewing all applicants as to their experience of working or contact with children, asking all applicants about any conviction for criminal offences against children and making appointments conditional on the successful completion of a probationary period; (ii) the arrangement of work and supervision to prevent opportunities for abuse; and (iii) the use of definite procedures for dealing with complaints or suspicions of abuse, including a system whereby children may talk to an independent person. At present there is, of course, no means by which the use of an excellent code such as this can be made a condition of the operation of a voluntary organisation. For some organisations these arrangements might be considered to represent an onerous burden. The more informal or infrequent a club the less likely it is to have the structure to implement such a code. The less "professional" a group the less likely it is to have a person who would be experienced in vetting or interviewing.

11.11 The recommendations in the code of practice to which I referred in the previous paragraph includes the advice that voluntary organisations should obtain at least one reference from a person who has experience of the applicant's work with children, whether paid or voluntary. This is in accordance with normal good practice. At present voluntary organisations in Scotland do not have direct access to the SCRO, although some have access to information informally through their local police force or more formally through local authorities for which they are providing services. Organisations are not encouraged to request applicants to obtain details of any record which is held in respect of them by the SCRO.

11.12 It has been proposed in the consultation document *On the Record in Scotland*, which was issued by the Home Department of The Scottish Office in June 1996, that the existing arrangements for access to the SCRO should be extended to, *inter alia*, voluntary bodies in respect of employees, trainees and volunteers whose duties involve regular contact with children. It is proposed that each organisation which wishes to obtain such a check would require to register with the SCRO, agree to abide by a code of practice to preserve confidentiality, and indemnify the police and the SCRO against any civil action arising from the use to which the information may be put. It is also pointed out that in order to avoid the SCRO being overwhelmed by requests for registration, it may be necessary to set a threshold of a minimum estimated number of checks per year below which an organisation would not be able to secure direct access. However, it would be open to smaller organisations to group together, perhaps using existing trade or professional associations, or to link with a larger organisation in order to meet the necessary conditions.

11.13 It may also be noted that in England but not in Scotland, the Department of Health provides a pre-employment consultancy service for social work authorities and voluntary organisations. According to The Scottish Office paper of June 1996 this service consists of a list which, apart from including the DfEE's list 99, notes the convictions of those who at the time of conviction were in child care work; and the names of persons formerly in such work who have been dismissed, or have resigned or been moved to other work, or left in circumstances which suggest that the safety or welfare of children was, or may have been, put at risk. A similar service is available in Northern Ireland through the Department of Health and Social Services. The effectiveness of this type of check is dependent on the provision of information by organisations to a specially qualified information bureau.

Is there a need for further measures?

11.14 Having considered the very wide field with which I started I propose to concentrate on situations in which children and young people under 16 years of age voluntarily attend clubs or groups for their recreation, education or development. I distinguish the cases in which they have no choice, such as the requirement to attend school, since in such cases there are well-developed systems for the scrutiny of those who have children and young persons under their charge.

11.15 I consider that it is preferable to take an approach which is directed to safeguarding children from the attentions of unsuitable people rather than to create additional offences to deal with problems after they have occurred.

11.16 It could be maintained that it is sufficient to leave each club or group to regulate itself, adopting whatever practice it chooses to limit the potential for abuse. Thus parents would have to assure themselves that the club or group was run on satisfactory lines and that there was no reason for them to think that the leaders or those who had unsupervised access to their children were unsuitable for the work.

11.17 However, if it is to be left to individual clubs or groups to carry out their own checks and to adopt whatever practice they please there would be no system for ensuring, or at any rate obtaining assurance, that the checks were adequate or that the practice was sufficient for the protection of those who attend their activities.

11.18 Further, it may be said that parents are not always in a position to make adequate enquiry into the way in which clubs or groups are run or their personnel are checked. Parents sometimes have to take a great deal on trust; and it is reasonable that they should be assured that the clubs or groups which their children attend have shown that they provide an adequate degree of protection against abuse. The children's safety is paramount.

11.19 The information which can be provided by the SCRO gives details of convictions and enables the enquirer to determine whether there is anything which makes the applicant obviously unsuitable. Such a check would reveal any offences committed against children and to this extent the SCRO record fulfils the role of a paedophile register. However, as I have already indicated, smaller organisations may face difficulties in obtaining access to this source of information. Apart from anything else, they may not be in a position to give an indemnity. In any event the interpretation of the information may create problems for them. Even if the SCRO check reveals nothing of significance it does not follow that there is no risk of abuse. It is common for a child abuser to have offended many times before he is detected. While the SCRO check provides information not only about convictions but also about pending cases it does not extend to other intelligence. In the case of Thomas Hamilton it would have revealed nothing, whereas the experience of the Scout Association with him was sufficient for them to "blacklist" him. These considerations point to the desirability of finding a means of assembling information which would alert any legitimate enquirer as to information about a person's past behaviour which indicates his potential unsuitability.

11.20 As matters stand there is no system for co-ordinating information between different areas of the country about persons regarded as potentially unsuitable for work with children and young people.

A new system

11.21 These considerations indicate, in my view, that a system should be instituted to ensure that clubs and groups which are voluntarily attended by children and young people for their recreation, education or development use adequate checks on the suitability of the leaders and workers who have substantial unsupervised access to them.

11.22 It is essential that if there is to be such a system it should avoid a bureaucratic approach and should be relatively easy for clubs and groups to work with, and for parents and others to understand and rely upon.

11.23 If there should be such a system, should it be directed to the scrutiny of the clubs or groups *or* to those who lead or work in them? Should the system be one for compulsory registration or for voluntary accreditation?

11.24 I do not consider that it would be practicable to have a system for the compulsory registration of leaders and workers in clubs and groups. This would involve a substantial overlap with the systems which larger voluntary organisations already operate. It would pose difficulties of defining which individuals were affected by the requirement to register, especially those whose services were given on an informal or occasional basis. There would be a risk of creating a bureaucratic system which would deter many from volunteering their assistance and which would not provide benefits commensurate with the considerable cost involved. It would be possible for someone who was minded to evade the system to do so.

11.25 A system for the voluntary accreditation of leaders and workers would not have all the drawbacks which I have mentioned in the last paragraph. However, it would still involve difficulty in determining the persons to whom the system was directed, having regard to the great variety of access to children and young people which occurs in one kind of activity or another. Further and more importantly, it would achieve only the accreditation of certain individuals. Parents might still know little more than the fact that one or more employee or volunteer was accredited. The system would not do anything to ensure that the club or group as a whole was run in such a way as to have adequate procedures for vetting or training recruits or for dealing with workers about whom there might be doubts.

11.26 I turn next to the compulsory registration of all clubs and groups. If all of them were required to be registered as a condition of being able to operate, there would again be a difficulty in defining the clubs or groups in such a way as to exclude informal or occasional arrangements. In the case of the latter parents should be able to determine whether the person who is providing the service is suitable or not and so there is far less need for such a system.

11.27 It might be possible to place some definite limit on the requirement to register which would be designed to cut out such cases. One example would be to restrict the requirement to cases in which payment was made. If the payment required to be a fee this would be unduly restrictive. It would also cause problems in determining whether a particular payment was a fee. In any event the mere fact that activities are provided at no charge or on an "at cost" basis does not mean there is no case for a protective system. Another possibility would be to exclude clubs or groups which had fewer than a certain number of members. However, it would be difficult to devise a figure which would be appropriate to a wide range of activities. Fluctuation in numbers would cause difficulties in applying the requirement. Further it could be said that the smaller the club or group the greater are the chances of a child finding himself or herself alone with an adult and hence potentially at risk. The task of detecting evasion in the case of such a system would be labour-intensive and expensive.

11.28   It is understandable that it should be thought that the greatest need for some independent system for protecting children and young people exists where parents are not in a position to keep an eye on the conduct of the activity, eg where their children are offered the opportunity of camping or attending residential courses away from home; or where club leaders are not personally known to them. No doubt this approach would seek to draw a clear line between what parents should be responsible for and what calls for independent assistance. However, it does not seem to me that such distinctions can be turned into a workable method of defining when a legal requirement does or does not apply.

11.29   These considerations lead me to put aside the option that there should be compulsory registration, and to turn to the option for voluntary accreditation. This would have the advantage of being much more flexible and certainly simpler to administer. In determining what required to be demonstrated in order to obtain accreditation the body could adapt its approach according to what was appropriate in the case of different types of clubs or groups.

An accrediting body

11.30   What should be the main functions of the body to which clubs or groups would be accredited? Should the body be a national or a local one?

11.31   Firstly, the body would have, in my view, the responsibility for drawing up or selecting guidelines for the recruitment, training and monitoring of leaders and workers who have substantial unsupervised access to children and young persons, with a view to minimising the risk of abuse. It would seek to collect information as to the best practice. For the larger organisations a code of practice at least consistent with the level of protection provided by *Protecting Children* would be appropriate. For smaller organisations or special types of activities different sets of guidelines would probably be required.

11.32   Secondly, the body would have a discretion to decide whether or not an individual club or group should be accredited to it. This would depend on whether it had suitable arrangements, including a code of practice, to enable adequate and appropriate checks to be carried out in recruiting and monitoring leaders and workers; and had proper arrangements for the reporting and investigation of any suspected abuse.

11.33   The checks which might require to be made could include checks on professional qualifications and affiliations, a check with the SCRO and other checks in order to exclude unsuitable characters.

11.34   As regards the SCRO it would, I consider, be for the body to determine how far, and at what stage in the recruitment process, such a check was necessary in regard to different types of club or group activity. I have already indicated that smaller organisations might have difficulty in obtaining or using information from such a check. In such cases it would be appropriate for the SCRO check to be commissioned by the body itself.

11.35   In the case of organisations which have relatively few leaders—such as clubs of the type run by Thomas Hamilton—it could prove difficult for them to demonstrate that an adequate and independent check had been carried out. For such cases it would be advantageous, if not essential, for the body to supervise the carrying out of the appropriate checks.

11.36   Thirdly, it would also be desirable if the body was able to collect accurate information in regard to any matter which might reflect on a person's suitability as a leader or worker with children and young persons. One of the difficulties which was illustrated by the evidence in the Inquiry was that information about Thomas Hamilton was not readily or fully available in a new area to which he had turned his attentions. If the information about Thomas Hamilton which was known to certain organisations had been available to such a body, other organisations could have been quickly alerted to be on their guard against him. The role which in England is fulfilled by the Department of Health or in Northern Ireland by the Department of Health and Social Services may provide a suitable model for such a function. It would be desirable that not only accredited clubs and groups provide such information but that "non-members" should be encouraged to do so. Great care would, of course, require to be taken in order to ensure that the information which was recorded was accurate. Whether and to what extent the information would be released to a "member" club or group official who enquired about a particular applicant or worker would depend upon what he needed to know. Special arrangements could be made for enquiries by representatives of statutory organisations.

11.37   Fourthly, such a body would also be expected to monitor the conduct of clubs and groups which were accredited, in order to see whether their performance matched the statement of practice. Where there was a significant failure the removal of accreditation could follow.

11.38   The system which I have described would, of course, require to be publicised in such a way that the identity and work of the body was well known, that clubs and groups had an incentive to become accredited, and that parents would be able to find out which clubs and groups were accredited and would have confidence in the reliability of the system. The owners of premises which might be used by clubs or groups, such as local authorities, would be encouraged to make accreditation a condition of any let.

11.39   The functions of the body and the need for its work to be well known clearly indicate that what is required is a national body. It is true that a local authority is readily accessible to parents. However, in the case of organisations which operate nationally or in several local authority areas there would be undesirable duplication if registration had to take place in every local authority area in which they were active. Further, the fragmentation of responsibility among a large number of bodies would make it difficult to achieve the collection of information about potentially unsuitable persons to which I referred in paragraph 11.36.

11.40 As regards the nature and structure of the body I have given some consideration as to whether it should be a private or public body of one kind or another. However, I have decided that I should not make a recommendation as to any particular type of body lest this inhibit consideration of the possible alternatives which are worthy of discussion.

11.41 It may assist, however, if I give an indication of a number of factors which I consider to be of importance and which may be significant in putting my earlier recommendations into effect.

11.42 The governing board of the body should reflect the width of all the interests which are relevant among the voluntary, private or charitable organisations which may seek accreditation, whether their interests lie in the field of recreation, education or general development of children or young persons. This is so as to ensure that the new body has the widest appeal to potential "members". For this purpose some form of consultation on appointments to the board would seem very desirable.

11.43 I do not see any reason why the work of the body should not be self-financing through the charges which it makes on its "members". However, it is obviously very important that charges are kept within the limits of what organisations can afford. There is a case for the Secretary of State being given the power, after due investigation, to supersede the level of charges which otherwise would have been made; and if appropriate, to pay grant-in-aid towards any shortfall arising from the reduction in charges.

11.44 While the body should, as I have already indicated, be responsible for ensuring that its standards for accreditation reflect the best practice, it is for consideration that the Secretary of State should have the right to require it to review these standards; and, in the event of the body's performance being unsatisfactory, have the right to commission that work from another source.

11.45 The body should publish an annual report giving not merely financial information but also details as to its standards and its procedures for dealing with applications and the monitoring of accredited clubs and groups, together with a statement of its objectives and a description of its past performance relative to previous objectives.

11.46 One consideration which underlies the last four paragraphs is that while the body would not be operating a compulsory system, it would be in effect occupying a monopoly situation. It is accordingly right that provision should be made for its public accountability. I leave it to the Secretary of State to determine how and when the new system should be established, as well as the exact details of its functions.

Training

11.47 A number of the submissions which I have considered have supported the development of professional courses for those who wish to lead in children's clubs. I agree with this. Consideration should be given to the development by SCOTVEC, the work of which will be taken over by the Scottish Qualifications Authority, of a Scottish Vocational Qualification on working with children, which would cover the organisation of clubs and child development and protection.

Children's Act 1989

11.48   I was invited in a number of submissions to express a view in regard to the proposals for altering the present scope of the requirement for registration. Since I have not recommended a system for compulsory registration, let alone an extension of the type of system for which the 1989 Act provides, I have not thought it necessary or appropriate to make any recommendation either way in regard to these proposals.

Chapter 12   Summary of Recommendations

In this chapter I will set out a summary of the recommendations which I have made in Chapters 8-11. Each recommendation in the summary is followed by a reference to the paragraph or paragraphs to which it is directly related and which provide further detail.

The certification system relating to section 1 firearms

The police   1. Officers carrying out enquiries should be supplied in advance with full information about any known change of circumstances and any reason for exercising particular caution (para 8.9).

2. The use of checklists by enquiry officers is endorsed, subject to the need for them to be alert to and report anything which could be relevant to the suitability of the applicant or certificate holder (paras 8.10-8.11).

3. Enquiry officers should be given as much training and guidance for their work as is practicable (para 8.13).

4. The power of search with warrant under section 46 of the Firearms Act 1968 should be extended to cases in which there is reasonable ground for suspecting that there is a substantial risk to the safety of the public; and to include in such cases the power to seize and detain any firearm certificate which may be found (para 8.15).

5. The power of search with warrant under section 46 of the Firearms act 1968 should be extended to any civilian licensing and enquiry officer who is authorised in writing for that purpose by the Chief Constable (para 8.15).

6. The powers enjoyed by police officers to inspect dealers' registers and premises and approved clubs should be extended to civilian licensing and enquiry officers who are authorised in writing for that purpose by the Chief Constable (para 8.16).

7. The steps being taken to enable police forces to hold and exchange information on computer as to the individuals who hold firearm certificates, and those whose firearm applications have been refused or certificates revoked are endorsed (para 8.23).

Good reason   8. The Guidance to the Police should advise that good reason implies intention; and that lack of past use *prima facie* indicates the lack of it (para 8.30).

9. Section 30(1) of the Firearms Act 1968 should be amended so as to provide for -

> the revocation of a firearm certificate on the ground that the chief officer of police is satisfied that the holder does not have a good reason for having in

his possession, or for purchasing or acquiring, the firearm or ammunition in respect of which the certificate is held; and for partial revocation; and

in the case of the revocation of a firearm certificate in respect of the ammunition to which it relates, the power to substitute different quantities (paras 8.31-8.33).

10. Each club which is approved for the purposes of section 15 of the Firearms (Amendment) Act 1988 should be required to maintain a register of the attendance of its members who are holders of firearm certificates, together with details as to the firearms which they used and the competitions in which they participated when they attended (para 8.42).

11. Every holder of a firearm certificate should be required to be a member of at least one approved club; and the firearm certificate should specify the approved club or clubs of which he or she is a member and the firearms which he or she intends to use in each of them (para 8.44).

12. Each approved club should be required to inform the police when a holder of a firearm certificate has ceased to be a member of the club for whatever reason (para 8.50).

13. Each approved club should be required to inform the police when a member who is the holder of a firearm certificate has not attended a meeting of the club for a period of a year (para 8.51).

14. The proposal that each club should appoint a person to act as a liaison officer with the police is endorsed (para 8.52).

15. Explicit statutory provision should be made for the laying down of criteria for the approval of clubs for the purpose of section 15 of the Firearms (Amendment) Act 1988 (para 8.53).

Suitability 16. The language of section 30(1) of the Firearms Act 1968 should be brought into full correspondence with that of section 27(1); and each revised in order to achieve a logical and consistent arrangement (paras 8.62 and 8.65).

17. Section 27(1) of the Firearms Act 1968 should include as one of the conditions on which the granting or renewal of a firearm certificate is dependent that the chief officer of police is satisfied that the applicant is fit to be entrusted with the firearm and ammunition to which the application relates (para 8.63).

18. It is desirable that the Guidance to the Police should contain advice as to the scope of "fitness" to be entrusted with a firearm and ammunition (para 8.64).

19. Each approved club should be required to inform the police of the receipt of an application for membership; and the outcome of the application (para 8.71).

20. Each applicant for membership of an approved club should be required to state whether or not he or she has submitted any prior application for a firearm certificate or a shot gun certificate which has been refused; and whether he or she has previously held such a certificate which has been revoked (para 8.73).

21. The current requirement for a counter-signatory of a firearm application should be abolished; and replaced by a system for the provision of two references (para 8.81).

22. The proposal by the Association of Police Surgeons for the provision by the applicant's medical practitioner of information as to the applicant's medical history and its consideration by a forensic medical examiner should be the subject of consultation with the interested bodies (para 8.90).

Decisions and appeals   23. Consideration should be given to the reform of the scope for appeal against decisions of the chief officer of police by restricting it to enumerated grounds which do not trench on the exercise of his discretion (para 8.119).

The availability of section 1 firearms

24. Consideration should be given to restricting the availability of self-loading pistols and revolvers of any calibre which are held by individuals for use in target shooting

preferably, by their disablement, while they are not in use, by either (i) the removal of the slide assembly/cylinder, which is to be kept securely on the premises of an approved club of which the owner is a member or by a club official; or (ii) the fitting of a locked barrel block by a club official (para 9.112);

or, if such a system is not adopted, by the banning of the possession of such handguns by individual owners (para 9.113).

School security

25. Those who have the legal responsibility for the health and safety of the teaching staff and pupils at school should prepare a safety strategy for the protection of the school population against violence, together with an action plan for implementing and monitoring the effectiveness of safety measures appropriate to the particular school (para 10.19).

26. It is desirable that the guidance provided by the Education Service Advisory Committee in regard to violence to staff in the education sector should be extended to encompass the safety and protection of the school population as a whole (para 10.26).

The vetting and supervision of adults working with children and young people

27. There should be a system for the accreditation to a national body of clubs and groups voluntarily attended by children and young persons under 16 years of age for their recreation, education or development, the main purpose of which would be to ensure that there are adequate checks on the suitability of the leaders and workers who have substantial unsupervised access to them (paras 11.21 and 11.29-11.39).

28. Consideration should be given to the development of a Scottish Vocational Qualification in respect of work with children, including the organisation of clubs and child development and protection (para 11.47).

Appendix 1 List of Parties and their Representatives

The Lord Advocate, the Right Honourable the Lord Mackay of Drumadoon

> The Lord Advocate; Iain Bonomy, QC; Jonathan Lake, Advocate

The families of the deceased children, the injured children, those absent from class on 13 March 1996, Mrs Eileen Harrild and Mrs Mary Blake

> C M Campbell, QC; Laura J Dunlop, Advocate; Levy & McRae, Solicitors, Glasgow

The family of Mrs Gwen Mayor and 29 members of the teaching staff of Dunblane Primary School (23 being members of the Educational Institute of Scotland; 6 being members of the Professional Teachers Association)

> Andrew T F Gibb, Solicitor, Balfour & Manson, Edinburgh

Stirling Council

> M S Jones, QC; Simpson & Marwick, WS, Edinburgh

Central Scotland Police

> James A Taylor, Solicitor Advocate, McGrigor Donald, Glasgow

†Mr Ronald G Taylor, Headteacher, Dunblane Primary School

> Martin S Stephen, Solicitor, Wright, Johnston & Mackenzie, Glasgow

‡Lothian and Borders Police and the Scottish Police Federation

> A R Hardie, QC, Dean of the Faculty of Advocates; Hughes Dowdall, Solicitors, Glasgow

In addition the following were permitted to make oral closing submissions:–

> *C N McEachran, QC* on behalf of The Scottish Target Shooting Federation

> *T B Cruickshank,* Solicitor, George Mathers & Co, Aberdeen on behalf of Stirling Rifle and Pistol Club, Callander Rifle and Pistol Club and their office-bearers and members.

> *M Scoggins*, Solicitor, Davies Arnold Cooper, London on behalf of the British Shooting Sports Council; together with the British Association for Shooting and Conservation, British Field Sports Society, Clay Pigeon Shooting Association, Gun Trade Association, Muzzle Loaders Association of Great Britain, National Pistol Association, National Rifle Association, National Small-Bore Rifle Association, The Shooting Sports Trust and United Kingdom Practical Shooting Association.

Notes:
The symbol † denotes that representation was only in relation to the events of 13 March 1996.
The symbol ‡ denotes that representation was permitted as and when the Tribunal deemed it to be appropriate.

Appendix 2   List of Witnesses

Adamson	John	Former Chief Superintendent
Aland	Margaret	Social Worker, formerly of Central Regional Council
Allan	Robert	Retired Chief Superintendent
* Allston	Roger P C	Acquaintance of Thomas Hamilton
* Anderson	Anne	Police Constable
Anderson	Derek	Police Constable, Lothian and Borders Police
Anderson	Ewen	Former Dunblane Boys Club Committee Member
Anderson	George	Telephone Engineer
Anderson	John	Detective Chief Inspector
Anderson	Katherine	Former Dunblane Boys Club Committee Member
* Anonymous		Former Boys Club Member
* Anonymous		Parent of Boys Club Member
* Anonymous		Parent of Boys Club Member
* Anonymous		Former Boys Club Member
Awlson	Agnes R	Assistant Head Teacher, Dunblane Primary School
Baird	John	Consultant Forensic Psychiatrist
Ball	Robert	Former Central Regional Councillor
Barker	Thomas	Deputy Director, Junior Police Training, Scottish Police College, Tulliallan
Baxter	George	Head of Centre, Woodmill High School, Dunfermline
Baxter	Michael	Forensic Scientist
Beattie	Dr Jack	Consultant Paediatrician
Bell	Lesley	Former Police Constable
Bell	Nigel K	Gun Club Member
Bennett	Graham	Deputy Chief Constable, Fife Constabulary
Binning	Iain	Police Inspector
* Blake	Mary	Schools Supervisory Assistant, Dunblane Primary School
Boal	Ian	Former Boys Club Assistant
Brown	John	Police Constable
Busuttil	Prof Anthony	Forensic Pathologist
Butterwick	Margaret	Journalist
Cameron	Roy	Chief Constable, Dumfries & Galloway Constabulary
Campbell	Robert O	JP
Campbell	William P	Competition Secretary, Stirling Rifle & Pistol Club
Capes	Graham	Acting Detective Constable
Cardle	James	Retired Procurator Fiscal, Dumbarton

Carrol	Paul	Police Constable, Lothian and Borders Police
Carruthers	Bruce	Former Boys Club Member
Carson	Archibald	Police Sergeant, Lothian and Borders Police
Carter	Patricia	Head Teacher, Bannockburn Primary School
Cassidy	Allan	Retired Police Inspector
Chisholm	Malcolm R	Scenes of Crime/Ballistics Officer, Tayside Police Force
Cobb	David	Former Depute Director of Admin and Legal Services, Central Regional Council
Cole	William	Shooting Club Member
Collie	Ian	Former Director of Education, Central Regional Council
Connell	Steven	Police Constable
Cooke	Prof David J	Clinical Psychologist
Cowan	Donald	Police Sergeant
Crawford	Gordon S	Secretary, Stirling Rifle and Pistol Club
Cullen	Francis	Former Shop Assistant
Dalgleish	Alexander W	Firearms Dealer and Gunsmith
Davies	Hugh D	Former President, Association of Police Surgeons
Deuchars	Robert C H	Former Scout District Commissioner
Dewar	Scott T	Police Computer Service Manager
Dickson	Allan	Area Community Education Officer, formerly of Strathclyde Regional Council
Drummond	William	Police Constable
Fairgrieve	Brian D	Former Scout County Commissioner
Fernie	Sandra L	Administration Assistant, Scout H.Q.
Fisher	Austin	Police Sergeant
Forsyth	Rt Hon Michael	Member of Parliament for Stirling
Gall	Charles	Journalist
Gallagher	William	Former Depute Procurator Fiscal, Stirling
Gardiner	James	Former Youth and Community Officer, Central Regional Council
Gillespie	James H	Acquaintance of Thomas Hamilton
Gillies	Karen J	Van Hire Receptionist
Goldie	Edward	Police Constable
Gordon	Frank A	Shop Owner
Gould	David J	Army Officer
Gouther	Robert	ScotRail Employee
Gunn	George	Police Constable
Hagger	Doreen	Mother of Boys Club Member
Haire	Leslie C G	Ambulance Technician
* Hamilton	Douglas	Detective Constable
* Hamilton	James	Adoptive father of Thomas Hamilton
Hanley	Dr Robert I	Thomas Hamilton's General Practitioner
Harrild	Eileen	Teacher
Holden	Joseph	Police Superintendent
Houston	William	Staff Development/Training Officer Stirling Council
Hughes	Paul	Chief Inspector
Hyde	Gary	Firearms Shop Manager
Isles	Ronald	Detective Constable
Jackson	Joseph	Retired Detective Superintendent, Strathclyde Police

Jeffrey	Allan A	Librarian
Jeffrey	Douglas	Senior Youth Education Worker, formerly of Lothian Regional Council
Jeyes	Gordon	Director of Education, Stirling Council
Johnston	Maureen	Firearms Certificate Disposal Officer, Central Scotland Police
Jones	David P	Parent of Boys Club Member
Keenan	Ann	Former Police Officer
Keenan	James	Police Superintendent
Kelly	Alistair	Former Reporter to Children's Panel, Fife Regional Council
Kindness	James	Retired Detective Sergeant
Kirkpatrick	Fiona	Police Constable
Lawless	Andrew	Detective Sergeant
Lister	James	Police Constable, Strathclyde Police
Loudon	Colin	Former Boys Club Member
Lynch	Douglas	Police Sergeant, Lothian and Borders Police
Lynch	Norman	Police Firearms Examiner, Central Scotland Police
McArthur	Duncan	Retired Police Officer, Lothian and Borders Police
McBain	Ian	Detective Inspector, Strathclyde Police
McCarthy	Terry	Hon Secretary, Scottish Pistol Association
McDiarmid	Ian	Police Photographer/Fingerprint Officer
MacDonald	David	Former Boys Club Member
McDonald	Garry	Former Boys Club Member
MacDonald	William J	Retired Police Officer
McFarlane	William	Former Police Constable
McGrane	Edward	Police Sergeant, Lothian and Borders Police
McGregor	Duncan G	Assistant Safety Officer formerly of Central Regional Council
Mack	Thomas A	Former Scout Leader
MacKenzie	Alastair	Police Constable, Lothian and Borders Police
MacKenzie	Ian	Former Superintendent
McLean	Kenneth	Police Sergeant
McMillan	Robert	Police Sergeant, Lothian and Borders Police
McMurdo	Douglas	Former Deputy Chief Constable
McNally	Sandra	Parent of Boys Club Member
Marshall	James	Chief Inspector
Martin	Isobel	Primary School Head Teacher
Matchett	George	Chief Superintendent
Mather	Colin	Chief Inspector
Mercer	Ronald	Community Centre Caretaker
Mill	Michael	Retired Police Officer
Millar	John	Retired Detective Superintendent
Mitchell	Charles	Detective Constable
Moffat	Allan	Detective Sergeant
Moffat	James	Chief Superintendent
Moffat	John	Gun Club Member
Moir	Robert	Acting Inspector
Morris	Arthur	Chairman, Scottish Council of B.M.A.
Morton	Heather	Neighbour of Thomas Hamilton
Neil	Janet	Sports Shop Manageress
Nimmo	Eileen	Retired Inspector

Nolan	David	Detective Sergeant
Ogg	John	Detective Chief Superintendent
Ogilvie	Grace J	Neighbour of Thomas Hamilton
Ovenstone	Susan	Journalist
Paterson	Hugh	Retired Police Officer
Paton	Alastair	Firearms Expert, Retired Inspector, Strathclyde Police
Pearson	Robert	Police Constable
Penman	Derek R	Detective Sergeant
Penn	David J	Chairman, Technical and Research Committee, British Shooting Sports Council
Perry	John	Former Assistant Director of Education, Lothian Regional Council
Pill	Brian W	Health and Safety Adviser, Stirling Council
Plain	David	Detective Constable
Ralph	Douglas	Police Inspector
Rattray	Lance	Retired Chief Superintendent
Reid	Raymond	Secretary, Callander Rifle and Pistol Club
Reilly	Janet	Acquaintance of Doreen Hagger
Renton	Janice	Deputy Commissioner for Local Administration
Rice	John W	Police Constable, Lothian and Borders Police
Richardson	James	Deputy Chief Constable, Strathclyde Police
Robertson	Alexander	Detective Chief Inspector
Robertson	George I McN	Parent of Boys Club Member
Ross	Callum	Police Constable, Lothian and Borders Police
Ross-Watt	Ranald	Parent of Boys Club Member
Roy	Malcolm	Police Sergeant, formerly Criminal Intelligence Officer
* Shaw	James R	Former Boys Club Member
Shelmerdine	David J C	Chief Executive, Scottish Scout Council
Smith	George	President, Stirling Rifle and Pistol Club
Smith	Michael F	Consultant Neurologist
Smith	Paul R	Former Boys Club Assistant
Somerville	David	Former Assistant Director of Education, Fife Regional Council
Speirs	Robert	Sports Shop Manager
Staden	George	Director of London Armoury Co Ltd
Sutherland	Sheila	Friend of Agnes Watt
Tavadia	Dr Hosie	Consultant Pathologist
Taylor	Gordon	Detective Sergeant
Taylor	Ronald G	Head Teacher, Dunblane Primary School
Thomson	William	Former Boys Club Assistant
Togneri	Robert J	Retired School Teacher
Ure	Robert M	Neighbour of Thomas Hamilton
Valentine	George	Head Teacher, St Francis Primary School, Falkirk
* Vannet	Alfred D	Regional Procurator Fiscal, Grampian Highland & Islands
Vass	John D R	Former Scout District Commissioner
Watt	Agnes G	Natural Mother of Thomas Hamilton
Watt	Elizabeth	Former Member of Parent Teachers Association, Alva Primary School
Williams	James	Parent of Boys Club Member
Wilson	John S B	Retired Police Officer

155

Wisdom	William S	Retired Chief Inspector
Wood	Jeffrey C	Gun Club Member
Woolhead	Donald P	Police Sergeant

Note: The symbol * denotes that all or part of the evidence of these witnesses was read to the Tribunal.

All police officers are or were members of Central Scotland Police unless otherwise stated.

Appendix 3   Discussion relating to decisions taken by Procurators Fiscal

On 24 June 1996 (day 19) Mr Bonomy on behalf of the Lord Advocate made a statement of the Lord Advocate's position in relation to that evidence and to the question of enquiring into decisions taken by Procurators Fiscal. The statement was in the following terms:

> It is a fundamental principle that prosecution decisions are taken independently of Government and that prosecutors, who act in a quasi-judicial capacity, are accountable for their decisions only to the Lord Advocate. The principle applies throughout the United Kingdom. It is recognised in the establishment of the Parliamentary Commissioner for Administration, or Ombudsman, and of House of Commons Select Committees.
>
> Accordingly, the prosecuting departments and matters relating to the commencement or conduct of criminal proceedings are not subject to investigation by the Parliamentary Commissioner for Administration, in terms of Sections 4 and 5 and Schedules 2 and 3, Paragraph 6 to the Parliamentary Commissioner Act, 1967.
>
> Similarly, the scrutiny of the Lord Advocate's Departments by the Select Committee of the House of Commons on Scottish Affairs specifically excludes "consideration of individual cases", in terms of a House of Commons Standing Order.
>
> The rationale for the principle is the importance of finality and fairness to a potential accused, to victims and to witnesses.
>
> The principle was clearly stated by Lord Justice General Clyde in *McBain v. Crichton* 1961 JC 25, 29: "The basic principle of our system of criminal administration in Scotland is to submit the question of whether there is to be a public prosecution to the impartial and skilled investigation of the Lord Advocate and his department, and the decision whether or not to prosecute is exclusively within his discretion". His Lordship went on "It is utterly inconsistent with such a system that the Courts should examine, as it was suggested that it would be proper or competent for us to do, the reasons which have affected the Lord Advocate in deciding how to exercise his discretion, and it would be still more absurd for this Court to proceed to review that soundness".
>
> The principle does not prevent an examination of the conduct of prosecutors. In the "Meehan" Inquiry Lord Hunter was able to examine the actions of prosecutors, although his remit excluded both firstly "the guilt or innocence of Mr. Patrick Meehan or Mr. Ian Waddell of the charges contained in the respective indictments against them", and secondly "the reasons for and justification of any decision taken by the Lord Advocate whether or not to institute, or concur in, any criminal proceedings".
>
> Equally, the Report of the Inquiry into an Allegation of a Conspiracy to Pervert the Course of Justice in Scotland by Messrs. W.A. Nimmo Smith, Q.C., and J.D. Friel made it clear that, although they had been instructed to

investigate whether decisions were taken by prosecutors for improper reasons, "there can be no question of our reporting on prosecution decisions in such a way as would facilitate public debate about their correctness".

The principle was reflected in the establishment and operation of the Waters Tribunal of Inquiry, the last Tribunal of Inquiry to be held in Scotland, in 1959. In that case there was a motion before the House of Commons that a Select Committee should inquire into the case of John Waters and advise, *inter alia*, in what circumstances it was decided that no prosecution should be instituted. The Government of the day brought forward a motion for appointment of a Tribunal of Inquiry into, *inter alia*, the action taken by Caithness Police. In explaining why it was inappropriate to examine the decisions of the prosecutor, the then Prime Minister, Mr. Harold McMillan, stated:

"It is an established principle of Government in this country, and a tradition long supported by all political parties, that the decision as to whether any citizen should be prosecuted, or whether any prosecution should be discontinued, should be a matter where a public as opposed to a private prosecution is concerned, for the prosecuting authorities to decide on the merits of the case without political or other pressure.

"It would be a most dangerous deviation from this sound principle if a prosecution were to be instituted or abandoned as a result of political pressure or popular clamour. In this case, my Right Hon and Learned Friend the Lord Advocate decided, after considering the evidence before him, that criminal proceedings would not be justified.

"In reaching his decisions the Lord Advocate's duty in Scotland, like the Attorney-General's in England, is to act in a quasi-judicial capacity, whether the person involved is a public functionary or a private citizen". That is a quotation from Hansard (HC Deb, 16 February 1959, col. 31).

Finally, in the North Wales Child Abuse Inquiry, which was announced in Parliament on 17th June, 1996, the terms of reference, which are very specific, include examination of "the response of the relevant authorities and agencies to allegations and complaints of abuse made either by children in care, children formerly in care or any other persons, excluding scrutiny of decisions whether to prosecute named individuals". That is a quotation from the Hansard report of the debate (HC Deb, 17 June 1996, col. 522).

Although the considerations underlying the principle against subjecting to critical scrutiny prosecution decisions apply most obviously to the interests of potential accused persons, they also affect victims and witnesses. Prosecutors are required to make judgements on their credibility and on the weight to attach to individual pieces of their evidence. Prosecutors are also entitled to take account of other information placed before them, which may be confidential. There are also related considerations applying to the integrity of the decision-making process itself. If decisions on criminal cases are not taken privately, without the pressure of public scrutiny and on the basis of an independent assessment of the quality of evidence and credibility of witnesses, prosecutors could be inhibited from taking difficult decisions, which they must take in the exercise of an independent discretion.

The Lord Advocate has considered the exceptional circumstances of this case, including the death of Thomas Hamilton, who was the principal subject of reports to the Procurators Fiscal. He has also borne in mind the fact that other persons named in these reports, as suspects, victims and witnesses, are still alive.

In the exceptional circumstances which apply, the Lord Advocate has concluded that it is entirely appropriate that evidence should be put before the Inquiry as to the investigation of the individual cases and that it was appropriate that the actual police reports—which would normally be wholly confidential to the Crown—should be made available to the Tribunal. He has also concluded that it is appropriate that the Tribunal should have a detailed account of the inquiries made by the relevant Procurators Fiscal.

He has considered that, in the exceptional circumstances of this case, it is also appropriate that the reasons for the decisions taken by Procurators Fiscal should be placed before the Tribunal, so that it is as fully informed as possible as to the facts surrounding Hamilton.

After Lord Cullen had been appointed to conduct the Inquiry, the Lord Advocate arranged for an independent senior member of the Procurator Fiscal Service—Mr. Alfred Vannet, the Regional Procurator Fiscal for Grampian, Highlands and Islands—to examine all the relevant case papers and to interview the members of the Procurator Fiscal Service who were responsible for taking decisions in the cases. Mr. Vannet has never worked in the Procurators Fiscal's Offices at Dumbarton and Stirling. Mr. Vannet had no prior involvement in any of the cases. He has produced a full review, which he has completed under the direction of Crown Counsel, setting out in detail the history of the dealings of members of the Procurator Fiscal Service with these cases and including the reasons for the decisions which were taken.

The Lord Advocate considers that presentation of this report to the Tribunal should enable the Tribunal to have a full account of the history of these cases and the reasons why decisions were taken.

The Lord Advocate trusts that Mr. Vannet's account will be sufficiently complete for the Tribunal's purposes. If the Tribunal so wishes, the individual members or former members of the Procurators Fiscal Service who dealt with enquiries concerning Hamilton are available as witnesses as to the facts set out in Mr. Vannet's review. It would, however, be incompatible with principle and the practice to which detailed reference has been made for the Tribunal to subject the soundness of the decisions made in relation to Hamilton to detailed examination in evidence or submissions at the Inquiry. For that reason the Lord Advocate's position is that evidence should not extend, so far as decisions are concerned, beyond informing the Tribunal what decisions were taken and what the stated reasons for these decisions were.

The Lord Advocate trusts that the Tribunal and parties appearing before it will understand and respect the position which he has adopted in the exceptional circumstances to enable the Inquiry to have a detailed account of the involvement of members of the Procurators Fiscal Service with Thomas Hamilton.

I gave the parties the opportunity to consider this statement along with Mr Vannet's report before hearing any submissions from them. On 25 June (day 20) I heard submissions from Mr Campbell and Mr Bonomy.

Mr Campbell accepted that in the exercise of his quasi-judicial role as public prosecutor the Lord Advocate should not be subject to political pressure. However, he was accountable to Parliament where his acts and omissions were open to scrutiny and comment. The rule that his decision-making should not be subject to outside pressure did not apply where a prosecution was not pending or underway. Mr Campbell pointed out that in regard to prosecutions the Lord Advocate and Procurators Fiscal enjoyed certain immunities *(Hester v MacDonald* 1961 SC 370; and Sec 170 of the Criminal Procedure (Scotland) Act 1995).

Mr Campbell's submission was that there should be no inhibition either in his submissions or in the Tribunal's report in regard to any criticism of the decisions taken by the Procurators Fiscal. As regards calling them as witnesses he was neutral and left this to the Tribunal to decide. In the present case the Crown had led evidence of fact which raised questions as to the soundness of the decisions. While he was not able to assert that there was no good justification for them there was no logic in denial of an opportunity to consider the merits of those decisions.

Cases which had been concerned with the question whether the High Court of Justiciary should exceptionally authorise a private prosecution did not demonstrate that the Lord Advocate could not be called upon to explain the reasons for the decisions taken on his behalf or that the merits of those decisions could not be scrutinised. In *J & P Coats Ltd v Brown* 1909 SC(J) 29 the Court embarked on a consideration of the merits of the case or at least the merits of whether or not there should be a prosecution. A distinction was drawn between matters of law and the review or re-examination of evidence. There would be very few cases in which the exercise of discretion would be interfered with. The passages in the opinion of Lord Justice–General Clyde in *McBain v Crichton* on which the Lord Advocate had founded were *obiter* in view of the fact that the complainer failed to show that he had a sufficient interest in the alleged wrong to sustain a prosecution. In any event they did not entail that there could be no comment on the decision itself. Any question of unfairness was outweighed by the public interest. In *Meehan v Inglis* 1975 JC 9 the distinction was again drawn between the application of judgement to all sources of evidence and questions of law or relevancy.

These cases did not deal with comment on past events. In any event they demonstrated a reluctance to embark on an examination of the decision-making process as opposed to an examination of the decision itself.

Mr Bonomy submitted that there was no justification for, on the one hand, refraining from interfering with a decision of the Procurators Fiscal while, on the other hand, engaging in a critical examination of that decision. The result of infringing the principle that the decision should not be open to review would be that every decision would be made under the threat that a decision-maker would be called upon to account.

The Court had observed a clear distinction between the question whether authority should be granted to bring a private prosecution and an investigation of the public prosecutor's decision and what lay behind it. The principle set out in *McBain v Crichton* applied also in the present case. According to that principle the Court refused to examine the reasons given by the Lord Advocate for the decision in question. However, if there were no reasons or if the stated reasons did not *ex facie* justify the decision, the Court was not prevented from making its own judgement in regard to the law and the relevancy of any charge (see *Meehan v Inglis* at page 14). There was no question of the Court ever stating that the Lord Advocate had erred in some way in the exercise of his discretion.

Mr Bonomy accepted that the relevancy of a charge was an area in which the Tribunal could properly be invited to make a decision, assuming there was sufficient available evidence on which to do so. It was one thing to say that a relevant charge could have been brought. It was another thing to submit that a charge should have been brought.

In the exceptional circumstances of the present case the Lord Advocate had presented material which was normally confidential. It was open to the Tribunal to assess what the substance of the available evidence amounted to, as opposed to reviewing the decisions which had been taken.

After the conclusion of these submissions I gave my decision in the following terms:

> Can I say first of all that I am most grateful to counsel for their very clear submissions to me in regard to the problem which has arisen at this comparatively late stage in the Inquiry.
>
> In considering the dispute which arises today, it seems to me that in the background there are two main considerations. The first is the consideration that in exercising his independent quasi-judicial role the Lord Advocate should not be subject to pressure or influence from outside sources. The *locus classicus* for that rule can be found in the speech of the Prime Minister, Harold McMillan, in the passage to which I was referred.
>
> Mr. Campbell has submitted to me, however, that this is not a case in which that arises, because we are not considering here a case in which a decision has not yet been taken or a case in which a decision is still open to re-consideration, nor are we dealing with pending proceedings.
>
> The second consideration which seems to arise is the question of confidentiality. It is I think well settled that information which becomes available to the prosecutor in the course of the performance of his work is and should remain normally confidential to him. That is referred to in the statement made by the Lord Advocate at the foot of page three, where he says "Prosecutors are required to make judgements on their credibility and on the weight to attach to individual pieces of their evidence. Prosecutors are also entitled to take account of other information placed before them, which may be confidential", and so on.
>
> Now, in this particular case Mr. Campbell did not seek to have the inward thinking of the prosecutors explored in this case, no doubt for perfectly good reasons. His submission was that he should be entitled to make comment on the decisions not to prosecute or in the case of one of the Procurators Fiscal the decision not to grant a warrant.
>
> Now, Mr. Campbell drew my attention to a number of cases dealing with those very special circumstances in which the Supreme Court has decided whether or not to allow a private prosecution to proceed; and he pointed out that in these cases the Court was able to reach its own view as to whether prosecutions should take place, in order to secure that justice was carried out. By implication I think he was suggesting that this was a comment on the Lord Advocate's decision to decline to prosecute. On the other hand, Mr. Bonomy has pointed out that in cases of that sort, while it was expected that the Lord Advocate should explain his reasons, he was not required to do so, and he pointed out that there was no question in these cases of the Court seeking to usurp the position of a prosecutor by reviewing his decision. He

accepted on the other hand that it would be open to the Court, and certainly open in this case, to consider what could be done on the basis of the material available. So in this case he accepted as I understood him that it would be open to this Inquiry to entertain submissions as to whether there was material on which a relevant charge could have been brought.

Now, it is plain that the material which is available to the Procurators Fiscal covers a considerable wide range, from, at the one end, matters of law, matters of available evidence, to, at the other end, various considerations where his discretion has wide room for play.

I am satisfied that it would not on the one hand be proper for this Inquiry to require the prosecutors to justify their decisions, or to entertain submissions as to the sufficiency of what was put forward in justification of those decisions. On the other hand, I see no good reason why this Inquiry should not entertain submissions based on the available evidence. I am not going at this stage to draw any hard and fast line as to what can and cannot be submitted on the basis of the available evidence. It would certainly include, on the basis of possible sufficiency, whether a relevant charge could have been granted or whether some other decision in the circumstances could have been taken. That is as far as I go. I merely illustrate what might be the subject of submissions.

I consider that in this case, as in any other case, where a submission can properly be made on the available evidence, there is no reason whatever why that should not be made. This is after all a free country. For that reason, therefore, I would not wish to inhibit submissions. But of course it has to be clearly understood that these submissions must be based on the available evidence and do not enter into a review in one form or another of the decisions reached by the prosecutors.

Turning to the invitation the Lord Advocate extended in his note, as far as I am concerned I am content that this Inquiry should not require the soundness of the decisions to be subject to detailed examination in submissions, but I do wish to hear submissions based on the available evidence insofar as submissions can properly be made on the basis of that evidence. Whether that can be described as a matter of fact, as Mr. Bonomy said, or whether it is not a matter of fact is of no consequence to me. I wish to hear what can properly be submitted on the evidence available.

That brings me to another matter. It is of course in a case of this sort for the Lord Advocate to decide to what extent he should adhere to any rule or principle against the disclosure of information available to or information about the prosecution system. That is a decision over which I have no right of control. In the present case, I note that the Lord Advocate's position is that it is appropriate that evidence should be available as to the information provided to and the inquiries made by the Procurators Fiscal and the decisions taken by the Procurators Fiscal and the stated reasons for these decisions.

I have seen Mr Vannet's report, and with his usual thoroughness he has set out a considerable amount of detail as to these matters, and I am certain that that report will be of significant assistance to this Inquiry. At the same time, in his note which Mr Bonomy read yesterday the Lord Advocate has given me an opportunity to invite individual members of the Procurator Fiscal Service who were concerned with these events in Mr Vannet's report. I consider that in general it is not necessary, but I consider it would be desirable to have evidence from two members of this service who are apparently able to give evidence in regard to certain matters which have already been explored at this Inquiry. These two persons are Mr Cardle—I am thinking in particular of his evidence in regard to a report which Mr Vannet refers to as report 1A—and secondly Mr Gallagher, as to the communications between him and Detective Constable Taylor in regard to report No 4.

I hope this is sufficient to enable the Crown to identify the matters about which I am interested, but I leave it entirely to Mr Bonomy to decide what further evidence in fact might usefully be taken from those two witnesses when they enter the witness box.

Appendix 4   List of Submissions

Source	Fire-Arms	School Security	Vetting of Adults
Action of Churches Together in Scotland	*		
Advertising Standards Authority, The	*		
All Wales Play Forum			*
Assoc of Chief Police Officers of England & Wales	*	*	*
Assoc of Chief Police Officers of Scotland	*		
Assoc of Christian Teachers Scotland		*	
Assoc of Deer Management Groups, The	*		
Assoc of Directors of Education		*	*
Assoc of Directors of Social Work	*		*
Assoc of Head Teachers		*	
Assoc of Police Surgeons, The	*		
Banking Insurance & Finance Union	*		
BMA-General Medical Services Committee	*		*
Boys Brigade, The			*
British Association of Social Workers	*		*
British Deer Society, The	*		
British Medical Assoc	*		
British Shooting Sports Council	*		
C.E.M. Firearms Ltd	*		
Callander Rifle and Pistol Club	*		
Calouste Gulbenkian Foundation		*	*
Cheltenham & Gloucester College of Higher Education-Prof C Brackenridge			*
Chief Constables' Management Committee-Regional Crime Squad (North East)	*		
Children 1st-Royal Society for Prevention of Cruelty to Children, The			*
Children In Scotland			*
Children's Law Centre (Northern Ireland) Interim Steering Group	*		*

Source	Fire-Arms	School Security	Vetting of Adults
Church of Scotland, The (Board of Social Responsibility)			*
City Of Glasgow Council	*		
Convention Of Scottish Local Authorities	*	*	*
CSV Education			*
Discovery Camps Trust			*
Dunblane Snowdrop Petition	*		
Educational Institute of Scotland, The	*	*	*
Firearms Consultative Committee, The	*		
Franks, Keith	*	*	
†Gabor, Professor Thomas	*		
Galbraith, Sam, MP			*
General Assembly of the Church of Scotland-Committee on Church and Nation	*		
Greater Gwent Authority			*
Greenwood, Colin	*		
Hammond, John	*		*
Hicks, P F	*		
Independence Institute	*		
International Shooting Sportspersons Liaison Committee	*		
Inverness Royal Academy School Board			*
IPA Scotland-International Assoc for Child's Right to Play		*	*
Irvine Royal Academy-School Board and Parent & Staff Assoc		*	
Jackson, P H	*		
Joint Child Protection Committee Clackmannan, Falkirk, Stirling	*		*
Kendrick, Steven William	*		
Kilwinning Academy		*	
Kilwinning Academy School Board		*	
Kingston Upon Thames Police & Community Consultative Group	*		
Labour Party, The	*		*
Law Society of Scotland	*		
Lawson, Dr Richard	*		

Source	Fire-Arms	School Security	Vetting of Adults
League Against Cruel Sports	*		
Lewis, Terry, MP (Worsley)	*		
Liberal Democratic Party, The	*		
Libertarian Alliance	*		
Long Preston Parish Council	*		
McLeod, Elizabeth			*
Moffat Academy School Board	*	*	*
Morecambe Rifle & Pistol Club	*		
Mosside & Hulme Community Forum	*		
Munday, Richard	*		
Nairn River Community Council	*		*
NASUWT		*	
National Assoc of Head Teachers		*	
National Association of Re-Enactment Societies	*		
National Farmers Union-Country Landowners Assoc, Scottish Landowners Federation	*		
National Foster Care Association	*		*
National Rifle & Pistol Assoc of Ireland	*		
National Steering Group on Services for Children Under 8			*
National Viewers & Listeners Association	*		
NCH Action For Children	*		*
North Ayrshire Council School Security Group		*	
North East Risk Management Group		*	
Office of Legislative Affairs	*		
Oliver, Dr Ian, QPM	*		
Penicuik Labour Party	*	*	*
Play Wales			*
Police Federation of England and Wales	*		
Preparatory Schools Rifle Association	*		
Principal Community Education Officers Group (Scotland)			*
Professional Assoc of Teachers		*	*
Ramsay, Alastair		*	
Religious Society of Friends in Britain (Quakers)			*

Source	Fire-Arms	School Security	Vetting of Adults
Religious Society of Friends in Britain (Quakers)-Meeting for Sufferings	*		
Right Reverend Vincent Logan, Bishop of Dunkeld	*		
Romsey Publishing Company Limited	*		
Royal British Legion Scotland, The	*		
Royal College of Psychiatrists, The	*		
SAGE-Society Against Guns in Europe	*		
Save The Children Fund, The Powys Project			*
Scottish Congregational Church	*		
Scottish Further and Higher Education Assoc	*		
Scottish National Party	*	*	*
Scottish Parent Teacher Council	*	*	*
Scottish Secondary Teachers Assoc	*	*	*
Scottish Sports Council	*		
Scottish Standing Council of Voluntary Youth Organisations			*
Scottish Target Shooting Federation	*		
Shooters' Rights Assoc-Scottish Committee	*		
Shooters' Rights Assoc, The	*	*	*
Slough Borough Council	*		
Society of Friends (Quakers)	*		
Sporting Shooters Association of Australia Inc	*		
Stepping Stones in Scotland			*
Stevenson, Mr Jan A	*		
Stirling Rifle and Pistol Club	*		
Summerfield, John	*		
Sussex Police Authority	*		
Suzy Lamplugh Trust, The		*	
Tayside Voluntary Organisations - Child Protection Group "All Our Children"			*
UNISON Scotland	*	*	*
Volunteer Development Scotland			*
Wandsworth Council-Crime Prevention & Public Safety Sub-Committee	*		
Watt, David			*

Source	Fire-Arms	School Security	Vetting of Adults
Watt, Mr & Mrs Fergus	*		*
West Wales Federation of Parent Teacher Assocs		*	*
‡Wilson, William, QPM, Chief Constable Central Scotland Police	*	*	*
Yardley, Michael	*		

†Submissions tendered by the legal representatives of the families or the deceased children, the injured children, those absent from class on 13 March 1996, Mrs Eileen Harrild and Mrs Mary Blake.

‡Submission tendered by the legal representatives of Central Scotland Police.

In addition to the above, Family Care provided a submission in regard to the importance of information about a person's family origins.

Appendix 5   Publications taken into consideration

Control of Firearms

Home Office leaflets on:
- (a) Firearm Security (1992)
- (b) Firearms: Approval of Rifle and Pistol Clubs (1995 FA4-95)

Firearms Act 1968:
- (a) Proposals for Reform (December 1987 Cm 261)
- (b) Report of the Working Party on the Administration of the Act (April 1984)

First, Second, Third, Fourth, Fifth, Sixth and Seventh Annual Reports of the Firearms Consultative Committee (1990-96)

Report of the Working Group on the Administration of the Firearms Licensing System (Home Office November 1991)

Report of the Firearms Rules Working Group (March 1994)

Report of the Working Group on the Criteria for Home Office and Scottish Office Approval of Rifle and Pistol Clubs (March 1995)

ACPO Crime Committee Working Group on the Administration of Firearms: Firearms Administration: An Executive Summary (1991)

The Council of the European Communities; Council Directive of 18 June 1991 on control of the acquisition and possession of weapons. (91/477/EEC-OJ No L 256 13 September 1991 p.51)

Coopers & Lybrand Deloitte and the Centre for Police and Criminal Justice Studies University of Exeter: Firearms Certification Study: A Report to The British Association for Shooting and Conservation (January 1991):
- (a) Executive Summary
- (b) Appendices
- (c) Report

HMIC Report on the Administration of the Firearms Licensing System (England and Wales) (1993)

Home Office Research and Planning Unit Papers:
- (a) No 79: Approval of Rifle and Target Shooting Clubs: The Effects of the New and Revised Criteria (1993)
- (b) No 84: The Theft of Firearms (1994)

Home Office Management Advisory Service Reports:
  (a) No 14 (1991/92): Feasibility Study to Establish the cost of a Firearms Control Board
  (b) No 14 (1993/94): Review of The Firearms Control Board

The Scottish Home and Health Department Police Circulars:
  (a) No 5 (1986)
  (b) No 11 (1993)

Devon and Cornwall Constabulary: Multi-force Firearms Scrutiny

The Scottish Office Statistical Bulletin Criminal Justice Series:
  (a) CrJ/1995/4 September 1995
  (b) CrJ/1995/8 December 1995
  (c) CrJ/1996/4 August 1996

Hungerford Shooting Incident:
  (a) Report of Colin Smith, Chief Constable of Thames Valley Police 29 September 1987
  (b) Written answer to Parliamentary Question no 419 of 27 July 1988, attaching a Summary of the Report and Recommendations of HM Inspector of Constabulary

School Security

Department of Education and Science. Building Bulletin 67:Crime Prevention in Schools: Practical Guidance. (1987)

HSE: Preventing Violence to Staff. B Poyner and C Warne The Tavistock Institute of Human Relations. (1988)

HSC Education Service Advisory Committee: Violence to Staff in the Education Sector. (1990)

HSC Education Service Advisory Committee: The Responsibilities of School Governors for Health and Safety. (1992)

HSC Education Service Advisory Committee: Safety Policies in the Education Sector. (1994)

HSC Education Service Advisory Committee: Managing Health and Safety in Schools. (1995)

HSE: Violence to Staff. (1995)

NAHAT: NHS Security Manual: Management Supplement (1995)

SHA: Managing Security in Schools and Colleges. K Cooper, formerly Assistant Chief Constable, and D Little, formerly Chief Superintendent of Northamptonshire. (1996)

DfEE Managing School Facilities Guide 4: Improving Security in Schools (1996)

Vetting and Supervision of Adults

The Scottish Office: Effective Intervention: Child Abuse (1989)

The Scottish Home and Health Department Police Cricular No. 4/1989: Disclosure of Criminal Convictions (1989)

Home Office, Department of Health and Welsh Office Circular: Protection of Children: Disclosure of Criminal Background to Voluntary Sector Organisations (1994)

Volunteer Development Scotland: Protecting Children (1995)

The Scottish Office Social Work Services Group Circular No SWSG 4/96: Child Protection: Local Liaison Machinery—Child Protection Committees (1996)

The Scottish Office Social Work Services Group; Deregulation and Contracting Out Act 1994—Supervised Activities and Holiday Play Schemes used by Children under 8: Consultation Document (1996)

Home Office: Sentencing and Supervision of Sex Offenders: A Consultation Document (1996)

Home Office: On the Record: The Government's Proposals for Access to Criminal Records for Employment and Related Purposes in England and Wales (1996)

The Scottish Office: On the Record in Scotland: Proposals for Improved Access to Criminal Records (1996)

The Scottish Office; Crime and Punishment (1996)

Appendix 6   Target Shooting Competitions for Handguns

The Appendix to the first submission by The Scottish Target Shooting Federation provides information as to the variety of competitions in which handguns are used, with an explanation of the rules as to the types of handgun, ammunition, targets and shooting procedures. That Appendix may be referred to for further detail but in brief the competitions can be considered by reference to the following groups:

A. UIT

These competitions are run under the rules of the Union Internationale du Tir (UIT) which regulates shooting events at the Olympic Games. It has also become the world governing body for a set of disciplines shot in continental championships, world cup series and the Commonwealth Games. The main types of events comprise:

   (i) Free Pistol (.22 rimfire single shot only);

   (ii) Rapid Fire (.22 short rimfire, five shot semi-automatic pistols only);

   (iii) Centrefire (five shot semi-automatic pistols or revolvers within a certain range of calibres);

   (iv) Standard Pistol (.22 rimfire, five shot semi-automatic pistols or revolvers); and

   (v) Sport Pistol (.22 rimfire, five shot semi-automatic pistols or revolvers).

B. Muzzle Loading

These events are run under the rules of the Muzzle Loading Association of Great Britain. They cater for antique firearms (or modern reproductions) of various types such as flintlock, percussion, single shots and revolvers. In general the firearms are of a type in use before the last quarter of the 19th Century. The events are held at levels up to international and world championship.

C. Classics

These events are shot under the rules of the Historic Breechloading Smallarms Association and cater for firearms made before the end of the First World War or those of identical type. The various classes of event are defined by reference to calibre, type (pistol or revolver) and the physical size of the firearm.

D. Long Range

These events are shot at distances of 100, 200 and 300 yards under the rules of the International Long Range Pistol Shooting Association. The various classes cater for pistols of differing types and calibres, ranging from blackpowder muzzle loaders through modern service and other pistols to specially built rifle-calibre firearms.

E. Police/Service

These events derive from police and army training procedures.

Police pistol 1 is shot at 25, 15 and 10 metre distances; and police pistol 2 at 50, 25 and 10 metres. These events were originally designed as revolver competitions. With changes in police firearms use policy they are now commonly shot with semi-automatic pistols. They are designed to test shooters' ability to shoot at various distances, in a variety of positions and under varying time constraints.

1,500 police pistol C is a more recent multi-stage development of police training procedures in the United States. It consists of five separate matches for revolvers shot at 50 metre down to 10 metre distances with a variety of shooting positions using either hand under time constraints.

The maximum number of shots in any one series within any of these competitions is 6.

Service pistol competitions call for the use of a 9 mm Browning semi-automatic pistol "as issued" in the British Army. Service pistol A is derived from the current army training course of fire. It consists of 40 shots in series of 10 with movement towards the target as part of the procedure at the commencement of each stage after the first. Service pistol B is derived from the former army training course of fire and consists of 30 shots fired in a series of 6. This competition is shot at levels up to international. To cater for shooters with other types of pistol the Open A and Unrestricted B classes have been developed.

F. Action

This is a group of competitions which do not fall easily into any of the above groups. It includes Practical Pistol which is for any pistol or revolver and is run under the rules of the United Kingdom Practical Shooting Association and internationally under the rules of the International Practical Shooting Confederation. International competitions are at all levels up to continental and world championships.

The courses of fire vary from standard exercises to individual procedures developed for specific events. The emphasis in this branch of shooting is on accuracy, speed and power. Results are calculated from a factor of score on target allied with time taken. Scoring on anything except a central hit is at a reduced level if the ammunition used is of a lower standard than "major" power factor, established from a formula taking into account bullet weight and velocity.

Man *vs* Man consists of two competitors shooting falling targets simultaneously against the clock in a knock-out league. There are separate classes for revolvers and semi-automatic pistols.

The Bianchi Cup, which is for any centrefire pistol, comprises four separate matches consisting of various types of target, shooting positions and distances all designed to test a shooter's ability to shoot with either and both hands under a range of conditions.

Printed in the UK for the Controller of Her Majesty's Stationery Office by The Stationery Office Limited, Dd 0293183 C70 10/96 (141756)